Megalithic Measures and Rhythms

Anne Macaulay

Megalithic Measures and Rhythms

Sacred Knowledge of the Ancient Britons

Edited by

Richard A. Batchelor

&

Vivian T. Linacre

Floris Books

First published in 2006 by Floris Books
© 2006 Estate of Anne Macaulay

British Library CIP Data available

ISBN-10 0-86315-554-5
ISBN-13 978-086315-554-3

Printed in Great Britain
By Biddles, King's Lynn

Contents

Editors' Preface

Universal assumptions governing prehistoric European culture and the origins of mathematics are exploded in this detailed geometric analysis of some two hundred — those of which enough has survived for accurate measurement — of the 'stone circles' that abounded in the British Isles and Brittany four thousand years ago. Anne Macaulay's rough typescripts and diagrams, representing twenty-seven years' work up to her death in 1998, have been thoroughly edited, amplified, refined and brought up to date, at the request of the family trust, by Richard Batchelor, a St Andrews University geologist, in collaboration with Vivian Linacre, a Perth surveyor.

Richard's principal tasks were to generally tidy up her calculations, reproduce her rough diagrams in proper form, select illustrations, and render her mathematics consistent (for instance, over the years she would adopt different historical values of 'π,' the dimension of a circle's circumference divided by its diameter, using variously 22 / 7, 25 / 8 or 16 / 5). Vivian's contribution was to rewrite and assemble the bulk of the text and knock the whole book into shape, under the publisher's most helpful guidance. Anne was a natural mathematical genius but would not have laid claim to any literary talent. Moreover, her mind was so quick and intuitive that she would leap to a conclusion as if it were obvious, leaving her editors to fill in the missing lines of figures or text.

Richard and Vivian did not meet until shortly after Anne's funeral — they were brought together by her family and by Ludivina How, her closest friend from school-days — but each had enjoyed the privilege of visiting her and falling under her spell during the last painful year of her life, when she was consumed with the need to find the right hands to which the work could be safely entrusted. Her passion for the harmonies of mathematics and music and their source in the early civilization of these islands was a revelation to all those about her — a revelation which the editors very much hope that readers may now share.

For Anne was primarily a musicologist; since mathematics and music are brother and sister. Her starting-point was the inspired recognition that the Pythagorean mathematics which apply to the tuning of the ancient Greek lyre, the 'cithara' (the forerunner of the guitar) also apply to the stone circles. She shows how our forefathers, during the period from *c.* 4000 to 2000 BC, freely adapted squares, circles, ellipses, pentagrams, hexagrams, and seven-, nine- and fourteen-pointed stars as the geometrical templates for the designs of their megaliths. Her perception of the standard units of measurement used in these geometric designs confirms the controversial discovery in the 1960s by Professor Alexander Thom that these common factors were the megalithic yard (MY) of 2.72 ft and the megalithic rod (MR) of 6.8 ft, so that 5 MY = 2 MR, and reveals, furthermore, that they used the 'Greek foot' of 0.97 ft as a third 'yardstick' — discerning not only that this was integral to many of the layouts but also that the authentic Greek fathom of 7 Greek feet exactly equals 1 MR (i.e. 7×0.97 ft ≈ 6.8 ft).

Another startling recognition was that the use of the pentagram must mean that megalithic builders were familiar both with the Fibonacci series of numbers — some 4000 years before publication by Leonardo of Pisa (popularly known as Fibonacci) of 'Liber abaci' in 1202, which has always been credited with the formula's 'discovery' — and with the 'magical ratio' or 'divine proportion' known as *phi* or the Golden Mean (often shown as 'ϕ'), which is calculated as $\sqrt{5} + 1$ divided by 2 or $(2.23607 + 1)/2 = 1.618034...$, because that is the ratio of the long side to the short side of a pentagram — and because it, too, is integral to the construction of many of the plans. Until now, this irrational number has always been attributable to the Pythagorean school of mathematics and proclaimed as one of its greatest accomplishments, but that did not develop until two thousand years later!

So did this original corpus of mathematical knowledge actually migrate from the Atlantic seaboard to the Eastern Mediterranean, there to be 'rediscovered' by the Ancient Egyptians and Greeks centuries later? Was the evolution of this branch of civilization not centrifugal, as we were all taught — from the Middle East outwards to the primitive periphery — but centripetal? The implications for conventional European pre-history are shattering. Anne Macaulay examined the evidence and speculated on the possible migration routes, as well as on the relationship between the geometry and the creation of the Titan Gods of Greek mythology.

She found powerful evidence to suggest that knowledge of mathematics was indeed generated in these islands. The legends of Apollo and the Hyperboreans have diffused this knowledge through the ages.

Richard Batchelor & Vivian Linacre

Chronological Table

c. 11000 BC   End of last Ice Age — wild grasses/corn harvested by hunter-gatherers in Greece, Anatolia and eastwards

c. 10000 BC   Start of farming; grain and domestic animals in Anatolia. Development of Indo-European languages and of villages and towns with growth of population

c. 4600 BC   Farmers established in the British Isles

c. 4000 BC   First rings and other buildings in stone — 'yardsticks' become established (some authorities date the first French Megaliths as early as 4700 and the first British Megaliths as early as 4500 BC)

3700–3200 BC   Callanish I – V

3600 BC   Square-cornered house at Westray (Orkney)

3100 BC   First stage (ditch and bank and 'Aubrey holes') at Stonehenge (p.51) — and 1st Dynasty in Egypt — and Newgrange (Ireland)

2800 BC   Maes Howe (Orkney) transition from Neolithic to Bronze Ages

2600 BC   First Pyramid in Egypt

2100 BC   The 'Beaker' vogue — first trace of organized tin working in Cornwall — and Bronze Age flourishing in Eastern Mediterranean

2100–1600 BC   Period of great activity in megalithic construction

1600 BC   Decline in stone ring construction (1623 Eruption of Thera in Greece)

c. 1400 BC   Abandonment of Stonehenge and other sites — Proto-Greek language written (Linear B) in Crete and Mycene

1159 BC Eruption of Hekla in Iceland — climatic changes throughout
Northern Hemisphere — collapse of many Eastern Mediterranean
kingdoms — the nineteen year 'Nuclear Autumn' in Britain (as
shown by dendrochronology and ice cores)

c. 1000 BC transition from Bronze to Iron Age

Note on Dating

The eastern Mediterranean archaeological sites have been dated according to the Egyptian king lists, but the accuracy of these lists is being questioned. They conflict with carbon dating. The west European sites are now being dated by carbon dating, dendrochronology (dating with tree rings) and ice cores from Greenland. Therefore the apparent parallels between Egyptian and megalithic dates may need to be revised.

The Clava site (p.134) has recently been re-investigated with the purpose of assessing the dates. The earliest date here was 2150 BC. Without these 'Clava Cairn' types, it would have been impossible to analyse the underlying geometry. In the past, many dates were suggested by scraps of pottery found on the site; but archaeologists were well aware that such few objects may have been deposited long after the building of the rings with which they are associated.

According to Heggie (1981):

> A factor which may affect the intervisibility of the components of an orientation is vegetation, especially trees. Unfortunately, even in specific cases there may be little direct evidence (without excavation) as to whether the trees were also there in megalithic times, or even if trees previously grew at a site which is now clear. Nor is it really enough to know that trees currently smothering a site were recently planted. Changes in the tree cover may have come about through two related causes: the extension of agriculture and climatic changes. According to the climatologist H.H. Lamb: 'there is now much evidence ... that between about 5000 and 2000 BC, forest grew much nearer to the open Atlantic coast of northwest Scotland than at any time since, and also in parts of the Hebrides and northern isles.' In fact the comparatively rapid decline of the woodlands is dated between 2600 and 1600 BC. To the extent that the orientations and the clearance of the forest can be dated at all, then, some

doubt is cast on suggested astronomical orientations that are very early, i.e. much before the end of the Neolithic, at least in certain regions. It has also been suggested that the need for horizons clear of trees may well have influenced the geographical distribution of some types of megalithic site.

But, of course, these observations, concerning the external orientation of some sites, do not affect the validity of their internal geometry.

Introduction: The Origins
of Megalithic Mathematics

by Vivian T. Linacre

Time and space are always measurable, yet suddenly, in our lifetime, cosmic visions of infinity and eternity are rapidly approaching to surround us! We are witnessing an unprecedented growth of knowledge, of both the origins and extent of the universe. Our past is receding as fast as outer space is expanding. By tracing background microwave radiation at a distance of almost fifteen billion light-years — nearly back in time to the 'Big Bang' — astronomers have reached virtually the edge of the known universe. NASA space probes, orbiting a million miles above the Earth, may prove either that the universe is indeed infinite in size or, on the contrary, that it is more compact than hitherto suspected and merely a part of a 'multiverse' — namely, there may be an indefinite series of 'fifteen billion light-year' horizons beyond our own.

In studies of our own past, human pre-history is somersaulting backwards, propelled by revolutionary discoveries that are continually revising backwards the birth-date of our species and the beginnings of civilization. The twin sciences of archaeology and anthropology, reinforced by the new science of archaeo-astronomy, have crucially freed us from reliance on documentary interpretation, breaking through into pre-literate, pre-recorded history, which has no chronological or geographical limits. In consequence, datings of (a) the earliest civilizations and (b) the beginnings of mathematics — whose marriage gave birth to metrology — are ever more remote. So now the scope for metrological research is as vast as it is for astrophysics and cosmology.

The latest DNA evidence shows that Neanderthals and modern humans diverged genetically at least 500 000 years ago, and as the human brain 100 000 years ago was the same size as today, it is inconceivable that — as historians traditionally assumed — throughout that vast period humans led a savage existence, foraging for food, and then, in a brief moment a mere 10 000 years ago, suddenly began to domesticate animals and cultivate the land in several different 'centres of origin' around the world!

The many applications of human intelligence — language, science, technology, mathematics, art and culture — are all very recent developments. The human species has had a recognizable concept of abstract numbers for at most 12 000 years. But that is nothing like enough time for the human brain to undergo major evolutionary developments. It took the human brain some 3 500 000 years to evolve to its present state, yet Einstein's brain differed little from that of men living long before mathematics existed.

Until as recently as 8 000 years ago, mathematics was just about numbers. Ancient Babylonian, Egyptian and Chinese mathematics consisted almost solely of arithmetic. But then, expanding beyond mere study of number, the mathematics of ancient Greece was more concerned with geometry. Indeed, the Greeks regarded numbers geometrically, to the extent that those measured lengths to which their numbers did not correspond were called irrational lengths. To the Greeks, mathematics was as much about shape as about number. So it grew from just a technique for counting into an academic discipline for measurement, with strong aesthetic and religious aspects. Mathematics continued to advance after the Greeks — mainly in Arabia and China — but its nature did not really change until modern times, when mathematics became the study, not just of number nor just of shape, but — overwhelmingly — of motion, change and space. All of these are defined by measurement, either directly by physical means or by processes of calculation and verification.

Around the sixth century BC, Pythagoras discovered the chief musical intervals and the relationships between numbers and the natural world. As we shall see presently, this was Anne Macaulay's starting point. Pythagoras and Aristotle had seen the invisible patterns of sound in music. A musician's eyes read straight through the musical symbols on the pages of the score to the sounds they represent, just as a mathematician reads straight through the mathematical symbols to the formulae and quantities they represent

Anne Macaulay contends in this work that the stone circles built in what are now the British Isles and Brittany from 6 500 to 3 500 years ago produce evidence of Pythagorean mathematical skills — far earlier than conventional wisdom would accept. It is vital then to explore the evolutionary background and consider when and how these faculties developed.

Let us start about 40 000 years ago, when humans began to use symbolic representations in cave paintings, rock carvings and decorative jewellery. When Picasso emerged from an examination of the wall-paintings in the caves at Lascaux he exclaimed: 'We have invented nothing!' The University of Texas archaeologist Denise Schmandt-Besserat discovered a highly advanced Sumerian society in Iraq that flourished 10 000 years ago, using small clay tokens of different shapes, including spheres, disks, cones, tetrahedra, ovoids and cylinders, as well as triangles and rectangles, for the purpose of counters in trade, each shape representing a certain quantity of a particular commodity. That period, between 40 000 and 10 000 years ago, covers what used to be called the Mesolithic and Neolithic Age and until recently was regarded as the dawn of civilization. So the 'prehistoric' label that is still attached to that era and the succeeding period known as the Bronze Age has become an absurd anachronism.

The discoveries at Blombos Cave, 180 miles from Cape Town in South Africa, announced in January 2002, included a pair of engraved pieces of ochre, the oldest examples of symbolic art found so far. They reveal that mankind was mentally sophisticated more than 70 000 years ago. The same dig has also uncovered evidence of the carving of specialized bone tools, standard markers of complex skills and modern thought processes, which date back just as far. *The Times,* reporting on these finds, commented:

> Though their function remains a mystery, they were created by human beings recognizably like ourselves. Art, science and religion seem to have emerged closer to the origin of our species, some 130 000 years ago, than had been thought.

In Australia, rock carvings resembling European megalithic cup and ring markings were discovered in association with artefacts found in dateable stratified debris, some 160 000 years old. Yet according to the textbooks humankind did not inhabit the Australian continent until almost 40 000 years ago. Ritually buried human remains of Caucasian origin have been discovered in the United States, dating back 9 000 years, yet according to the textbooks Caucasians (the earliest Viking explorers) did not arrive in North America until little more than 1 000 years ago. Evidence of man's seafaring and navigational skills has been deduced from many sites and artefacts found spread among the East Indies, reliably dated back 70 000 years; epochs before the conventionally accepted dates for such progress.

Remains of a 'Lost City' have been discovered, 120 feet below sea-level in the Gulf of Khambhat, 40 miles off the coast of Gujurat in western India; from which fragments of pottery, carved wood, bone and beads dating back over 9 500 years have already been recovered. Every ancient culture nurtures myths such as Atlantis and Noah's Ark. The idea of cities constructed during the Palaeolithic Age will compel a drastic re-evaluation of orthodox pre-history.

For the latest calculations show that over ten million square miles of fertile coastal land — which is obviously where the earliest civilized tribes would have settled — were inundated by catastrophic tides resulting from the great glacier melt of around 11 000 years ago. Evidence of thousands of cities, villages, temples and fortresses may lie beneath the shallow seas around every continent, especially where formerly land-bridges linked an island to the mainland.

What lies around the Hebrides and — bearing in mind that the largest concentration of stone circles outside the British Isles is in Brittany — beneath the English Channel? Could the remains of hundreds more circles lie off our shores, whether of stone or — like the Norfolk 'Seahenge' — of timber, preserved by the salt-water? Ultimately, will we learn of civilizations that possibly existed even prior to that last Ice Age but were destroyed by it — when most of the Earth's northern latitudes became covered by ice up to two miles thick?

Certainly, some fresh hypothesis is necessary to provide a background for the otherwise inexplicable emergence of a universal system of measurement around 3 500 years ago. To quote John Neal (2000):

> One cannot begin by trying to explain metrology from the point of view of an evolutionary development, because the earliest known measures prove to be part of a completely developed system that on analysis is extremely sophisticated and identical to numerical systems, the evidence suggests, universally.

Likewise, from the great B.L. Van der Waerden's *Geometry and Algebra in Ancient Civilizations:*

> We have seen so many similarities between the mathemati-
> cal and religious ideas current in Neolithic England, in
> Greece, India and China in the Han period, that we are
> bound to postulate the existence of a common metrological
> doctrine from which all these ideas derived.

Thus, we are immediately confronted with the mystery as to the
location and period of the prime source of a number of related systems
in far corners of the Earth. For, as Knight & Lomas (1999) point out,
either it was just a huge coincidence that humankind across the globe
spontaneously developed all of these great advances at the same time, or
else the knowledge of such advanced matters had already evolved naturally over a far greater period of time, but for which the archaeological
evidence remains inaccessible. Is not the latter much more likely?

Opposing schools of thought on the origins of measurement systems
are personified by two great Greeks, the historian Herodotus (*c.* 484–
424 BC) and the philosopher Aristotle (384–322 BC). The former held that
geometry originated in Egypt from the practical necessity of resurveying
after the annual flooding along the Nile valley, whilst the latter argued
that it was devised by the leisurely priestly class for ritual practice and
for its intellectual mystique. Pursuing the latter, it may be that all mathematics evolved from a proto-mathematics that germinated in ritual
practices, just as science evolved from mythology and philosophy from
theology and astronomy from astrology. That is certainly consistent with
Anne Macaulay's outlook. To quote from Boyer & Merzbach's *History
of Mathematics* (1991): 'That the beginnings of mathematics are older
than the oldest civilizations is clear.'

In the present debate, conflicting theories are advanced on the one
hand by writers such as John Michell and John Neal (both eminent
authorities and admirers of Anne Macaulay's work) who argue that
the digit represented by the 'megalithic inch' corresponded to ancient
Egyptian and Hebrew measurements. On the other hand, we have the
followers of Alexander Thom who hold the megalithic system to be
original and self-contained, maintaining that it was the very fountain-
head from which different streams flowed into the emerging civilizations of the Eastern Mediterranean. Professor Thom was Professor of
Engineering Science in the University of Oxford from 1945 until his
retirement in 1961, following which he devoted the rest of his active
life to conducting precise engineering surveys of some 200 of those

megalithic stone circles whose remains are still clearly defined. He was assisted latterly by his son, Dr A.S. Thom, senior lecturer in the Department of Aeronautics and Fluid Mechanics in the University of Glasgow. It was these surveys that inspired Anne Macaulay to discern their hidden geometry and crucial significance, mathematically and culturally.

To Anne Macaulay, with the benefit of her musicological studies, harmonizing the Pythagorean mathematics of megalithic building with the origins of stringed instruments, reinforced her conviction that the élite of the megalithic Britons actually became the proto-Greeks.

It is as if mathematics, like music and time, was not actively invented nor even discovered by our remote ancestors but was passively revealed unto them, as if these measures and ratios had always existed, inherent in nature, and imperceptibly came into use once the demand arose — as it did, almost spontaneously, for the construction on the Atlantic seaboard of the phenomenal megalithic monuments. The notion of mathematics diffusing into the world of the ancient Greeks, for instance, is supported by David Fowler who wrote in his *The Mathematics of Plato's Academy:*

> ... surely no one can believe that there was not some rich prehistory to what we find in Euclid's *Elements*. But nothing of what was then written has survived in its original form; still less can we, or could the later commentators, know of the conversations in the garden of Academe and elsewhere. In the case of early Greek mathematics, the important informal tradition has been lost ...

If some primal system were supposed to have spread by slow dissemination, it could not possibly have done so from other, already established, cultural centres such as Sumer or Egypt but would have had to have done so in the millennia before those civilizations arose! Considering how constrained geographically were each of those early civilizations and how distinctive — even alien — their respective cultures, it is inconceivable that they all spontaneously adopted interrelated systems of measurement. At first blush it sounds perfectly plausible to say: 'There's nothing unique about megalithic units; the relationships are easily reconcilable with the Babylonian/Egyptian/Greek ...' — but that leads directly to the implausible question: if the whole network of ancient European and Middle Eastern metrologies can be unravelled, who wove the network in the first place? Where did it all begin and when did the great diaspora occur? The presumption — whether conscious or not — of some remote progenitor is inescapable. Was the Britain-Brittany phenomenon an autonomous one-off or was it itself that 'remote progenitor' or, if not, then where was it and when?

It is another paradox that, although the theory implied by Thom and propounded by Anne Macaulay — that megalithic Britons devised and perfected this advanced system of measurement in isolation — sounds insular and inordinate, there is no actual conflict with the opposing theory if the megalithic system does prove to be that 'remote pro-genitor'! Moreover, the 'mono-megalithic' theory does eliminate the otherwise intractable problem of antecedents altogether; and it allows for the growth of its own culture over ensuing millennia — with the development of associated and secondary units, hybridization and adaptation of Roman and Germanic units, and so on. Whatever the truth, it remains very remarkable that the ancient civilization which flourished between the Tigris and the Euphrates produced cuneiform tablets, illustrating primitive mathematics, that date from 3000 BC; while the Step Pyramid at Sakkara (preceding the Great Pyramids at Gizeh) was built around 2900 BC, and the earliest sites of the Mayan civilization in Central America also date from about 2700 BC.

Were these all merely haphazard concurrences, random manifestations of a universal evolutionary process, or direct derivatives of a common creative source somewhere? We know that the original idea of denoting numbers by having a small collection of basic symbols and stringing them together to form terms — numerical expressions similar to words — did most definitely come from Babylon, around 4000 years ago. Because it was constructed on the base 60, the Babylonian system was too cumbersome and so did not gain widespread acceptance, although it was adopted universally in geography for measurement of latitude and longitude and also for measurement of time, for all of which essential purposes it has proved ideal. (After all, the number 360 is divisible by every number between 1 and 10 apart from 7.) The Arabic number system was an extraordinary human invention. It is very concise and easily learned, it allows us to represent numbers of unlimited magnitude and apply them to collections and measurements of all kinds, and — most important of all — it reduces computation with numbers to the routine manipulation of symbols on a page, whether by hand or in print.

But meanwhile, on the northwest Atlantic seaboard, thousands of great stone circles were built between 6 500 and 3 500 years ago, ostensibly without benefit of any numerical system!*

They were planned primarily as astronomical observatories, as well as for ceremonial purposes. These megalithic monuments are miraculous feats of engineering, constructed concurrently and to an identical repertoire of precise geometric designs by isolated tribes who had no known means of intercommunication! Yet Anne Macaulay's analyses of Thom's engineering surveys reveal that these megalithic builders were using standard units of measurement — the precursors of the yard, foot and inch — and that they knew the shape and dimensions of the Earth. She demonstrated, moreover, that they must have had knowledge, not only of advanced geometry but also of rudimentary algebra and trigonometry. Considering the handicap suffered through their lack of a rational numerical system, which did not reach Europe until several millennia later, their mathematical prowess and sheer power of abstract thought amount to cultural genius.

To quote Euan Mackie in *The Megalithic Builders* (1977):

> If the European Megaliths ... are older than the oldest towns, then it is difficult to see how urban societies could have played any significant part in the great social processes which were under way in Atlantic Europe between 4500 and 2500 BC ...

It appears, then, that the megalithic Britons were evidently a pastoral people, who built stone circles as all-purpose observatories, temples and community centres, without any associated urban settlements. The religion of this pastoral society was pantheistic, unlike the deistic religions of the hierarchical societies in the Middle East, and its wealth was measured in land rather than in slaves or livestock or precious metals. It is doubly amazing that not only were their feats of engineering apparently accomplished by isolated tribes but also in isolated places, without the support of

---

* Incidentally, the term 'stone circle' or 'stone ring' must be distinguished from the term 'cromlech' which is sometimes, especially in Brittany, used to mean the same but more properly refers to a prehistoric structure consisting of a large flat unhewn stone resting horizontally on three or more upright stones, found especially in Ireland, Wales and SW England; often called 'table-stones.' But these in turn are sometimes, again mostly in Brittany, known by the alternative term 'dolmen.'

urban social structures or resources. It appears that our megalithic ancestors invented these mathematical techniques independently. So, it seems, did Islamic civilizations, and also probably the ancient Chinese, but each of these was based on an urban civilization. In the megalithic West, as Anne Macaulay shows, mathematics originated and continued to progress as a sacred art in order to design and develop these sacred sites; whereas mathematics in Mesopotamia, ancient Egypt and elsewhere was practised for secular — commercial and political — purposes.

The megalithic Britons ('Beaker folk') are otherwise known as 'Groove Ware People' because of the style of ceramic artifacts they left behind — a very distinctive class of pottery decorated on the surface with many grooves — found in profusion on all the main sites in Southern England and on Orkney. The same grooved pattern is found on large stone structures in Ireland, Wales and Scotland — what are called the 'cup and ring' marks — as well as on stone balls mentioned later. This is further powerful evidence, not only of the artistic and technical skills of the people but also of their high level of organization and cultural unity throughout the British Isles, despite a sparse population and complete absence both of recorded knowledge and of means of communication.

Within the foregoing intellectual chronology, how did metrology itself evolve? Naturally, the beginning of measurement in every early society was always time. Measurement of the seasons of the year — the solstices and equinoxes — was vital for spiritual and ritual purposes. The lives and beliefs of 'primitive' peoples were governed by the heavens. (Even today, astrology still exerts an appeal to many!) Ability to calculate the time of day or night was an advantage usually confined to a superior caste. Later, measurement of the seasons became even more important as agriculture developed.

A knowledge of music and rhythmic movement accompanied this development, for music and dance are measurement of time in another form. It expressed itself in ceremony and ritual. Also, in pre-literate societies, sound was vital as the only available medium for transmission of knowledge from one generation to the next. Therefore measurement of music and time must have have originated very early, if we base our thinking on the fact that the first sensation experienced by the foetus is its mother's heartbeat — representing sound and rhythm.

Next came measurement of length — for timber to build shelters and great stones for temples, and measurement of territorial boundaries. Time and distance provided for planning of journeys. Then followed calculation of areas, for the laying out of fields and planning of larger buildings. That was the point reached in the megalithic period.

Of course, as Anne Macaulay emphasizes, all that the dating of the megalithic monuments proves is the period within which the builders had acquired the engineering skills to erect these massive structures. The mathematical knowledge required for planning and design could well have been acquired much earlier.

Then the calculation of height, for more ambitious buildings, provided the third dimension for the purpose of measuring cubic capacity. Fluid volume naturally followed, for wine and water; and finally, with the growth of trade and nationhood, the calculation of weight, to measure produce and accordingly to levy taxes. That was the natural sequence — the necessary order governing the gradual application of number to humanity's working environment.

A consciousness of time and a compulsion to devise means of measuring it — the lunar cycle and the seasons of the year — were what essentially marked the emergence of humankind. Laying out of sacred sites, for astronomical and ritual purposes, gave expression to this need to measure the passage of time; but that presupposed a sophisticated knowledge of geometry and arithmetic, as Anne Macaulay demonstrates — a knowledge that was put to good use during the period of great activity in megalithic construction from 4 500 to 3 500 years ago.

The largest megalithic monument in the world is the alignment known as Le Ménec at Carnac in Brittany, consisting of some 3 000 megaliths in eleven rows that stretch across the countryside for a distance of some three quarters of a mile. It was constructed around 5 000 years ago. Many of the lines appear to encode the directions in which bright stars rose during that era. Similarly, two lines of megaliths at Callanish on Lewis in the Hebrides marked the rising directions of the bright star Capella and the Pleiades star cluster between 3 800 and 3 750 years ago. Clearly, the respective populations were impelled to plan these vast monuments in order to encode the directions of the rising and setting of the Sun, Moon and bright stars.

The largest structure in Britain is at Avebury in Wiltshire, enclosing an area of over 28 acres, with an outer circle of 400 yards diameter, surrounded by a ditch 30 feet deep and connected to the mound at Silbury Hill several miles away. Yet it wasn't recognized until 1648, because it is so big that nobody could realize its shape, and because nobody was interested anyway. As a subject for study, the stone rings were totally neglected for thousands of years; pillaged by farmers for the stone and dismissed by historians as the work of savages.

Ironically, after centuries of scorn and neglect, we are suddenly over-whelmed by 'megalithomania' — by glossy coffee-table books and TV programmes devoted to highly speculative and pseudo-mystical theories surrounding the Late Stone Age and its great monuments — all of which could damage the credibility of the scientific pioneers, the Thoms and Macaulay, who devoted half their lives to the subject. The inescapable truth, of course, is that this whole area of enquiry, which plumbs the springs of human culture, is still quite new! Against the current back-ground, we have all the more reason to appreciate the value of Thom's rigorous surveys and Macaulay's analyses.

Aubrey Burl (1976) estimated that of the 900 rings still standing in Britain, about 600 are circles, 150 flattened circles, 100 ellipses (see Glossary) and 50 ovoid (egg-shaped). Quoting Burl, Anne Macaulay points out that:

> Those chosen by Thom were picked mostly from the stony and upland parts [of the country]. It has become clear that in lowland England — that is, the fertile, Eastern side — the same sort of sacred, megalithic sites were created and marked with tree trunks instead of stones. Tree trunks rot in time and ploughing subsequently obliterates these lowland sites ...

(Erosion of the East coast must also have left scores of timber circles under the North Sea.)

Thom said that altogether there are probably well over a thousand remaining stone rings still visible in Britain (quite apart from those in Brittany), ranging very widely in scale.

> As the megalithic culture lasted for some 2 000 years, ample time existed for the knowledge of geometry to develop; and develop it certainly did, so that, long before the Greeks, peo-ple in NW Europe were setting out ellipses and other much more complicated geometrical shapes. (Thom 1978, p.17)

Anne Macaulay's analyses of about 180 of Thom's sites reveal 21 dis-tinct types of plan. It is unlikely — even if most of the remaining 800 or more were surveyed in the future and the data eventually analysed — that any new, hitherto unidentified type of plan could materialize. These results are tabulated, with numbers of each type, in Appendix 8.

On 21 March 1982, Professor Thom wrote to a fellow researcher, Margaret Ponting:

> For over 60 years I have cruised in the waters of the Hebrides, exploring out-of-the-way places, many of them normally inaccessible by public transport. On the 1933 cruise in the sailing yacht 'Hadassah,' with my son and four friends, we had finished a long day's sail in the North Atlantic. Having left the Sound of Harris that morning, we arrived in East Loch Roag, a beautiful secluded inlet in NW Lewis. I was seeking a quiet anchorage for the night, and navigating with care between rocky islets and promontories, I finally made up my mind to anchor as far up East Loch Roag as my chart allowed safely. As we stowed sail after dropping anchor, we looked up and there, behind the stones of Callanish was the rising Moon. Since I had been concentrating on navigation as darkness approached, I did not know how close we were to the main Callanish site. After dinner we went ashore to explore. I saw that by looking at the Pole Star there was a North/South line in the complex. This fascinated me, for I knew that when the site was built no star of any magnitude had been at, or near, the Pole of the heavens. Precession had not yet brought Polaris as nearly due North as it now is. I wondered whether the alignment was a chance occurrence or whether it had been deliberately built that way. If it had been deliberate, North/South alignments would probably be found at other megalithic sites. The Outer Hebrides have a charm of their own, not the least being their remoteness. To realize that megalithic man had lived and worked there as well as on mainland Britain aroused my interest in the workings of his mind and my interest stirred, I have ever since made detailed surveys of all the sites I could find.

Thom and Macaulay were equally brilliant, original and single-minded. But whereas Thom's gifts were providentially and indispensably concentrated on astronomy and mathematics, Anne Macaulay's were catholic and holistic, embracing every subject relating to her ideas: geometry and metrology, archaeology and anthropology, history and mythology, astronomy and music. Who else could have speculated that the sexagesimal system which governs geometry, geography and horology, may have sprung from musical scales (e.g. 12 notes in a chromatic scale and 6 in a whole-tone scale) as may the 365 days of the year — 360 days plus 5 intercalary days for pagan festivals?

Both researchers would certainly have agreed that the importance of the study of megalithic mathematics is reflected in the universality of the knowledge that it yields. It was Anne Macaulay's special studies in Greek musicology and numerology that suddenly revealed the potential for enlarging upon Thom's megalithic geometry. She saw that the first 7 of the 18 main types of plan (out of 21 in all) are all contained within pentagrams — i.e. regular pentagons. Indeed, over a third of all the sites analysed contain pentagrams. The pentagram is featured also in early Babylonian art and was regarded as a mystic symbol throughout pre-history. From that initial break-through, she could visualize — using a combination of archaeo-mathematical skill and sheer intuition — and reproduce complex geometrical diagrams from Thom's meticulous survey material.

Throughout these analyses, as may be seen in Part I, she gives Thom's actual measurements alongside the dimensions calculated from her own theoretical formulae, and the difference ('error') in each case, which is never substantial. Obviously, discrepancies could arise, depending on which side of large stones the measurements were taken from, or where stones had fallen or were missing, or as the result of 'soil creep,' tree growth, frost action or human spoilage.

A flavour of Thom's methods may be given by this passage from the Preface to the last of his three major works (1978), reflecting on the two earlier publications (1968, 1971):

> Since the publication of these books, we have extended the investigation to France in addition to surveying a number of important sites in Britain. As a result we now have highly accurate plans of the thousands of stones in the Carnac alignments with most of the nearby menhirs [Breton for 'long stone'] and we have precise plans of Stonehenge, Brogar in Orkney and Avebury. These surveys necessitated six visits to Orkney, one to Shetland, and five to Carnac

where, in some years, we had as many as ten to twelve help-
ers. The analysis of the resulting mass of material required
years of desk-work. For example, the plan of the Kermario
alignments was over 8 ft long and took several months to
plot. Our Avebury survey demanded more than a plotted
plan and, accordingly, we have given the coordinates of
the centre of every stone. The work in Carnac has shown
that the erectors of standing stones in Brittany made use of
the same units of measurement and the same geometry and
were investigating the same astronomical phenomena as the
erectors in Britain.

Then Thom's Conclusion to the same 1978 book begins:

Our method of working depends entirely on measuring
lengths and angles and, while occasionally we use a rod
or a bayonet to prod, we do not dig. In this we differ from
archaeologists whose major weapon is the spade. We have
established that a universal unit of length was in use from
Shetland to Brittany and we have shown that most of megalithic man's constructions of circles, rings and alignments
were designed to definite rules.

He called this unit of length the megalithic yard (MY).
In his first major work, Thom had demonstrated that this standard
measurement of 2.72 ft was a component of the design of practically
every stone circle; and in his last book he commented: 'More powerful
methods of analysing the diameters listed have been given by Kendall
and by Freeman' and concluded that there are in Britain

four strong indications, if not proofs, of the reality of the
MY — (i) these analyses of the diameters; (ii) Avebury,
(iii) histograms of distances between stones and distances
between circles, and (iv) the perimeters of ellipses, egg-
shaped rings, etc. Consider also the histogram of observed
diameters and the reality of the egg-shaped rings and of
ellipses that depend on right-angled triangles built from
integral numbers of yards — and consider the evidence
from the Brogar ring. It seems impossible to combine the

results ... so as to give an overall probability level, but philosophically the conclusion is quite clear. There cannot be any doubt about the reality of the MY.

There followed a summary of derived values, producing a mean of 2.722 ft.

Thom carried out an entirely fresh and extremely accurate survey of the vast Avebury site, to verify the megalithic yard beyond question. The test was to compare the results from physical measurements in the field with independent geometrical and algebraic calculations. The Thoms reported (1978):

> Both of us have considerable experience in setting out roads and railways using modern equipment and we know that even using such equipment it would be quite a task to complete this ring satisfactorily. Any engineer asked today to do this would begin by making a number of trigonometrical calculations. The erectors did it without theodolites, without steel tapes, and without trigonometrical tables.

They added that, in view of the extreme care taken with the Avebury survey and analysis, and the perfect fit of the field-work with the postulated geometry, there could be no doubt that 'the most accurately determined value of the megalithic yard was indeed 2.722 ft.'

Thom also demonstrated a second standard unit: the 'megalithic rod' of 6.80 ft or 2.5 MY. Thus, 5 MY = 2 MR.

To illustrate the Avebury data, the Southern inner circle has a diameter close to 340 ft, i.e. 50 MR. That is also, astoundingly, the exact diameter of the Brogar ring on Orkney. Thom believed that the reason for using 50 MR or 125 MY is that such a diameter makes the circumference 392.699 MY — approximating to 392.5 MY or 157 MR — implying a value for π of 3.140.

These two 'yardsticks,' as the megalithic yard and the megalithic rod are collectively known, remained constant from before 3700 BC until after 1500 BC. Now the first farmers in what became the British Isles, whether immigrants or native, started sowing grain around 4500 BC: they evidently used the 3-4-5 right-angled triangle for laying out fields. Even if they were not already using MR/MY for measuring boundaries, and there is no evidence suggesting they were not, they were soon using them for designing stone rings, which are the oldest surviving large-scale, man-made structures in the world.

Because the only units required for analysis of the geometry of the stone circles were the megalithic yard and rod and the Greek foot (see below), Anne Macaulay's text makes no mention of Thom's additional discovery of the megalithic inch, measuring $^1/_{40}$ of 1 MY or $^1/_{100}$ of 1 MR — i.e. between 0.816 and 0.817 (just over $^4/_5$) Imperial inch. However, some mention of the 'MI' does further reinforce proof of the integrity as well as the antiquity of the megalithic measurement system. For instance, Bronze Age wooden measuring staves from Borum Eshoj and Borre Fen in Denmark have notches marking lengths of 1 MI; and bone artefacts from excavations at Balbirnie, Dalgety and Patrickholm in Scotland measure 1 MI. Other bone artefacts have been found near Callanish in the Outer Hebrides with zig-zag markings on one edge, every four zig-zags measuring exactly 1 MI.

The megalithic inch is important because it was the common unit of measurement (at least in Scotland and Northern England) for a vast array of the curious 'cup and ring' marks that were cut into rocks and large stones throughout Europe; sometimes only cups or holes scattered about the surface, or concentric rings round the cups, or spirals, or egg-shaped or yet more intricate patterns.

Thom commented: 'Instead of using dividers or compasses as we would today, the designer probably used beam compasses or trammels with the points set at fixed distances apart.' Furthermore,

> the terms of reference to which the designs were made were identical to those used in setting out the rings of standing stones. In both we find integral values of the unit used and in both the designs are usually based on right-angled trian-gles with all sides integral. Sets of cup-marks are also found in Brittany where there are again examples of complicated petroglyphs [pre-historic rock-carvings] in some of the tumuli [burial mounds or barrows].

Integral lengths, he emphasized, were the key to megalithic geometry. Graduated rules were unnecessary.

Less than fifty years later, it is hard to imagine the hostility and ridi-cule that greeted Thom's discoveries. Historians were still teaching that savages inhabited these islands until shortly before the Romans arrived. The notion that Neolithic Britons, 5 000 or more years ago, possessed an advanced knowledge of mathematics and astronomy, was mocked by the media and contemptuously dismissed by most archaeologists and anthropologists.

In 1969–70 the BBC produced a series of documentary programmes featuring Thom's work; one including a long interview between Thom and Magnus Magnusson during which Thom aired his theory concerning the 'cup-and-ring' markings that appear so frequently on megalithic monuments, saying: 'I have an idea — entirely nebulous at the moment — that these markings were a method of recording, of writing, that may indicate — once we can read them — what a particular stone was for.' Whereupon Magnusson replied: 'Your theories about Stone Age Einsteins have got up the back of some archaeologists. The idea that the cup and ring markings were used as writing has got up the backs of a lot more. Does it worry you?' To which Thom mildly answered: 'Not in the slightest. I just go on recording what I find.'

Towards the end of his life Thom wrote: 'I have shown elsewhere that megalithic man had a highly developed knowledge of geometry. It now appears that his knowledge of how to apply that knowledge puts him in line with the greatest civilizations of antiquity.'

'Caveman calculator' was another of the jibes flung at Thom's numerate megalithic man. As recently as 1984, scientists were still criticizing Thom's yardstick. Barnett and Moir (1984) stated: 'After reassessment of Thom's data on mensuration and geometry, we find that the quality of the surviving remains is not sufficiently high to give positive support for his hypothesis.' However, since then a revolution has occurred in attitudes. Of course, until 30 or 40 years ago the national media were limited in range, resources, status and self-confidence: their task was to serve and disseminate received opinion. Culturally they were largely conformist, transmitting academic orthodoxy. But since then the media have vastly grown in scale and influence, and hence in assertiveness — dominating rather than deferring to opinion — with an insatiable appetite for sensational discoveries and for debunking old beliefs — for innovation and iconoclasm. Consequently, under these popular pressures, certain areas of the academic establishment have become more open-minded.

Furthermore, scholars in every related discipline have meanwhile come to recognize the explosion in human knowledge that occurred

between 6 500 and 3 500 years ago — throughout the period that coincided precisely with the stone rings' building boom. The very earliest
forms of writing — ranging from the cuneiform tablets of Sumer and
Babylon to Mayan hieroglyphs and solar calendars — and the development of Proto-Indo-European languages, the introduction of the wheel
and domestication of the horse, all resulted from that explosion. As the
historian Arnold Harvey has said: 'Practically everything we know has
happened to man has happened since 3000 BC.'*

In the light of so many revelations of a rapidly advancing state of
civilization in different parts of the world over 4 000 years and more
ago, Thom's discovery of megalithic geometry seems almost mun-
dane and even Anne Macaulay's startling deductions and speculations
begin to appear quite plausible. After all, the dating of the stone rings
is irrefutable, as is their sheer size and number. Nor can there be any
doubt that the main function of the stone rings was astronomical. As
Thom wrote:

> A statistical analysis of the sites shows that they were so
> carefully erected that we can deduce (1) the inclination of
> the ecliptic, (2) the inclination of the lunar orbit, (3) the mean
> amplitude of the lunar perturbation and (4) the mean lunar
> parallax — with an accuracy better than one arc minute.

(An understanding of such astronomical technicalities is not required
in order to follow Anne Macaulay's work!) Moreover, Thom's identifi-
cation of the megalithic yard and rod is now universally accepted, or at
least acknowledged, however grudgingly in some quarters.

Macaulay was generous in acknowledging Thom's achievements. In
the draft typescript for this book, she wrote:

> His approach to astronomy led to the understanding of the
> ancient calendar with the quarter-days that still exist today!
> He surveyed very many sites with great accuracy, from
> which he was able to deduce the ancient yardsticks that

---

* In 1991 the 'Ice Man' was found in a gully on the Southern Alps, near the Austrian bor-
der; a freeze-dried mummy who had lain there, in a marvellous state of preservation,
since his death around 3000 BC — as exhaustive examinations showed — yet well-
shod, elaborately clothed and equipped, and having evidently enjoyed a varied diet.

they used: these have turned out to be identical to the later ancient Greek fathom and foot.* Professor Thom worked on the geometric plans that underlie the egg-shaped, elliptical and flattened rings. He also worked on the micro-geometry found in many places. Without the accurate and pioneering work of Professor Thom and his ability to approach the megalithic remains without the limitations of the standard theories, this research [of mine] would have been impossible.

This lengthy introduction has been necessary because Anne Macaulay, with the impatience of genius, plunges straight into her discoveries with precious little preamble! The Greek foot, her 'third yardstick,' provided the key to unlocking the complex system of distinct geometrical types represented by the whole range of stone 'circles.' She also demonstrated that, in addition to the primary yardsticks — the megalithic yard and rod and the Greek foot — the megalithic builders used two secondary yardsticks: the square root of 3 and the Golden Mean — of which, again, much more later — from which derived the Imperial foot.

Just as both Socrates and Aristotle were taught by Aspasia — the 'first lady of Athens' — and Pythagoras himself was taught mathematics by another woman, Aristoclea, so we all have a great deal to learn from Anne Macaulay.

---

* They hadn't simply 'turned out to be identical': she is being characteristically modest here — this was her second breakthrough, as we shall see later. EDS.

PART I

The Geometry of the
Megalithic Monuments

The geometry of the ancient megalithic Western Europe seems to have started, at the latest, early in the fourth millennium BC in what is now northern France, spreading to the British Isles before 3000 BC. From the beginning, all the sites were evidently designed on geometric figures. But this early mathematics was very different from the early mathematics that has been uncovered in ancient Mesopotamia (modern Iraq) and Egypt. For the early mathematics of the Near East was developed for practical purposes, to serve the growth of trade and political structures including systems of taxation; whereas mathematics in the megalithic West evolved as a sacred art and was used to lay out the plans for their sacred sites.

Numeracy was required by all early civilizations with the coming of farming. Moreover, numbers were looked upon as possessing distinctive qualities: e.g. number one represented the quality of oneness. Studies of symbolism contain frequent references to the ancient symbolism of numbers. But in the megalithic West, they were also exploring the shapes associated with various numbers. Hence they developed the art of geometry, working out how to create polygons accurately, based on as many as 14 sides.

Thom's conclusions from his surveys of the many megalithic rings in the British Isles and north-west France aroused much controversy — particularly his claim that the builders were using specific 'yardsticks' and defining the sites by means of geometry. But an intriguing discovery emerges from my further researches, revealing that the 'megalithic rod,' as worked out by Thom, is identical to the ancient Greek fathom, which measures exactly seven Greek feet — a known length — and a search through Thom's plans quickly demonstrated the presence of this Greek foot in megalithic Britain. This is detailed in Chapter 1, to establish the yardsticks precisely.

In Chapter 2, the explicit geometry is analysed. The sites in this group are of the 'Clava cairn' type, where there are three concentric circles and, exceptionally, with a certain number of (almost) equally spaced stones. Because of the three circles, a series of exact measures becomes apparent, clearly showing the methods used by these ancient geometers. The four types of flattened circles are examined in Chapter 3. All of them contain pentagrams.

But the most surprising feature that I found is that all the pentagrams — whether in flattened circles or in a full circle — were designed on Fibonacci ratios (see below), yet using different units of length to create the desired overall size for each site. The methods employed are explained more fully in Chapter 4. The plain circles (without inner circles), the ellipses and pairs of geometrically related circles have a chapter each: 5–7. Then in Chapter 8, pairs of circles that imply a larger geometry are investigated. These lead naturally to the egg-shaped rings in Chapter 9. Finally, Chapter 10 is made up of very exceptional 'one-offs.'

In all, about 180 site plans are analysed. The source for the diagrams is, of course, Professor Thom's work. He surveyed well over 200. He took extraordinary care with his surveys, measuring to all four corners of each stone and normally taking the average to establish the radius or other appropriate dimension — and marking the stones that were in their original position by shading. If a site is so ruinous that he could not determine the radius exactly, it is marked, for instance: ± 3'. There are, alas, many sites that Thom said could only be measured accurately from excavation in order to unearth the exact original setting. Burl estimates that of the 900 rings still standing in Britain, there are about 600 circles, 150 flattened circles, 100 ellipses and 50 eggs. So the choice of rings on which my work is based was very largely Thom's. There are plenty more megalithic rings waiting to be explored!

Those chosen by Thom were picked mainly from the stony and upland parts of the British Isles. It has become clear that in lowland England — that is, the fertile, eastern side — the same sort of sacred megalithic sites were created and marked with tree trunks instead of stones. Tree trunks rot in time and ploughing subsequently obliterates these lowland sites, though remains are occasionally found. A circle comprising 55 oak stumps was exposed off the Norfolk coast in 1998–99 (see Appendix 7).

Stonehenge (p.51) is the exceptional site in that they used stones which, by an immense feat of engineering, were brought there from southern Wales, to give permanence to that extremely important site.

The term 'megalithic' rings is used to cover the whole period from perhaps as early as 3800 BC until about 1200 BC during which time these sacred sites were developed. However, the dates of construction are not easy to assess. In only a few cases, such as Stonehenge — 3100 BC — has there been the luck to find the tools used in their making which can be carbon-dated. Hence the dating is not so accurate as the archae-ologists would like. Besides, dating the constructions merely tells us when the people had acquired the engineering knowledge to erect them; for all we know, they might have possessed the mathematical knowledge to plan and design them much earlier. That remains a mystery, because we are dealing with pre-literate history, of which the only record consists of artefacts that cannot cast any clear light on anything so coherent and intellectual as the state of mathematical knowledge.

Meanwhile, what we can deduce from the geometry represented by these great monuments — the oldest of all man-made structures — is astonishing enough. Most astonishing is the realization that the builders were already, at least prior to the start of this vast construction pro-gramme along the Atlantic seaboard, sophisticated geometers who, for instance, were familiar with the Fibonacci series, five millennia before it was first published by Leonardo of Pisa, popularly known as Fibonacci ('the son of Bonaccio') in 1202, and familiar too with the Golden Mean (or Golden Section) or *phi*. Since they feature prominently in my analy-ses of the diagrams, these are explained here.

The Fibonacci series begins with 0, 1, 1, 2, 3, 5, 8, 13, 21, 34, 55 ... where each term (after the first two) is the sum of the two immediately preceding terms. It has numerous fascinating characteristics, and governs not only the ratios of many dimensions in megalithic geometry (particu-larly pentagrams) but also those in many natural phenomena, including the laws relating to the multi-reflection of light through mirrors, the rhythmic laws of gains and losses in the radiation of energy, the ratios of males to females in honey bee hives and the breeding pattern of rabbits — a symbol of fecundity. The product of these ratios grows towards, until it approximates to, the value of 1.618034, which is the Golden Mean or *phi*. Thus, $5/3 = 1.666666$, $21/13 = 1.615$, $144/89 = 1.618$, $233/144 = 1.618055$, etc. Now this ratio *phi* governs universal laws of

Plan	Type	Number analysed
1	Type A flattened ring	2
2	B flattened ring	3
3	B modified flattened ring	2
4	D flattened ring	1
5	Circles containing pentagrams	1
6	Circles containing pentagrams enclosed in a pentagon	1
7	Pentagrams in decagons	0
8	Circles containing pentagrams enclosed in hexagrams or hexagons	3
	(All of the above contain pentagrams)	
9	Circles containing hexagrams as main geometry	3
10	— containing 7- or 14-pointed star on formula 51-46-22	5
11	— containing two geometries	1
12	— containing 8-pointed star on formula 13-12-5	2
13	— containing 9-pointed star on formula 14-9-(10.72) or circles (equilateral triangles with side 14 units — both methods were used)	3
14	— containing 11-pointed star on formula 37-20-(31.128)	2
15	Ellipses on Pythagorean triangles	1
16	Ellipses on ± 1 triangles	2
17	Ellipses on square root of 2 using the series 12-17-24-34	0
18	Pairs of circles geometrically related	0
19	Pairs of circles that are the centres of unmarked larger geometries	4
20	Egg-shaped rings (illustrated in Chapter 9)	16
21	Exceptional one-offs	4
	TOTAL	56

Table 1

proportion; discernible in marine shells, spiralling plants (phyllotaxis), classical architecture and the human frame. (It is classically illustrated by Leonardo da Vinci's drawing of 'Vitruvian Man' and discussed later)

Phi is most simply defined as the ratio of each of the longer sides to the shortest side in a triangle in which the angle at the narrow end is 36° and each of the other two angles is 72°; i.e. the larger is to the smaller precisely as their sum is to the larger. It is expressed as: $(\sqrt{5} + 1)/2$. Thus $(2.23607 + 1)/2 = 1.618034$.

However, this unique factor is also expressed by its inverse; i.e. $(2.23607 - 1)/2 = 0.618034$. Two further marvellous equations arise. One is that these two versions multiplied $(1.618034 \times 0.618034)$ produce precisely 1.000. The other is that 1.618034 squared $(1.618034 \times 1.618034)$ produces 2.618034.

The same symmetrical and harmonic patterns have been recognized in modern times in atomic structures, quantum and wave mechanics, hydrodynamics, electrochemical reactions and molecular bonding. The discovery that megalithic geometry embodies these twin mathematical keys reveals a degree of knowledge among the inhabitants of these islands some six thousand years ago that is far beyond what had ever been previously suspected.

I have analysed 56 sites in this book, comprising the 21 identified types of plan, as in Table 1.

Fig.1 The Arundel stone

1. Megalithic Yardsticks

Thom worked out two of the 'yardsticks' (i.e. fixed standards for measurement) that were used by the megalithic builders, the megalithic yard (MY) and the megalithic rod (MR). Though the megalithic yard has been recognized by a few scientists, it has received no general acceptance. Archaeologists believe that societies living in Britain were in too primitive a state and too fragmentary to have maintained any common standard. Even those few scientists who acknowledge the MY do so tentatively, since so many of the sites have diameters that are clearly not in exact megalithic measures. But the reasons why sometimes the diameters may not be in precise megalithic units emerge once they are analysed.

The two yardsticks deduced by Thom are, then:

The MEGALITHIC YARD (MY) = 2.72 Imperial feet = 0.8288 metres
The MEGALITHIC ROD (MR) = 6.80 Imperial feet = 2.072 metres

It occurred to me, however, that there is an exact equivalent of MR in the ancient Greek fathom. The ancient Egyptians and Romans made copies of their standard units in stone, but the Greeks did not, and so few records of their standard measures survive. The precise length of the Greek fathom remained unknown until Professor Fernie re-examined the Arundel Stone (see Fernie 1981). This is an Anatolian Greek stone pediment, as if to hang over a doorway or a lintel, depicting in shallow relief

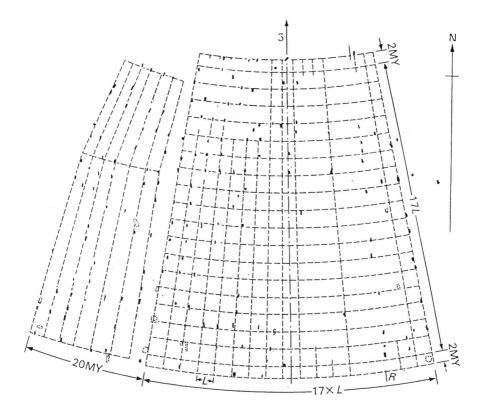

Fig.2 Mid Clyth, N 1 / 1, showing layout of sectors

a left-facing male head above front-facing shoulders and outstretched
arms and hands (his left broken off above the wrist) and, incongruously,
a bare footprint planted above his right shoulder (see Fig.1). It dates
from well before 400 BC.

The Greek fathom is defined from fingertip to fingertip of the male
figure's outstretched arms; the Greek foot by the length of the carved
footprint. This fathom is given as 2.07 metres long, but as the sculp-
ture is broken it cannot be measured precisely. The Greek foot is 0.296
metres. Now Fernie quotes the size of the Greek foot and recognizes that
$7 \times 0.296 = 2.072$ metres, but hesitates to claim that the Greek fathom
consists of exactly seven Greek feet because there is no other precedent
for a unit of length being divided into seven sub-units. But the MR as
calculated by Thom — his larger unit — coincides with this Greek

fathom — again the larger unit. (The margin of error is only 0.64mm.) Furthermore, the Greek foot itself appears in many megalithic sites. So here in Britain is the precedent for the Greek fathom comprising seven Greek feet.

$$1 \text{ Greek ft} = 0.97142 \text{ Imperial ft}$$
$$7 \text{ Greek ft} = 6.8 \text{ Imperial ft} = 1 \text{ MR}$$

The best example of the Greek foot is at Mid Clyth (see Fig.2), a fan of stone rows. The spacing of the rows both from north to south and along the southern edge is given as L, which is given by Thom as $20/7 \times \text{MY}$. Since $1 \text{ MR} = 2/5 \times \text{MY}$, then this is equal to $8/7 \times \text{MR} = 8$ Greek feet.

The Greek foot, therefore, was used by the megalithic builders as a distinct unit on its own.

(This provides an unexpected piece of evidence in the debate as to whether or not the megalithic designers actually used measuring rods.) The relationship between the MR and the Greek foot, conversely, enables the MY as representing $^2/_5$ of the Greek fathom, to fall comfortably into place.

Accordingly, to Thom's two megalithic yardsticks we can now add a third: the Greek foot of 0.971428 Imperial feet or 0.296 metres or $^1/_7$ MR.

In the analysis of the geometry, it is the proportion of the parts that is the essence of the design; therefore, in order to create the whole site on an appropriate scale, any multiple or fraction of these units could be used, as with customary units today.

2. The Explicit Geometry
of the Megalithic Rings

The explicit geometry emerges mainly from the Clava Cairn type of megalithic constructions which were designed with three concentric circles. I discovered that drawing tangents from the outer circle to the main circle produced exact polygrams, and then tangents from the main circle to the central space produced other exact polygrams. One cannot produce these sorts of polygrams with just any pair of concentric circles, so I realized that the polygrams had been laid out carefully by the original designers.

By comparing the measurements defined by Thom, it became clear how the designers achieved certain types of polygram. Squares and hexagrams, as the main geometry, appear only rarely. In these cases, the square or the triangle was first prescribed for the chosen site, after which the circle was described. And with pentagrams, the first arm of the chosen size was laid out before the enclosing circle was defined. Knowledge of the Golden Mean or *phi* is essential to an understanding of pentagrams, for all regular pentagrams are made up of five tangent triangles, revealing the *phi* ratio as defined earlier (the ratio of either of the longer sides to the shorter side of a triangle containing the two angles of 72° and one of 36°).

Some of the earliest megalithic sites are flattened circles, with pentagrams in them based on Fibonacci pairs; therefore it is undeniable that an understanding of Fibonacci ratios for laying out pentagrams was commonplace by 3200 BC, by which date construction of stone rings was well under way. This advanced mathematical knowledge must have been familiar even earlier in Brittany, where megalithic building started before 4000 BC. (The ancient Greeks, the Pythagoreans themselves, never appeared to use the Fibonacci series although indirect evidence suggests that they were aware of it; maybe the knowledge disappeared after the Western megalithic era until Leonardo of Pisa — Fibonacci — rediscovered it.)

Also in this chapter are a very few sites that are surrounded by a specific number of stones that turn out to hold the polygram simply defined by the number of stones themselves.

The Clava cairns and passage graves are basically all the same shape when geometry is involved. There is the central area for the deposition of burials or cremated remains. The shaded area was built up and filled with stones, beyond which is the functional area marked usually with a few tall standing stones.

The crucial measurements are: the inside edge of the inner ring, the outside edge of the main circle, and the centres of the few stones of the outer circle. This method presumes that the ancient geometers had laid out accurately the various polygons on the ground with string, but, apart from this specific group, it was only the circles surrounding them that were permanently marked out in stone. No straight lines were ever marked in stone, but that was for a practical reason — there had to be an open space where the people could congregate.

For all the geometric measures in the ensuing geometries, the error — quoted as the difference between my calculated length by use of trigonometry and Thom's measurement on the ground — is shown in inch decimals. Thom used feet and tenths of a foot, therefore any error under ± 0.6 in. (i.e. $^1/_{20}$ of one foot) is negligible — safely attributable to inaccurate setting out. It is remarkable how many of Thom's 'errors' fall inside this trivial fraction of an inch. This degree of exactitude, however, cannot be sustained for the more dilapidated sites, where many of the stones have been either removed or strewn meaninglessly out of their original settings. For in the past 4 000 and more years, there has been much damage, mainly since the Reformation when so many of these

Fig.3 Milton of Clava

supposedly 'pagan' sites were despoiled, particularly on Skye, Iona and along the west coast of Scotland. Also, in modern times, farmers have used the sites as quarries for stonewall building.

Milton of Clava, Inverness
(Figs.3–4, Thom ref. 248)

This structure represents a pentagram based on the 5 / 8 Fibonacci numbers, unit 1 MR, with outer hexagram. These remains of a Clava cairn lie in the Nairn valley about half a mile upstream from the main Clava cairns. There is only one stone remaining of the outer circle, recently blown over by a gale.

	Thom's measures	Calculated	Error
Diameter of main circle	57.8' (8.5 MR)	57.84' (8.5065 MR)	0.53"
Diameter of inner circle	22.0'	22.095'	1.14"
	Burl's measure		
Diameter of outer circle	c. 100'	100.19'	2.28"

If the main circle has a diameter of 8.5 MR, then the enclosed pentagram has arms of 8 MR wide and a foot spacing of 5 MR.

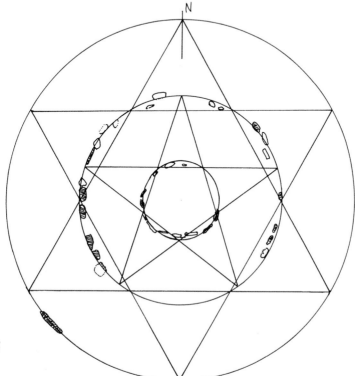

Fig.4

Castle Dalcross (Dalcross Mains), Inverness
(Fig.5, T254)

This represents a pentagram based on Fibonacci numbers 8 / 13, unit 3 GF, with outer hexagram.

	Thom's measures	Calculated	Error
Diameter of main circle	39.2'	39.66'	5.52"
Inner circle (no measure is given but it is drawn in)		12.26'	
	Burl's measure		
Diameter of outer circle	c. 70'	68.69'	1.31'

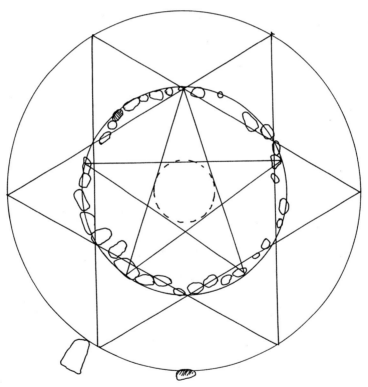

Fig.5

Loch Mannoch, Kirkcudbrightshire
(Fig.6, T282)

A pentagram on Fibonacci 3 / 5, unit 1.5 MY (4.08'), lying on a slight plateau six miles west of Castle Douglas and two miles ENE of Loch Whinyeon. It comprises a circle of ten equally spaced stones.

	Thom's measures	Calculated	Error
Diameter of main circle	21'	20.82'	2.16"

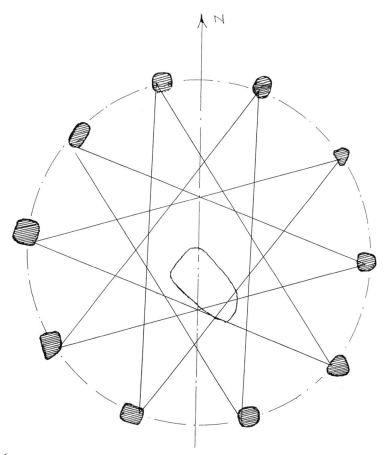

Fig.6

Comment on the pentagrams

The Milton of Clava pentagram is made using Fibonacci numbers and
the central circle is formed by the junction of the arms of the pentagram.
The Castle Douglas pentagram is also made using Fibonacci numbers,
with the inner circle tangent to the arms of the pentagram. The Loch
Mannoch site, which is marked by 2 × 5 stones, was created simply by
use of Fibonacci numbers.

From this material, it is already clear that the designers of the
geometric plans had some means to hand of defining the pentagram,
and that they were using the Fibonacci series. The actual method
that they used to draw out these accurate pentagrams emerges when
the 'flattened circle type B modified' is examined — see Chapter 3:
Whitcastles (p.69).

Comment on the hexagrams

Two of these sites have hexagrams forming the outer ring. There are others, however, that have an extension of the pentagram in the form of a
ten-pointed star, or sometimes an unrelated polygon. The hexagon and
hexagram are the most commonly used figures for defining the outer ring
throughout all the figures analysed. The advantage of using the hexagon
or hexagram is clear. After the inner geometry was defined, the surrounding circle was marked out; so they had already achieved the radius which
could be used to mark off the six equal divisions of that circle in order to
define a complete hexagon or hexagram. Evidently they knew the method
of dividing a circle into six equal parts that is used today. No exact measurements and no metrical calculations were required — just accurate
geometric drawing!

Heptagrams and 14 Stars

River Ness (Kinchyle of Dores), Inverness
(Fig.7, T272)

This is a 14-pointed star, based on a unit of $^1/_2$ MY. It is a Clava passage grave, situated $4^1/_2$ miles SW of Inverness.

	Thom's measures	Calculated	Error
Diameter of outer circle	25.4 MY (69.1')	$51 \times MY / 2$	3.1"
Diameter of inner circle	10.85 MY (29.5')	$22 \times MY / 2$	5.04"

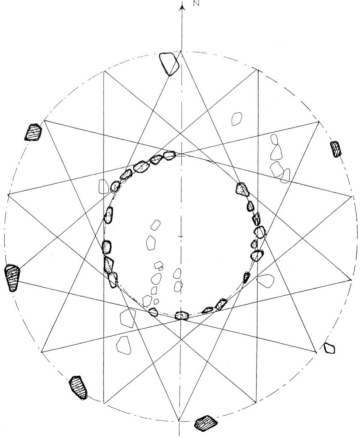

Fig.7

Before going any further with this example, comparison with a second site is helpful.

Tomnagorn, Aberdeen
(Figs.8–10, T220)

This is a heptagram, unit MY / 3. It consists of a rather dilapidated recumbent stone
circle, located four miles NNE of Torphins.

	Thom's measures	Calculated	Error
Diameter of outer circle	*c.* 27 MY (73.44')	81 × MY / 3 (74.16')	8.64"
Diameter of main circle	17 MY	51 × MY / 3	exact
	Burl's measure		
Diameter of central stone-linedspace	*c.* 12'	11.35'	7.8"

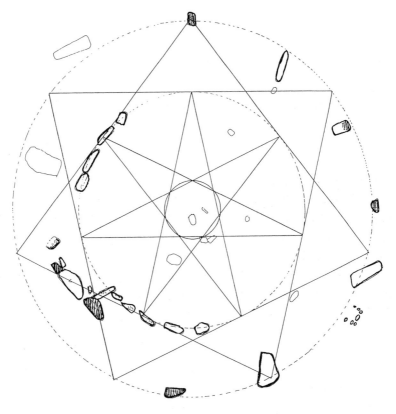

Fig.8

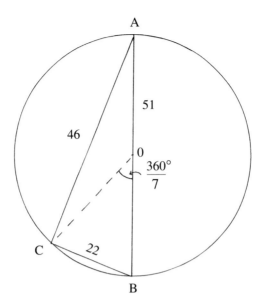

Fig.9

Take the main circle as 17 MY. If the unit is taken as ¹/₃ MY, then there are 51 units in the diameter — the same number of units as the circle at River Ness. The outer circle is formed by drawing tangents at the 7 points of the star on the outside of the main geometry and terminating at the second junction.

Now return to the River Ness site. The diameter of the main circle *AB* is 51 units. The diameter of the inner circle is 22 units and, when projected onto the larger circle *CB*, forms a right-angled triangle *ABC* with *AC* tangent to the inner circle.

Therefore $AC = \sqrt{51^2 - 22^2} = 46.010868$ and $22/51 = \sin CAB$, which, × 2, gives the angle *COB* at the centre: i.e. $22/51 = \sin 0.431372 = 25.554697°$

$25.554697° \times 2 = 51.109394°$ (the angle at the centre '0')

NB $360/7 = 51.42857°$

Following directly from this, the line *AC* covers ⁵/₁₄ of the circle in the angle *AOC*.

So from any circle with a diameter of 51 units, they could use a chord of 22 units length, to mark off seven equal divisions on the circumference (as at Tomnagorn), or else, by using a chord of 46 units, they could mark off 14 equal spaces (as at River Ness).

Fig.10 Tomnagorn

Having marked off the desired number of points on the main circle, they could join these points in a variety of ways, according to the desired size of the central circle. At Tomnagorn, they chose the heptagram and joined every third point on the circumference. At River Ness, they marked out all 14 points by using the cord of 46 units, and joined every fifth point, making a 14 point star. The central ring at this site is too destroyed even to hazard a guess as to its measure — but judging by other sites it would also have had internal geometry.

Presumably by trial and error the ancient geometers had worked out a set of three whole numbers, 51-46-22, which were used to mark the division of a circle into 14 or 7 equal parts. Note that $51 \times 51 = 2\,601$, while $(46 \times 46) + (22 \times 22) = 2\,116 + 484 = 2\,600$.

It is now clear how these ancient geometers were able to lay out circles on the various polygrams. Their method for making 7 and 14-pointed stars did not stop here. They had also discovered pairs of numbers or triangles for dividing circles into 8, 9 and 11 equal parts.

Fig.11 Stonehenge

Octagrams
The megalithic geometers were so proficient that I even suspected they would define the octagram by drawing a nominal north/south line and then an east/west line, as they were able to do in other geometries, and then halve the quarters to form the octagon. But that was not so.

Stonehenge

This is a very early site, dated to 3100 BC. But that date applies to the first stage when the ditch and bank, as well as the 'Aubrey' holes were created. What was originally placed in the central area remains unknown. On excavation by Atkinson, the central area was found to have multiple traces of reworking and resetting of stones, so numerous that no patterns could be detected. The stone settings to be seen today are the unfinished last reworking of the site before it was virtually abandoned about 1400 BC.

The Aubrey holes are a series of pits, 56 in all, that were filled with pieces of white chalk, apparently the original filling and without any signs of having either wooden posts or standing stones in them. They are named after John Aubrey, a seventeenth century antiquarian, who detected them beneath dense vegetation.

Keith Critchlow, the well-known authority on sacred architecture, recognized the presence of both an octagram and a heptagram on the Stonehenge plan, reinforced by the pattern of Aubrey holes: $7 \times 8 = 56$.

The diameter of the Aubrey hole circle is given by Thom as 104 MY. If the unit is taken as 8 MY, there are 13 units in the diameter. A perfect Pythagorean triangle, 13-12-5, can be fitted into the diameter. The position of the octagram is clearly defined by the four station stones. Constructing an octagram generates a central circle with diameter of 5 units, spanning 40 MY. This central space was the inner sanctum of the site within which most of the constructions of different periods were sited. The 13-12-5 triangle was consistently used to produce octagrams in other sites.

Fig.12 Stonehenge

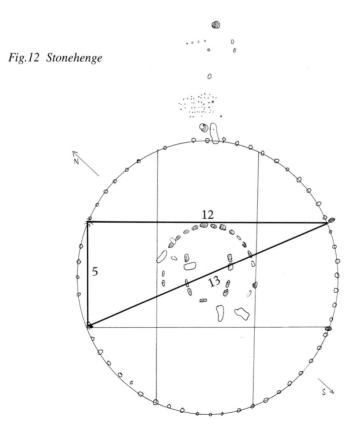

$5/13 = 0.384615 = \sin 22.6199°$

Therefore the angle at the centre is $45.2397°(360/8 = 45°)$

As there are 56 Aubrey holes (i.e. 7×8), there is the suggestion that a 7-pointed star was also present. By calculation, the outer intersection of the arms of the heptagram measures 37.11717 MY $= 100.96'$, the error for 37 MY being $3.82''$. The inner and outer faces of the sarsen circle are given by Thom as having circumferences of 45 MR (112.5 MY) and 48 MR (120 MY) respectively.

The diameter of the inner face is 35.8098 MY and of the outer face 38.1972 MY. So the diameter of the centre of this circle is 37.003 MY, which is the same size as the circle formed by the heptagram.

The sarsen circle was a feature of the later alterations to the site at Stonehenge: that they chose 37 MY as the central diameter for this circle indicates that the original geometry of the octagram and 7-pointed star was still remembered. Note, however, that the centres for the various additions were altered, so that the position of the early circle of the heptagram is slightly squint on the sarsen circle.

Fig.13 Stonehenge

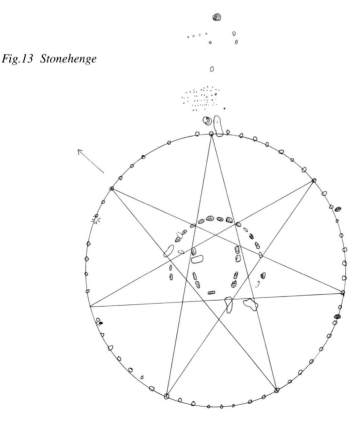

Easter Delfour
(Fig.14, T256)

An octagram surrounded by a hexagram, unit $^5/_3$ MY (or $^2/_3$ MR) and using 13-12-5 triangle, situated 4 miles SSW of Aviemore.

	Thom's measures	Calculated	Error
Diameter of inner ring	not given	22.666' = 5 × $^5/_3$ MY	
Diameter of main ring	max. 22 MY		
	min. 21.01 MY		
	mean 21.666 MY	58.933' = 13 × $^5/_3$	MY10.9"
Outer circle	104.6'	102.075' = 15 MR	2.525'

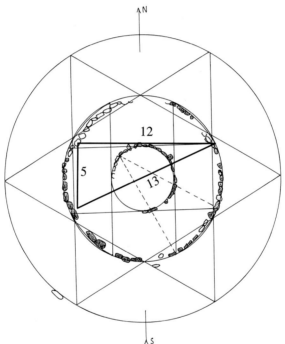

Fig.14

The main ring, however, is not a true circle. The four main divisions, N/S and E/W, are enclosed in its circle, but the remaining four divisions are slightly flattened by drawing an arc centred on the opposite side of the central circle. That is, the NW side was centred on the SE of the central circle, and so on for the four flattened parts of the main circle.

This device emphasizes the effect of the cross, placed in this site due N/S and E/W. The proportions of this cross (equivalent to the station stones at Stonehenge) are shown on the diagram. The outer circle, of which only one standing stone survives, is formed by a hexagram.

Nine Stars

Loch Buie, Mull
(Fig.15, T320)

There are nine nearly equally spaced stones around this site.

	Thom's measures	Calculated	Error
Diameter of circle	44.1'	43.97'	1.56"

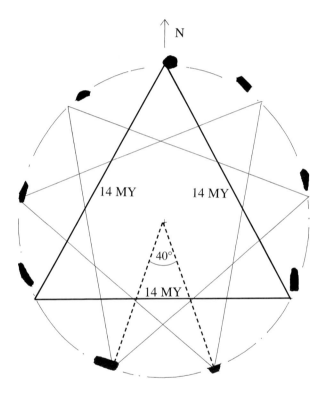

Fig.15

This geometry turns out to be extraordinarily illuminating, with even a touch of humour! The nine equally spaced stones suggest it might contain a 9-pointed star. The circle is the right size to contain an equilateral triangle with sides 14 MY in length. In this design, each point of the three triangles would lie on one of the stones. The angle subtended at the centre to each of the 9 points would be $360/9 = 40°$. Coincidentally, $14 \times \sin40° = 8.99903$ MY; or, conversely, other way round, $9/14 = 0.6428 = \sin40.0052°$.

But first a clue to the solution emerges, at a later date, in Minoan Crete. Around 1700 BC onwards, among the many carved seal stones in the Heraklion Museum, there appear some with geometric designs on them. These are directly comparable to megalithic geometry. There are at least two examples of another geometry formed by an equilateral triangle with circles placed on the three points. Exploring the possibilities here, two figures emerge:

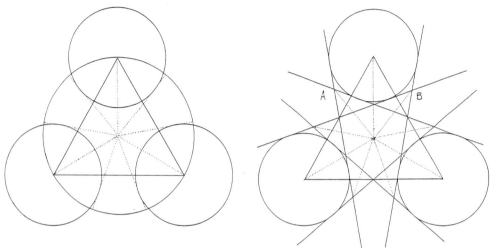

Fig.16a and 16b

Figure 16a:
* Define a triangle with sides 14, and draw a circle enclosing it.
* At each point of the triangle, define circles with a diameter of 9.
* Draw tangents to the small circles, omitting those in the centre and those outside the circle.
* The points *A* and *B,* where the two tangents intersect, are now joined to the centre point, with angles of 40° at the centre.

However, there is an easier method.

Figure 16b:
* Define a circle diameter 14, and mark off the three equally spaced points.
* Draw a circle with a diameter of 9 at each of the three points on the circumference.
* Draw tangents from the centre to the small circles.
* Using trigonometry, the angles at the centre are sin 9 / 14 = 40.0052°.

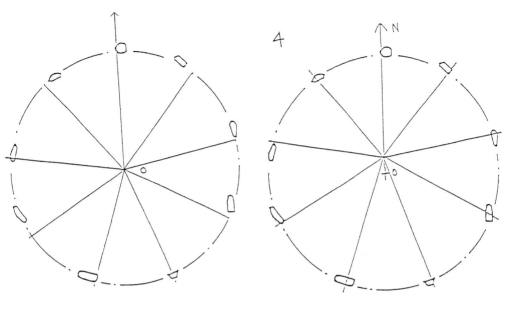

Fig.16c and 16d

Figure 16c:
The nine stones fail to fall exactly on the nine 40° divisions.

Figure 16d:
Now move the centre to the north and use Figure 16b. If the site was
planned and laid out on the plan of Figure 16b with the centre nearer
north, then all the nine divisions fall on stones or at the side of stones.
The latter were presumably astronomical site lines.

Decagrams
No case of a decagram as the main geometry has emerged, yet it does
appear as a secondary to the pentagram or a pair of pentagrams. There
seems no method for distinguishing between a single pentagram (or pair
of pentagrams in the case of the Loch Mannoch circle with ten stones)
and a few others.

There are, however, two examples using divisions by ten for the outer
circle (Figs.19 and 20).

Fig.17 and 18 Farr West

Farr West
(Figs.17–19, T266)

This is based on a pentagram and decagram. The centre is a 'type B flattened circle' surrounded by a star, created on the 5 / 8 Fibonacci numbers, with the unit 1 MR. The ten points for the decagram can be achieved from the pentagram. The site is located in Strathnairn, 12 miles south of Inverness.

	Thom's measures	Calculated	Error
Diameter of outer circle	113.2'	112'	1.2'
Diameter of inner circle	66.8'	66.4	4.8"

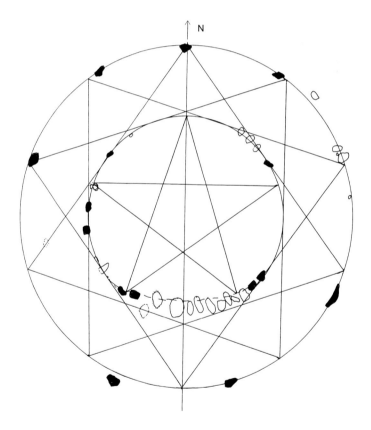

Fig.19

Loanhead of Daviot
(Figs.20–22, T190)

Here a decagram encloses a pentagram, which is made on the Fibonacci 3 / 5 pair, with the unit 11 GF. It is located 4 miles west of Old Meldrum in Aberdeenshire.

	Thom's Measures	Calculated	Error
Diameter of main circle	54.4' (8 MR)	55.88'	1.48'
Diameter of outer circle	68'	68.77'	9.2"

Burl's measurement

67.25'		1.52'

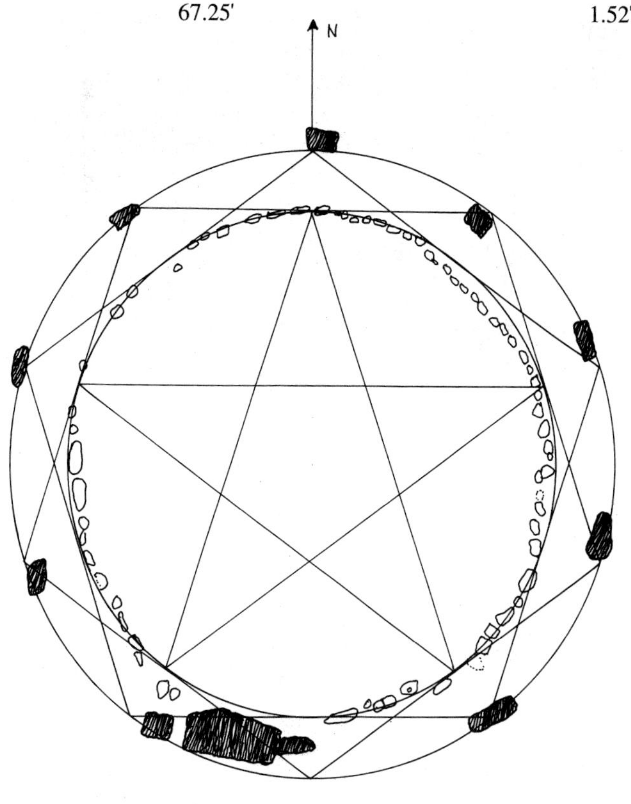

Fig.20

The outer circle is created by drawing tangents to the points of the pentagram — i.e. a pentagon — and then by drawing a second pentagon halfway between the first five points. As at Loch Mannoch, there are ten stones in the outer ring. It is impossible to be sure whether in both cases there were two pentagrams implied or not. In reality, the decagram in this site consists of two pentagons.

Fig.21 and 22 Loanhead of Daviot

Seven Stars

Aquorthies Manor, Aberdeenshire
(Figs.23–24, T162)

This is one of the rare sites where the number of nearly equally spaced stones in
the circle — 11 in this case — gives the clue to the internal geometry of the site:

(i) the diameter of the circle is 37 units of $^1/_4$ MR;
(ii) the triangle used is 37 / 31.128 / 20 — not a true Pythagorean triangle but still a
   right-angled triangle — $37 \times 37 = 1\,369$ while $31.128 \times 31.128 = 968.95238 +$
   $(20 \times 20) = 1\,368.95238$;
(iii) 20 / 37 = sin32.72044° = 2 × 32.72044° at the centre;
(iv) 360 / 11 = 32.7272.

	Thom's measures	Calculated	Error
Diameter	63.0'	62.9'	1.2"

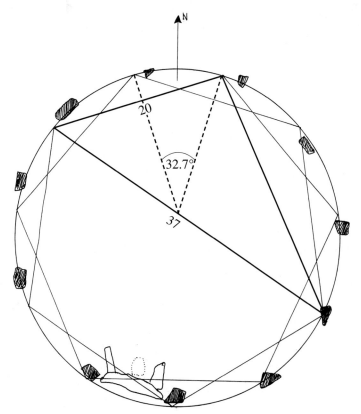

Fig.23

Fig.24 Aquorthies Manor

If a line 20 units in length is drawn as a chord within a circle of 37 units diameter, and walked round the circle, then it divides the circumference into 5.5 parts and 11 on the second round.

Twelve-pointed Star

No twelve-pointed star has emerged so far. It would, however, have been easy enough to make, simply by halving the angles of the hexagram. But the hexagram does not seem to have been used as an internal construction for main circles except on rare occasions — it is normally external to the central geometry.

Twenty-six-pointed Star

Aquorthies, Kingausie, Kincardine
(Figs.25–26, T226)

This is a heptagram and 26-pointed star, based on unit 1 GF, creating a fine recumbent stone circle, situated $4^1/_2$ miles SE of Peterculter. The 51-46-22 formula is used to mark out the seven equal divisions on the main circle, while the 26-point star was fashioned from the 51-77 formula, by taking a chord 51 GF long and marking off units on the circle of diameter 77 GF, three times round, until 26 points are made.

Each point subtends an angle of $360/26 = 13.846°$ at the centre.

$51/77 = 0.6623 = \sin 41.47°$ which, divided by $3 = 13.823°$.

Thus, the use of strong 51 and 77 units creates a 26-pointed star.

	Thom's measures	Calculated	Error
Diameter of outer circle	76.9088 GF (74.7114')	75.1'	4.66"
Diameter of main circle	51 GF (49.5428')	49.7'	1.88"

Burl's measure

Diameter of inner circle	11.348 GF (11.024')	11.00'	0.288"

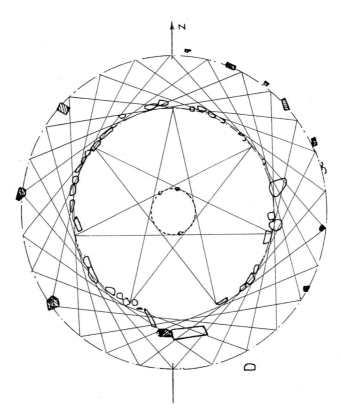

Fig.25

Comments on the methods used in the explicit geometry

It was a great surprise to discover so much about the techniques and practices used in the designs of the explicit variety of standing stone circles. So much information has emerged about the methods from (a) the sites with three rings and (b) some of the sites with an exact number of stones equally spaced on the circle, that the question arises whether all the standing stone structures in the British Isles were laid out in a similar way and — further — whether they were using the same yardsticks.

Stonehenge is the only site in southern England to have markers — i.e. an outer and an inner ring to mark the heptagram and the station stones to mark the octagram — which might be taken to indicate a special relationship between Stonehenge and the Clava cairn types in the north-east of Scotland. But it may merely illustrate the variable practices for setting out sites that are found in many different areas.

In the next chapter the flattened circles are re-analysed. This sector discloses even more surprising evidence of the expertise of the megalithic geometers.

Fig.26 Aquorthies (Kingausie, Aberdeenshire)

3. Re-analysis of Thom's Flattened Circles

It was only after most of the other sites had been analysed that re-analysis of the flattened circles became comprehensible. Many other circles, of different types, contain various polygrams, which seems to have been their purpose. What then was the original purpose in creating these odd-shaped rings that we call flattened circles?

There are estimated to be about 150 remains of them in the British Isles, widely spaced throughout the standing stone areas. Burl equates the early flattened circles as comparable to the henges, both in use and time. It is presumed that the larger ones are earlier than the smaller; but the flattened circles were first constructed in hilly areas, particularly the Lake District, whereas the henges were built on more even, lower ground. The first appearance of flattened circles precedes the elliptical forms in Britain, yet their design continued to be used long after the newer shapes had been incorporated into the canon.

Thom then worked out that there were four types of flattened circle, which he identified as Types A, B, B (modified) and D. On re-analysis, 'Type B modified' is by far the most important form, with Type D coming second. All the flattened circles contain pentagrams, all made on Fibonacci pairs of numbers, as described in Chapter 2.

'Type B modified' is the most important because it has the exact construction to produce the Golden Mean *(phi)* and must have demonstrated the method to be used for achieving this relationship in all the other sites. Type D is the next most important because it can produce *phi* but only correct to three decimal places and by a different formula that was too elaborate to have been used generally. Types A and B were 'celebrations' of the pentagram, differing little from the many other pentagrams enclosed in complete circles. Type A is a pentagram enclosed in a circle; Type B is a pentagram enclosed in a hexagon. Essentially, the curves that join the 'flattening' to the circle are purely aesthetic in the other three types but in the 'B modified' type this curve is a fundamental part of the geometry.

One third of all the rings analysed here have pentagrams as the central geometry. Therefore, the use of Fibonacci numbers was widespread in both space and time.

Thom conjectured that flattened circles related to the gradual increase in accuracy of megalithic man's understanding of the incommensurable relationship between the length of the circumference and the diameter of a circle (π = 3.14159265... etc.). For it was perhaps taken originally to be 3, then about $3^1/_8$; hence the fact that there are more circles with a diameter of 8 MY than any other number. He points out (Thom 1978) that: 'The product of $3^1/_8 \times 8 = 25$ and so the circumference was assumed to be 10 MR of $2^1/_2$ MY each. Still later it was obviously realized that $3^1/_8$ was not perfect; witness that at Brogar (p.94) a value of 3.140 was accepted. It is shown in Thom (1967, p.47), that when the diameter was irreconcilable with the circumference in integers it was often slightly adjusted in order to make both approximately integral.'

The four types of flattened circle as defined by Thom are:

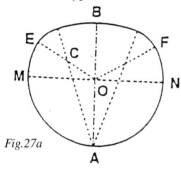

Fig.27a

Flattened circle type A
< EOF = 120°   OC/OE = $^1/_2$
AB/MN = 0.9114

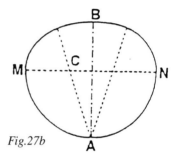

Fig.27b

Flattened circle type B
MC/MN = $^1/_3$ *AB/MN* = 0.8604

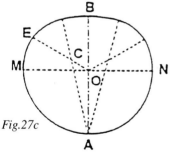

Fig.27c

Flattened circle type D
OC/OE = $^1/_3$ *AB/MN* = 0.9343

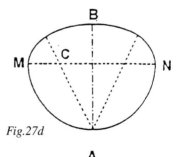

Fig.27d

Flattened circle type B modified
MC/MN = $^1/_4$ *AB/MN* = 0.8091

Though Thom had no idea what these figures were about, he scrupulously measured the relationship of the flattening to the diameter, *AB/MN,* and his figures are quite remarkably similar to those that emerge from careful calculation of the new analysis.

All the flattened circles turn out to contain accurate pentagrams. The most important type — B modified — defines the method of creating an accurate triangle with the narrow end containing the angle of 36° and the other two angles being 72°. This triangle is essential to define an accurate pentagram. Once this first triangle is achieved, it can be enclosed in a circle, and then the other four similar triangles filled in. This procedure involves quite sophisticated techniques, yet they had achieved an even more surprising sophistication by always using the Fibonacci numbers in order to create their pentagrams.

Re-analysis of the four types of flattened circle

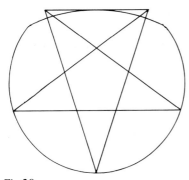

Fig.28a

Flattened circle type A

AB/MN = 0.9045

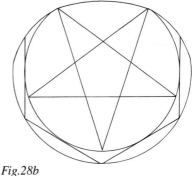

Fig.28b

Flattened circle type B

AB/MN = 0.8906

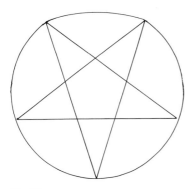

Fig.28c

Flattened circle type D

AB/MN = 0.934258

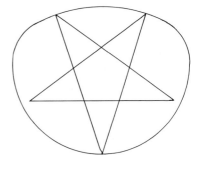

Fig.28d

Flattened circle type B modified

AB/MN = 0.8090

Though the megalithic geometers used Fibonacci numbers, they naturally tended to take the short side as accurate, realizing that the long side might be slightly different from its Fibonacci pair. In the Summary Table at the back of this book (see Appendix 8), there are only three exceptions where, in using the 3-5 pair of Fibonacci numbers, they have started with the '5' measure, leaving the '3' measure to be derived from $5/phi$ — i.e. $5/1.618034 = 3.0902$ — in other words, not an exact measure.

Re-analysis of the 'type B modified' flattened circle

Whitcastles, Dumfriesshire
(Figs.29–31, T300)

This is a pentagram on Fibonacci 34/55 and unit 1 MY, located 6 miles north of Lockerbie.

	Thom's measures	Calculated	Error
Length of main radius	34 MY	34 MY	exact
Short diameter	55 MY	55.013 MY	0.424"

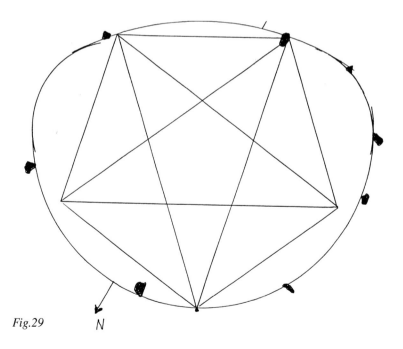

Fig.29   N

Fig.30 Whitcastles

The method of laying out pentagrams and the Golden Mean in 'type B modified' rings:

Having chosen the site, the size and direction in which it is to be laid out, they would first prepare the ground. By archaeology, it has been discovered that a few sites were ploughed to level the ground before building started and a very few sites had to be cleared by burning.

At Whitcastles, the chosen orientation was marked out by placing *COD* at right angles to *AB*. At centre *O* a circle diameter was defined by *GJ* measuring 34 MY. Then at centre *E* a second circle diameter *OB* was defined — also — 34 MY; and two lines (shown dotted) were marked out, tangent to the *O* and *E* circles, and touching *CD* at *G* and *J*.

Then, with centres *G* and *J*, two more circles were described, each diameter 34 MY, aligning *BGK* and *BJN*.

If we let the measure 34 MY equal 1 unit, then in the triangle *GOB*, $OG = 0.5$ and $OB = 1$

Therefore, $BG = \sqrt{(0.5^2 + 1^2)} = \sqrt{1.25} = 1.118033989$

Then add $KG = 0.5$: therefore $BK = 1.618033989$, which is the correct figure today for the Golden Mean.

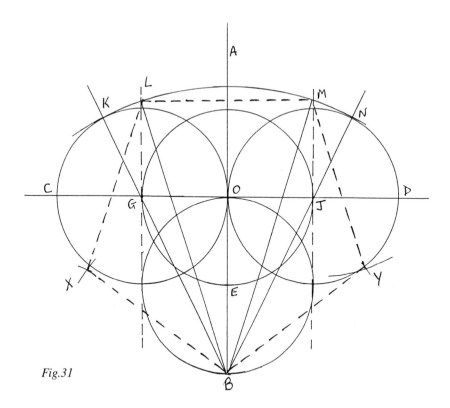

Fig.31

To create the triangle with the exact angle 36°, with centre *B* and radius *BK*, swing an arc *KLMN* over the top of the figure. As *LM* = 1 and *BK* = *phi*, the triangle *LMB* forms one of five triangles that make up the pentagram; or, in original measurements, *LM* = 34 MY, *BK* = 55 MY.

Accordingly, with centre *L* and length *LM* (=1), swing a small arc below *K*.

Next, centred on *M*, repeat arc below *J*.

Centred on *B*, mark an arc to both small arcs (*X* and *Y*).

The intersections represent the other two corners of the pentagram.

Finally, connect *LMYBXL* to complete the pentagram.

Pobull Fhinn, North Uist
(Fig.32, T316)

This is a type B modified flattened circle, using the 8 / 13 Fibonacci pair and unit 8 GF.

(Hadingham comments: 'An intriguing monument by the shores of Loch Langass, less than a mile SE of A867 and about 6 miles from Lochmaddy. Walk there via Barpa Langass chambered cairn which is extremely well preserved.')

	Thom's measures	Corrected	Error
Diameter	125'	128 GF = 124.343'	7.9"

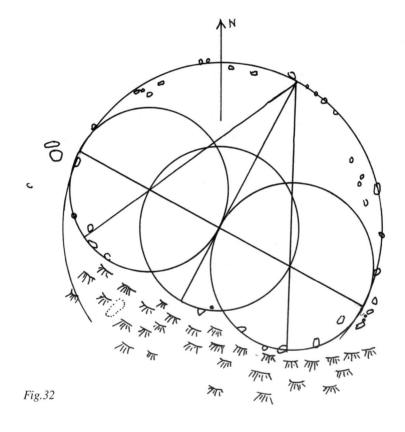

Fig.32

Like all this type, the diameter is twice the shorter of the chosen Fibonacci pair of numbers, and the length of the lesser diameter is the chosen lower number multiplied by *phi* exactly.

When Thom drew out the geometry of the various types, he used the least possible markings. It is obvious from the construction of this site that the small equal circles could be drawn on the greater diameter, but did the megalithic designers draw all these circles forming two vesicas? (A vesica, or *vesica piscis,* due to its fish shape, is a pointed oval figure, the sides of which are properly parts of two equal circles passing through each other at their centres.) In this case the site was deliberately laid out so close to a steep downward sloping bank that there is no space for the flattened side to be marked out and so the outline of the three small circles is defined instead.

Flattened circle type D
Type D, like type B modified, produces a formula for achieving the *phi* relationship, correct to three decimal places, but different to the normal method. The type D version is:

$(\sqrt{13} + 2) / (2 \times \sqrt{3}) = 5.605551275 / 3.464101615 = 1.618176.$
phi $= 1.618034$ (a difference of 0.000142!)

There are only two examples of type D in Thom's surveys: Seascale (T46) and Rough Tor (T86), but two more have emerged. In all of them, the Fibonacci series was used, the individuality of the *phi* relationship being:
Seascale $^5/_8$, unit 1.5 MR   Rough Tor $^8/_{13}$, unit 4 MY

Construction of the flattened circle

Step 1
Choose a pair of Fibonacci numbers, select a unit of length, and lay the lower number out on the chosen ground, at the chosen orientation, *AB.*

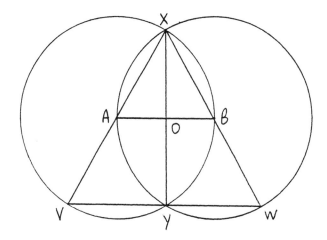

Fig.33

Step 2

Using *AB* as a radius, draw two intersection circles centred on *A* and *B*, generating a *vesica piscis,* with apices *X* and *Y.*

Now extend *XB* to right-hand circle *W,* and extend *XA* to left-hand circle *V,* and join *XY.*

Since *XB* = *BW* and the angle *XYW* = 90°, therefore — by congruent triangles — *YW* = 2 × *OB* = *AB,* therefore $XY^2 = XW^2 - YW^2$

If *YW* = 1 and *XW* = 2, therefore $XY^2 = 4 - 1$, and therefore $XY = \sqrt{3}$

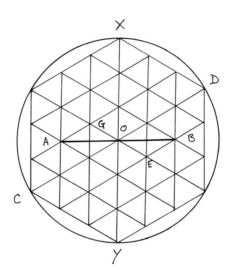

Fig.34

Step 3

With centre *O,* at the intersection of *AB* and *XY,* and using radius *OX* or *OY,* define a circle, and mark off the six equidistant points of a hexagon starting at *X* or *Y,* and draw in the hexagon.

Step 4

Define the three main diagonals of the hexagram, by joining opposite corners *CD, XY, MN.* Draw a line parallel to *CD* passing through the point *B,* and then complete the triangular web throughout the hexagon. Next, define an intersection of the hexagonal web, *G,* between *A* and *O.*

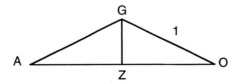

Fig.35

If $OG = 1$, then (by the geometry of hexagon equilateral triangles) $GZ = \frac{1}{2}$

Therefore $OZ^2 = 1^2 - GZ^2 = 1 - \frac{1}{4} = \frac{3}{4}$

Therefore $OZ = \sqrt{3}/2$ Therefore $AO = \sqrt{3}$

Now, let $OG = 1$, the basic unit, then $AO = \sqrt{3}$ and $AB = 2 \times \sqrt{3}$

So the whole figure has been reduced to basic proportions.

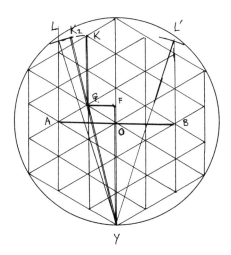

Fig.36

Step 5

Let F be a point a half-cell width above O.

Since $AO = \sqrt{3}$, therefore $GF = \sqrt{3}/2$

Join $FY = 3.5$, thus forming the triangle GFY

Then $(\sqrt{3}/2)^2 + 3.5^2 = GY^2 = 13$

Therefore $GY = \sqrt{13}$

Step 6

Join GK (which is 2 units) and swing round a radius to be in line with $YGK(2)$. So $GK(2) = GK$

Step 7

Extend the lines at right angles to AB from A and from B to cut the circle perimeter; with centre Y and radius $YK(2)$ swing this length to cut the A vertical line at L. Repeat with centre Y and radius $YK(2)$ to cut the B vertical line at L'

Thus $LL' = AB$

The triangle $LL'Y$ is one side of a pentagram. The upper angles YLL' $= YL'L = 72°$, and the lower (pentangle) $LYL' = 36°$

The points *L* and *L'* lie inside the original circle, so the centre for the circle enclosing the pentagram is slightly below that of the main centre.

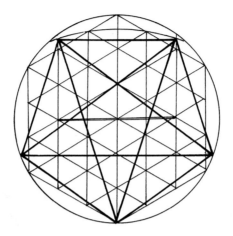

Fig.37

The only part of the pentagram that touches the original circle is at the bottom. The next two higher points do not touch the circle but are so close that they appear to do so.

The only measured element in the whole figure is *AB,* which was the lower of a pair of Fibonacci numbers. With this construction, the length *AB* is developed in such a way that the two incommensurable figures — $\sqrt{3}$ and *phi* — could be defined on the ground.

If the diameter of the outer circle is 6, then *YL* is 5.605551275 (the flattened element).

Now, 5.6055515 / 6 = 0.934258 whereas Thom's figure is 0.9343.

So not only did the builders define the whole arc of *YL* to *YL',* they also drew attention to this feature by flattening the circle.

Flattened circle type D (not standard)

Loch nan Carragean
(Fig.38, T260)

Based on Fibonacci 13/ 21 and unit 1 MY, this unusual site is located near Aviemore. Such rare examples of non-conforming geometries have an appeal of their own.

In this case, it is the circle containing the pentagram that has been used for 'flattening' the circle. This provides confirmation of the method that was used for the type D flattened circles. Thom tried and failed to make this figure into an ellipse.

	Thom's measures	Calculated	Error
Large diameter (north to south)	22.5 MY	22.51666 MY	0.543"
Small diameter (west to east)	21.93 MY	22.1169 MY	6.10"

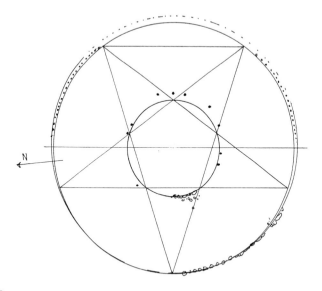

Fig.38

The two arcs joining the east section with the western half seem to have been made with the larger radius, since its centre was moved towards the west.

Type D flattened circles are easy to detect because, by their construction, the outer circle is formed by multiplying the lower Fibonacci number by √3, in this case, the shorter side of the pentagram, 13 MY.

Comment on type B modified and type D flattened circles
The type B modified represents a straightforward construction that is correct today in mathematical terms for producing the Golden Mean. The type D flattened circle is very surprising; for without the web of equilateral triangles, they would not be able to define √13, nor the '2' which is deducted from it to produce a figure approaching the Golden Mean. Thus, √13= 3.6055, minus 2 = 1.6055 (close to 1.618034).

Here then are two methods for producing the *phi* relationship. This demonstrates that the builders knew how to produce that relationship, as necessary for making pentagrams. That they were also using the Fibonacci series is equally astonishing.

The web used in the type D flattened circle is the same web as was used later in Greece and elsewhere. The Pythagorean Tetractys [the sum of the first four numbers: $1 + 2 + 3 + 4 = 10$] is constructed on this same web as well as for their other configurate geometries.

The purpose of the type B modified and type D flattened circles was to define the pentagrams accurately. The other two types — A and B — are, as it were, a celebration of the accurate pentagram.

Burn Moor
(Fig.39, T40)

A type A flattened circle, based on the 21 / 34 Fibonacci pair and unit 3 GF. It is situated up in Cumbrian hills.

	Thom's measures	Calculated	Error
Diameter of main circle	104.5'	1.4.1196'	4.56"

The main circle is defined by the enclosed pentagram, while the flattening is determined by a straight line connecting two adjacent points of the pentagram.

Nearby are the remains of several smaller rings. Thom measured four of them (T36 & T38).

Circle A	Octagram	13×2 MY	Circle B	Heptagram 51×1 GF
Circle C	Nine star	14×4 GF	Circle D	Pentagram $^8/_{13}$, unit 4 GF

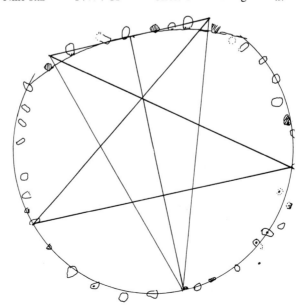

Fig.39

Fig.40 Aviemore, Inverness-shire

Flattened circle type A
This is the simplest of all the flattened circles. It is the circle containing a pentagram and the flattening marks the height of the arm of the pentagram inside the circle.

The relationship of the short to the long diameter is given by Thom as 0.9114. My method of calculation gives 0.9045.

Aviemore, Inverness–shire
(Figs.40–41, T258)

The central circle contains a type A flattened circle, based on the 13 / 21 Fibonacci pair and unit 2 GF, surrounded by a hexagram.

	Thom's measures	Calculated	Error
Inner circle	43'	42.97'	0.36"
Outer circle	76'	74.426'	1.57"

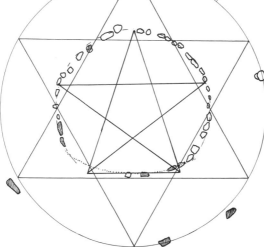

Fig.41

Flattened circle type B

Like type A, type B flattened circles are not attempting to define the means of creating the *phi* relationship but simply exploit it as a proportion of the pentagram. The pentagram was laid out in a circle and a hexagon placed outside it, forming the outer circle. The flattening marks the length of one arm of the pentagram swung round to form an arc. The relationship of the main diameter to the flattened part by this method of calculation = 0.850723. Thom's figure is 0.8604.

Bar Brook, Derbyshire
(Fig.42, T18)

This is a type B flattened circle based on the 5 / 8 Fibonacci pair and unit 5 GF.

	Thom's measure	Calculated	Error
Outer circle diameter	47.7'	47.7091'	0.0091"

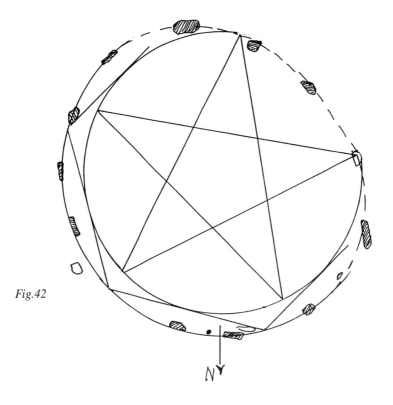

Fig.42

Fig.43 Long Meg

Long Meg
(Figs.43–46, T42)

This Cumbrian (off the Little Salkeld to Gamblesby road) flattened circle type B is based on Fibonacci 21 / 34 and unit 9 GF. It is supposed to be one of the oldest sites in Britain.

	Thom's measure	Calculated	Error
Diameter	359'	360.68'	1.68'

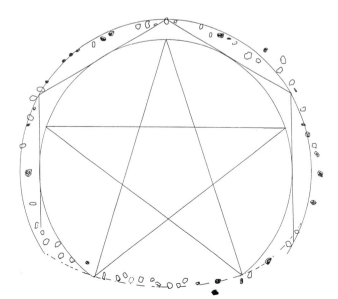

Fig.44

Fig.45 and 46 Long Meg

Comment on flattened circles

All the flattened circles involve use of a pentagram which, without understanding the Golden Mean, could not have been laid out as accurately as it certainly was. The most important type is the 'B modified' holding the accurate geometry of *phi* = ($\sqrt{5}$+ 1) / 2.

The Fibonacci series — 1, 1, 2, 3, 5, 8, 13, 21, 34, 55... etc. — was used in all the pentagonal geometries whether in a flattened ring or in a complete circle. The flattened circles appear amongst the earliest of the various rings — *c.* 3200 BC. This indicates that by then the ancient megalithic builders were already advanced in their knowledge of geometry and use of accurate yardsticks.

There is nothing to indicate why the flattened circles were all marked by the 'flattening.' There are many more circles containing pentagrams, both with and without the hexagon, that have no flattening.

How could they have laid out pentagrams on site?

(i) They could have used a template for the angle of 36° that is so necessary to the pentagram;

(ii) They could have laid out on a small scale the essential part of the flattened circle 'type B modified' to give the correct angle;

(iii) They could also have made two special yardsticks representing the basic measures and *phi*, which could have been carried about.

4. A Review of the Ancient Geometers' Methods

The results of the analysis of the explicit geometry in Chapter 2 and the flattened circles in Chapter 3 show that most of the ancient geometers' methods have become apparent.

Professor Thom was aware that these sites were laid out on geometric principles and worked on the hypotheses that they used megalithic yards for diameters of the rings and calculated circumferences in megalithic rods. This was a good enough starting point but not the correct answer.

Why are some diameters of circles not in whole numbers of megalithic yards? Many people have asked that question and the apparent inconsistency in Thom's many measurements has led to the general abandonment of the theory that consistent yardsticks were ever used. However, the answer to this question has now become clear.

1. They were using not two but three yardsticks for diameters — Greek feet as well as megalithic yards and rods.
2. They were also using 'units' of either fractions or compounds of the basic measures, in order to make the final plan of the desired shape and size.
3. By wrapping the central geometry in a polygon — either in a hexagon or hexagram, for instance — as is quite common, the $\sqrt{3}$ factor comes in and, as $\sqrt{3}$ is incommensurable, the outside circle must have an incommensurable diameter.
4. The circle enclosing a pentagram can never be a whole number of any yardstick because they always used the Fibonacci series to create the pentagram.
5. They were using measured units as the starting point in all the sites but those measures may be hidden. For instance, see Loch Mannoch (p.45), where the measured starting point was the base of a pentagram with the chosen unit and a Fibonacci number; or at Easter Delfour (p.54), where the main circle has the diameter $13 \times 2 \, MR / 3 = 8 \, ^2/_3 \, MR$.

*The ancient methods used to create polygons and polygrams
in the western European megalithic period*
The explicit geometry has shown how these ancient geometers were
achieving the various polygonal geometries. There are, however, two
types of figure: the hexagram and the square as the main geometry,
which only appears in the following chapters.

Equilateral triangles / hexagrams and hexagons
In the three cases where hexagrams appear as the main geometry, it
becomes obvious that they started by first laying out an equilateral triangle with a chosen length of the side. Next they placed a circle on the
triangle and then completed the hexagram.

   To make a hexagon or hexagram on a given circle, they used the radius
of the circle to mark off six equally spaced points for the six-sided figure.

Squares and √2
For squares, and for doubling or halving the area, they used the series:
... 12, 17, 24, 34, 48, ... They also occasionally used this series for
ellipses.
   Thus, $\sqrt{2} = 1.414213$ $17/12 = 1.41666...$ $24/17 = 1.41176$
   A second series comes to mind: 5, 7, 10, 14, which looks simpler but
is not so accurate. Thus: $7/5 = 1.4$ $10/7 = 1.2857$
   This demonstrates the accuracy of the arithmetic that the megalithic
builders were using.

All the other polygrams (trigonometry)
All the polygrams, other than the pentagrams, hexagrams and squares,
were created in the same way, using a simple form of trigonometry. After
much trial and error, they had discovered exact whole figures that could
be used to divide a circle into the desired number of equal divisions.

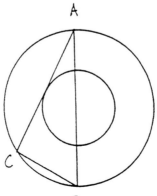

Fig.47

For heptagrams and 14-stars they used the numbers 51-46-22. If the diameter of the circle (AB) is 51 units, then by using a chord (CB) of 22 of the same unit, it can be stepped round the circle to mark off successively seven equal divisions on the circle. So the figures emerge:

for heptagrams and 14-stars	51 / 46 / 22
for octagrams	13 / 12 / 5
for enneagons	14 / 9 / (10.723)
for 11-stars	37 / 20 / (31.128)
for 12-stars	from the hexagon
for 26-stars	77 / 51 / (57.688)

There is no material available to allow us to discover whether they were using the notion of degrees in circles or triangles. However, using modern methods, it is easy to work out their accuracy.

For instance, in the heptagram, $22 / 51 = 0.431372 = \sin 25.55469°$
Now multiply by 2 for the angle at the centre $= 51.109394°$
$$360°/ 7 = 51.42857°$$

Whether the ancient geometers generalized this method into the 'science' of trigonometry to measure land distances or the distance of the stars, sun and moon, must remain tantalizingly unknown.

Pentagrams

Pentagrams appear in four main forms:

1. Occasionally as pentagons for the outer circle
2. As the main geometry of circles
3. As the geometry of flattened circles Types A and B
4. In the flattened circles Type B modified and Type D, which demonstrate the means of creating the pentagram

In Type D flattened circles, the method produces a value for *phi,* correct to three decimal places, but — as we saw earlier — it is a very elaborate figure to construct and probably not much use for creating pentagrams on new sites. The main factor of interest is the use of the triangular grid. Triangular grids were adopted for general use much later to configure geometric figures, yet here they were devised by megalithic builders for this type of circle.

Type B modified flattened circles are — again, as we saw earlier — the most significant. They produce the exact construction for the Golden Mean of $(\sqrt{5} + 1) /2 = 1.618033989$. Not only this, but they had also achieved the Fibonacci series of whole numbers approaching *phi*.

It has now become clear, not only that all the pentagrams were created using Fibonacci pairs of numbers, but also that throughout the megalithic builders employed a consistent set of yardsticks. No new geometric practices emerge in the final chapters, but there are some new applications of this familiar geometry, notably in the egg-shaped rings.

5. Implicit Geometry

The explicit geometry, where the main geometric features are marked by circles of stones or a specific number of equally spaced stones, allowed an approach to the actual geometry itself. There are far more sites, however, that are marked only by the outside ring of stones. Did these circles also have a geometric basis?

So much has been learned from the explicit group, that every possibility has already become known. Accordingly, an attempt was made to analyse these single rings. All three yardsticks were used: the megalithic rod, megalithic yard and Greek foot, or obvious fractions or multiples thereof.

The possibilities:

(A) To detect the polygrams, the values used have already been found. If the diameter is in whole numbers of one of the measures or an obvious fraction, it can be divided by the numbers that are known. The diameter should be divisible as follows:

For a seven star	divisible by 51
eight	13
nine	14
eleven	37

(B) If the diameter is an irrational number, there are only a limited number of possibilities:
   (i) that the circle encloses a pentagram;
   (ii) that the geometry is hexagonal (the arm of the hexagram turns out to be the measured starting point;
   (iii) that the internal polygram is wrapped in a polygon or polygram.

Unfortunately, the plain rings, with no internal features, do not indicate how they used the polygrams, although some of the details have emerged. But more details have also emerged in Chapters 7, 8, 9 (the egg-shaped rings) and 10. For instance, for circles with a diameter of 51 units, with no internal layout recorded, it is impossible to tell whether it is a 14-star or a 7-star.

(There is only one example of the square as the main geometry. It appears as an egg-shaped figure in Brittany.)

Pentagrams

Stanton Drew, Somerset
(Fig.48, T116)

A pentagram enclosed in a hexagram, based on Fibonacci numbers 13 / 21 and unit 10 GF, this is the second largest circle in Britain, second only to Avebury. It is located about 6 miles south of Bristol. The cove and the centres of the two circles lie on a line running approximately NE-SW.

	Thom's measure	Calculated	Error
Diameter	372.4'	372.13127'	3.22"

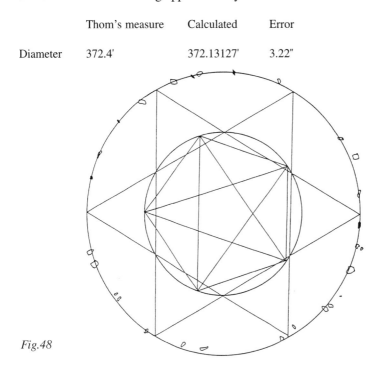

Fig.48

This very large circle is in a group of ancient remains. There are also two ellipses and a stone-lined avenue.

Very recently, the site at Stanton Drew was examined using geophysical techniques. This has revealed that originally the interior of the stone ring had nine concentric circles of wooden tree trunks. This new position can be compared with Woodhenge (p.141) and The Sanctuary (p.144). For Stanton Drew, the minimum geometry has been drawn in, whereas at Woodhenge their methods for making extra rings is clear, and so this figure could be treated similarly.

Figs.49 and 51 (opposite page) Oddendale, Westmorland

Oddendale, Westmorland
(Figs.49–51, T62)

The geometry here is made up of two hexagrams, the arms of the larger one being 11 MR. There has been some slippage on the west side of the central ring — Thom chose the wrong half!

	Thom's measures	Calculated	Error
Outer ring	*c.* 86'	86.37'	*c.* 4.44"
Central ring	*c.* 24'	24.933'	*c.* 11.2"

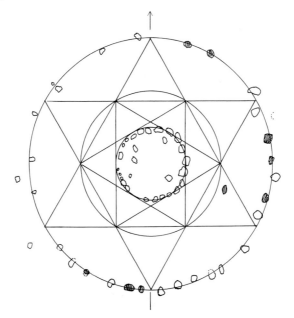

Fig.50

7- or 14-Star

The Rollright stones, ('The King's Men'), Oxford
(Fig.52, T136)

This is a 7/14-pointed star on the 51/22/46 formula and using unit ³/₄ MY. The construction of the 7-pointed star is based on that for Tomnagorn (p.48), using a diameter of 51 units and chord of 22 units. It is located beside a minor road off the A436 to Great Rollright.

	Thom's measures	Calculated	Error
Diameter	103.6'	104.04'	5.28"

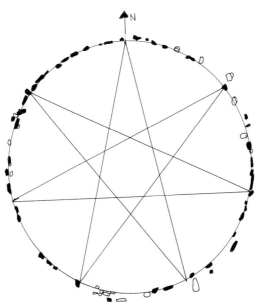

Fig.52

Octagrams

The Hurlers, Cornwall
(Fig.53, T74)

The unit used here is 13MY. This is one of a group of three circles, situated roughly on a line from Minions village to the Cheesewring — approach along B3254.

	Thom's measures	Calculated	Error
Diameter	39 MY	39 MY	exact

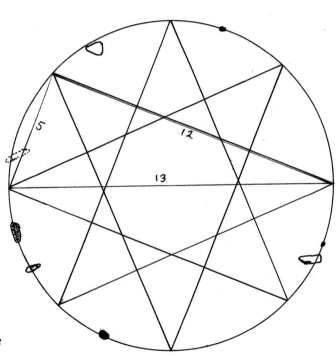

Fig.53

9-Star Circles

Latheron Wheel, Caithness
(Fig.54, T324)

This is a large circle, diameter 188.447' designed by the unit 12 GF.

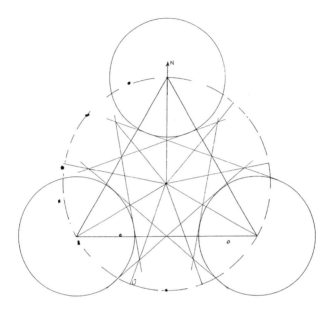

Fig.54

To create this figure:
1. Draw an equilateral triangle, each sides measuring 14 units. Here the unit is 12 GF.
2. Enclose the triangle in a circle.
3. At the points of the triangle, define a circle whose diameter measures 9 units.
4. Define tangents between the small circles, but not the central nor the outer ones.

The 6 'pointed' junctions along with the 3 intermediary diameters divide the circle into 9 equal parts. But there is an easier method of dividing a circle into 9 equal parts:

In a circle of 14 units diameter, define an equilateral triangle. At each of the 3 points of the triangle define a circle whose diameter is 9 units. Draw tangents from the little circles to the centre of the large circle, and join the centre of the main circle to the centres of the little circles. Now the large circle is divided into 9 equal parts. $(9/14 = \sin 40.0052°)$

Brogar, Orkney
(Figs.55–58, T323)

Located 4 miles NE of Stromness, beside the B9055, this is a 9-star ring, based on Fibonacci numbers 89 / 144 and unit 2 GF, enclosed in a hexagon.

	Thom's measures	Calculated	Error
Main circle: 9 star	50 MR (340.02')	50 MR	exact
Inner circle not marked — the pentagram		43.2617 MR	
Enclosing hexagon		49.954 MR	3.75"
Inner edge of ditch formed by 9 star	53 MR	53.208 MR	1.4'
Outer edge of ditch: pentagon on 50 MR	63 MR	61.803 MR	8.14'

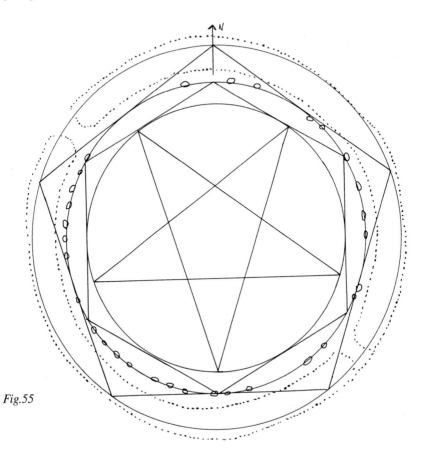

Fig.55

Figs.56 and 57 Ring of Brogar

This is a major site and one of very few cases with evidence of two geometries. It was constructed on a sloping site, with the older site — the 'Stones of Stenness' — just across the narrow part of the loch. The famous site of Maes Howe lies in the near distance.

The pentagram in the centre is made on the Fibonacci pair 89 / 144 — the highest pair of numbers to be used in any of the megalithic structures so far discovered — and as such the closest approximation (1.6179775) to the value of *phi* (1.618033).

The ground beneath the site is a sheet of stone which only supports grass and heather. The holes for the stones and the ditch had to be dug from stone. In the interval of 4 500 years since it was made, there has been much damage both from rain and frost and from domestic animals. Thom's plan of the ditch shows it to be far from circular, with various bulges due to weathering and disturbance by domestic animals.

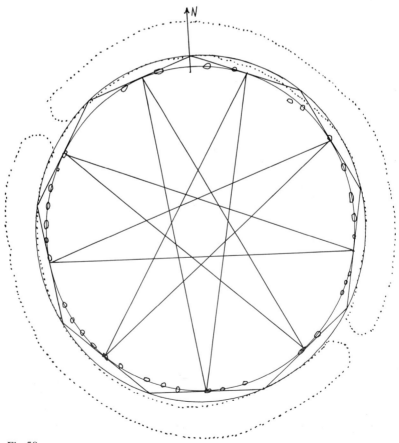

Fig.58

11-Star Circles

Nine Maidens, Ding Dong, Cornwall
(Fig.59, T92)

Using the 37-20 formula — unit 37×2 GF — the geometrical basis of this circle is $360/11 = 32.72$ and $\sin(20/37) = 32.72°$

	Thom's measure	Calculated	Error
Diameter	71.6' ± 0.3'	71.88'	3.36"

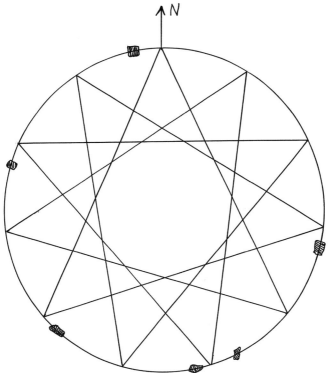

Fig.59

Comment on the implied geometry of simple circles
The geometry underlying the plain circles uses the same yardsticks and the same rules as were found in the explicit geometry. But the explicit geometry allows us to realize much of the detail that is absent in the plain rings, because there are no inner rings to indicate whether, for instance, the Rollright Stones (p.91) was a 7-star or a 14-star construction.

There is, however, more labour involved in analysing these circles because of the possibility that the central geometry had been wrapped in another polygon/polygram. As it turns out, the geometry of the plain rings — especially in southern Britain — generally lack the more complicated figures of the Clava Cairn types.

6. The Ellipses

Professor Thom was working with the disadvantage of not knowing the third yardstick — the Greek foot. Of the 24 elliptical geometries shown by Thom, there are actually only 16 true ellipses. The other 8 turn out to be different figures.

Much controversy has surrounded the construction of ellipses. There could have been other ways of laying out these sites, and it is claimed that megalithic Britons would not have been technically competent to plan and measure out the ellipses scientifically. The material shown here has already demonstrated the quality of the megalithic designers' geometrical theory and practice. As shown at Stanydale (p.115), the curved sides of the egg-shaped rings were constructed with elliptical curves, without the need for Pythagorean triangles. They would, therefore, realize eventually that they could use the same method to construct the ellipses, which are also egg-shaped. And for those ellipses they chose special triangles — i.e. right-angled triangles with whole numbered sides. For in polygonal geometry there is earlier evidence — prior to the use of ellipses — that geometers had explored the application of right-angled triangles.

For dividing the circle into 7 and 14 parts, they used the triangle:51-46-22

For dividing the circle into octagrams, they used: 5-12-13

Of the 16 ellipses analysed, there are 9 on true Pythagorean triangles; 5 on ($\pm$ 1) — i.e. imperfect — triangles, such as the 51-46-22 and 2 exceptions, which are both $\sqrt{2}$ triangles, using the 12-17-24-34 series. These two exceptions are built on squares, using the side of the square of 12 and the diagonal of 17, since $12 \times \sqrt{2} = 16.9706$.

Pythagorean triangles: In the ellipses, the triangle in the proportions 3-4-5 appears twice, in the proportions 5-12-13 it appears four times, and only once each in the proportions 8-15-17, 12-35-37, and 28-45-53.

($\pm$ 1) triangles: These triangles appear once each: 43-41-13, 37-29-23, 21-19-9, 13-11-7, and 12-9-8.

Construction of ellipses

Using Stanton Drew as an example, an ellipse based on the 5-12-13 Pythagorean triangle can be constructed using three posts and a long rope. First, the centre is marked with a post *C*, then along a straight line passing through *C* are placed two posts *A* and *B*, each exactly 5 units distant from *C*.

Next, a rope of length 13 units is used to mark an arc from *A* and then from *B*. The arcs intersect at *D*. The distance *CD* will be 12 units long, because in either of the identical triangles *ACD* or *BCD*, 13^2 minus $5^2 = 12^2$.

Then a length of rope *ACBDA* = 5 + 5 + 13 + 13 = 36 units, is made and tied end to end. The post at *C* can be removed and a scribing tool [used for marking an outline, as with one point of a pair of compasses] is held at *D*. Holding the rope taut and moving the tool *D* around the two foci, *A* and *B*, an ellipse is formed with a major diameter of 26 units and a minor diameter of 24 units. The choice of unit varied around the country, depending on local custom or space restrictions.

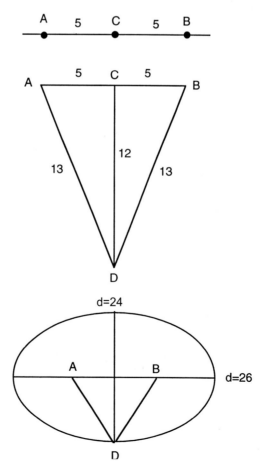

Figs.60–62

Stanton Drew, Somerset
(Figs.63–64, T116)

Two ellipses were formed here, both on 5-12-13 Pythagorean triangles, the larger using unit 1.5 MY and the smaller using unit 1 MY. Thom analysed these correctly because of familiarity with MY units.

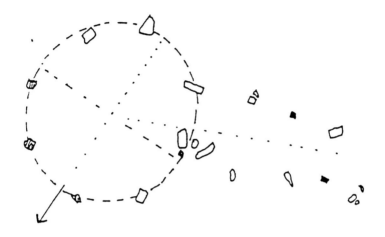

Figs.63 and 64

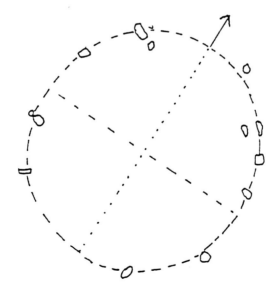

Ettrick Bay, Bute
(Fig.65, T154)

This is an ($\pm$ 1) ellipse, based on 37-29-23 and unit MY / 4.

	Thom's measures	Calculated	Error
Radius of major axis	18.5 MY	$37 / 4 \times 2 = 18.5$ MY	exact
Radius of minor axis	14.5 MY	$29 / 4 \times 2 = 14.5$ MY	exact
Foci	11.5 MY	$23 / 4 \times 2 = 11.5$ MY	exact

Mathematical calculations: 37^2 minus $29^2 = 1\,369 - 841 = 528$
Now $\sqrt{528} = 22.9782$ (say 23) which squared $= 529$
That yields a negligible error of 0.18".

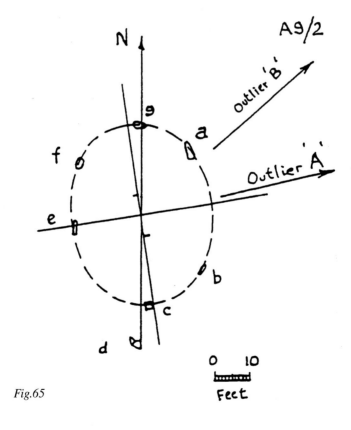

Fig.65

South Ythsie, Aberdeenshire
(Fig.66, T168)

This is a Pythagorean (3-4-5) triangle, based on unit 3 GF. It is a small site with comparatively huge stones: they are so big, indeed, that the enlargement for the diameter makes the error irrelevant. The stone in the south and its neighbour on the south-west are 8 ft high, that on the east is 6 ft high and the other three are 5 ft high.

   Note that the two smallest stones lie tangential to the ellipse. The hypotenuse (5) of the 3.4.5 triangle forms the major axis radius, while the side (4) forms the minor axis radius.

	Thom's measure	Calculated	Error
Major axis	28'	29.1428'	1.14'
Minor axis		23.314'	

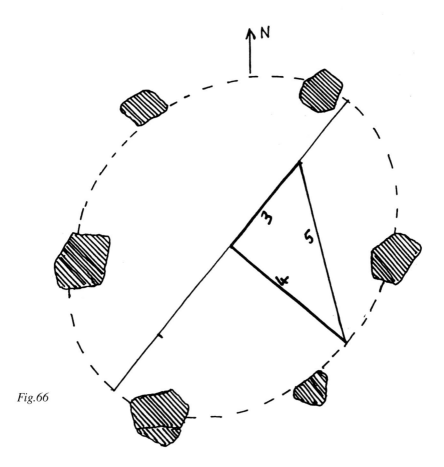

Fig.66

Comment on the ellipses

In view of the sophistication of the previous geometries shown here, and the choice of triangles used for ellipses, there is no doubt that they were well aware of the method(s) required to form ellipses. Likewise, their knowledge of Pythagorean triangles as well as those in the form of *A* squared + *B* squared = C squared ± 1 need not be a surprise.

There are just a few more features that demonstrate their arithmetical abilities — as does the use of the series 12-17-24-34 for √2. For the ellipses show that they could work out square roots and Pythagorean triangles — and also show how slight was the error on the ground of triangles in the form of $A^2 + B^2 = C^2 \pm 1$.

7. Pairs of Smaller Circles

This short chapter produces no new geometry; but it does show another aspect of the ancient geometers' practices.

Ringmoor East and West, Dartmoor
(Fig.67, T110)

This is a pair of circles, the east circle containing a hexagram, each arm being 37 GF with a smaller hexagram inside it. The west circle is identical to the inner circle of the east circle, having a diameter of 37 / 3 GF.

	Thom's measures	Calculated	Error
Diameter of east circle	41.4'	41.503'	1.24"
Diameter of west circle	12.0'	11.98'	0.23"

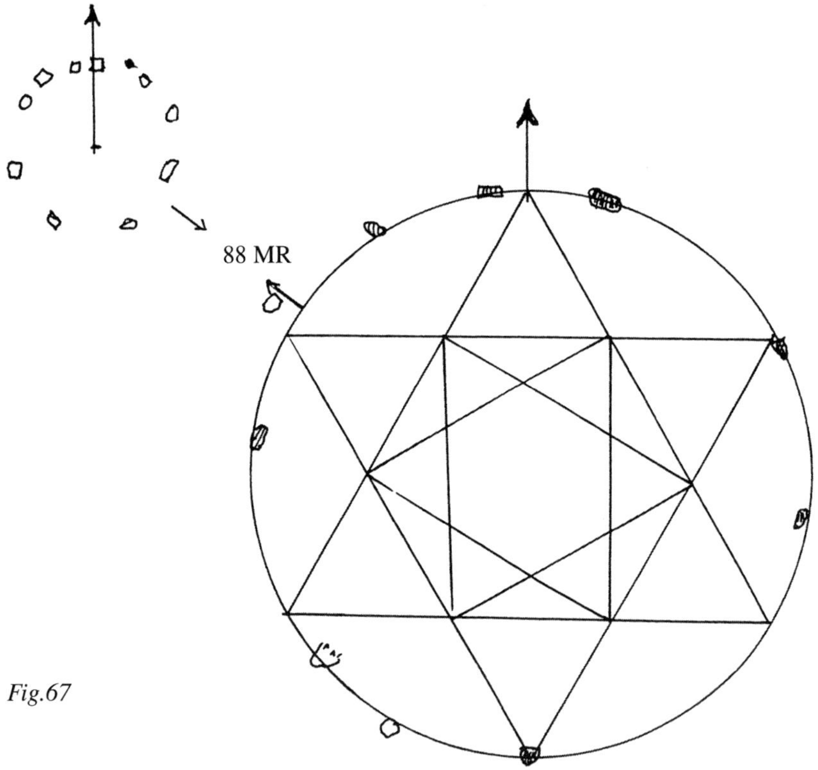

88 MR

Fig.67

The Loupin Stanes, Dumfriesshire
(Fig.68, T296)

	Thom's measures	Calculated	Error
Circle Q: type A flattened circle based on 13 / 21 and unit MR / 4	37.7'	37.598'	1.22"
Circle P: very dilapidated	44'	43.42'	c. 7.00"
Distance between centres: 1½ times diameter of circle P	65 ½'	64.63'	c. 10.40"

The distance between the circle centres is 38 units

Fig.68

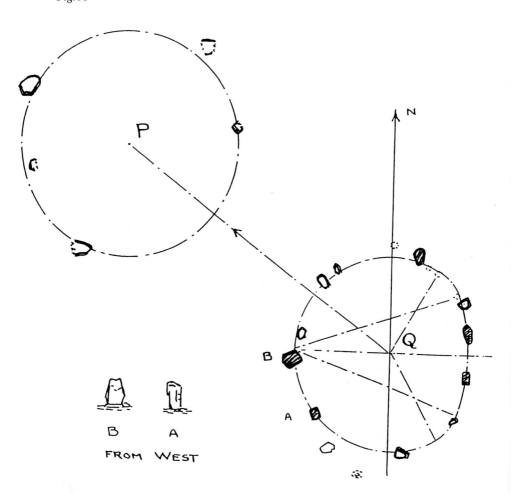

Penmaen-Mawr, Conwy
(Fig.69, T372)

This is an ellipse of the '± 1' variety, based on the triangle 43-41-13 and unit 1 GF, a nearby small circle with diameter measuring 13 GF

	Thom's measures	Calculated	Error
Long axis	31 MY / 84.32'	83.54' (86 GF)	c. 9.33"
Short axis	29.5 MY/80.24'	79.66' (82 GF)	c. 6.96"
Foci	9.5 MY / 25.84'	25.26' (26 GF)	c. 6.96"
Small circle	c. 13'	12.628' (13 GF)	c. 4.46"

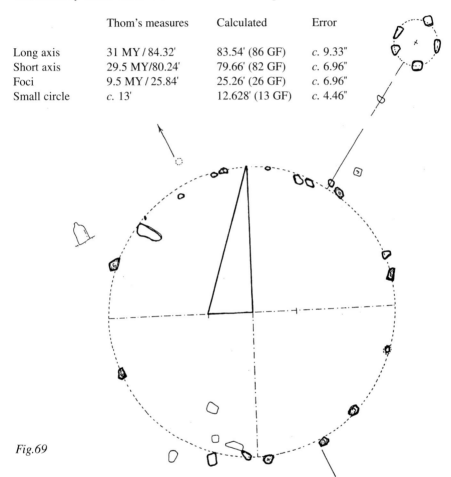

Fig.69

The diameter of the small circle equals the size of the short side of the triangle of the ellipse.

Note. Heggie (1981) points out that the basic triangle is very close to being Pythagorean in units of $\frac{1}{4}$ MY, and also that the perimeter is 95.06 which is very close to a multiple of $2\frac{1}{2}$ MY. He adds that the sides of the relevant triangle are half the major and minor axes and the focal separation — hence the unit of $\frac{1}{4}$ MY.

Loch Nell (Strontoiller), Argyll
(Fig.70, T140)

Two circles and a standing stone, enclosing a heptagram, using the unit $1\frac{1}{3}$ GF
and based on the 51-46-22 triangle, where the 51 unit represents the diameter of
the circle, which in turn forms the hypotenuse of the Pythagorean triangle.

	Thom's measures	Calculated	Error
Diameter	65'	66.057'	12.68"
Small circle diameter	*c.* 14'	14.7'	*c.* 8.40"

The small circle is the same size as the central circle of the heptagram

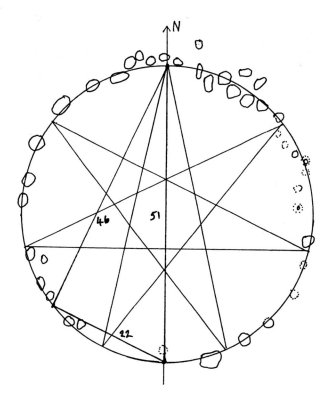

Fig.70

8. Pairs of Small Related Circles

There are only four examples of this type of paired small circles from Thom's surveys, though it appears that there are more still to be surveyed. There is a great deal more geometry to these apparently insignificant small sites than at first appears. Tangents drawn across the pairs produced significant angles: at Tullybeagles 60° and Shianbank 45°. This gives the clue to the geometry of these sites.

These pairs of smaller circles form the central circles of two much larger rings that are tangent to each other yet which were seemingly never marked with stones.

These geometries turn out to be very similar to the internal geometry of some of the egg-shaped rings (Chapter 9). One is bound to wonder whether the outer edges of these sites were marked with wooden posts.

Tullybeagles, Perthshire
(Fig.71, T342)

Two 6-pointed stars, tangent; hexagrams — a very dilapidated site, with only five stones in their original settings.

	Thom's measures	Calculated	Error
Large circle diameter	32'	31.408'	7"
Containing circle, unmarked		62.82'	
Small circle diameter	23.2'	23.556'	4.27"
Containing circle, unmarked		47.112'	
Distance between centres	54'	54.964'	11.57"
Overall length of the geometry		109.928'	

The distance between centres is 54.964' which equals 8.08 (± 0.07) MR. Was this distance meant to correspond with the length of the arm of the larger hexagram?

It has now become clear that these stone circles marked the inner rings of two complete hexagrams, touching each other at the crossing

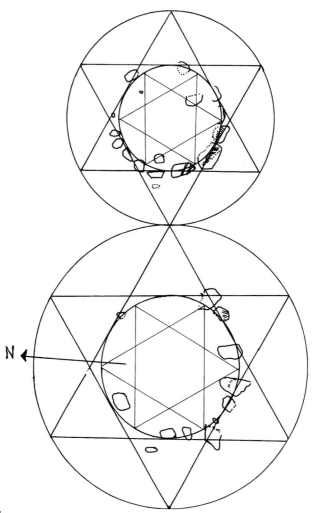

Fig.71

of the tangents. The larger hexagram has arms 8 MR in length; the smaller hexagram has arms 6 MR in length. The tangents are formed by the hexagrams extended.

The length of the whole geometry figure is 109.928 feet, at its widest being 62.816 feet. There are, however, no surviving stones to mark the whole geometry. They might have marked the outer rings with tree trunks, which would have rotted away quite soon.

Shianbank, Perthshire
(Fig.72, T358)

Two 8-pointed stars, tangent; based on 5-12-13 triangle and unit 2 MY — in this example the two circles are identical. (An apparently chaotic site, it is nevertheless of considerable astronomical significance, since the line joining the two centres defines a solstitial alignment in one direction and a calendrical one in the other.)

	Thom's measures	Calculated	Error
Diameters of the two circles	27'6"	10 MY (27.2')	3.5"
Distance between centres	70'6"	26 MY (70.72')	2.64"

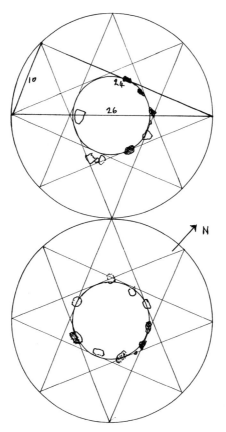

Fig.72

The angle of the tangents is 45°. The centres of the two small circles are also the centres of the two larger circles, each with a diameter of 26 MY.

The length of the whole figure is 52 MY = 141.144 feet, and the width of 26 MY = 70.72 feet.

Shin River, Lairg, Sutherland
(Fig.73, T36)

Two 11-pointed stars, tangent; based on units 4 GF and 8 / 3 GF. In this example the circles are much farther apart.

	Thom's measures	Calculated	Error
Larger circle	20'6"	20.46'	0.48"
Smaller circle	13.6'	13.64'	0.48"
Distance between centres	1198'	119.8095'	0.114"

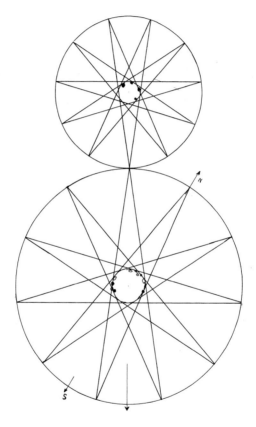

Fig.73

Thom's accuracy in measuring this site is remarkable.

Like the first two examples, these two circles form the central geometry of two very much larger circles. The larger outer circle is 37 × the unit of 4 GF (143.77'); the smaller is 37 × the unit of $2^2/_3$ GF (95.847'). The formula of 37 / 20 for dividing a circle into eleven equal parts has already been seen. So the geometry is a pair of 11 stars, tangential to each other, one's diameter being $1^1/_2$ times larger than the other.

The original (unmarked) geometry for this site is 239.619' long and 143.77' wide; which is a very large figure, but this NE area of Scotland contains other surprisingly large figures — e.g. Latheran Wheel (p.93) and Ring of Brogar (p.94).

Carnousie House, Aberdeen
(Fig.74, T234)

Like the previous examples, Thom's survey shows the central geometry of two large tangent circles. The larger is 14 units of 18 GF (244.8'), while the smaller is 14 units of 6 GF (81.6').

	Thom's measures	Calculated	Error
Diameter of larger circle	84'	81.6'	2.4'*
Diameter of smaller circle	27' (?)	27.91'	10.92" (?)
Distance between centres	163.1'	163.2'	1.2"
Total length of figure		326.4'	

* This is an extraordinarily large geometry and suggests that an unaccountable error has been committed in the survey measurement, requiring a fresh scale drawing or re-examination on the ground.

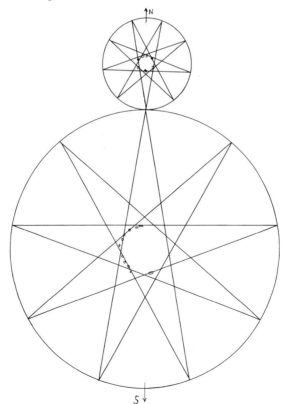

Fig.74

Comment

These four pairs of small circles, on analysis, are transformed from ugly ducklings to fully fledged swans (except for the last, slightly lame duck)! But it is difficult to imagine that the original designers of these sites did not mark the much larger outer rings. Would it be possible to examine the position of the unmarked outer rings with technologically advanced instruments, in order to search for possible wooden post holes? Is this not an urgent, highly appropriate and eminently desirable project for one or several of our national heritage and conservationist bodies to undertake?

Neither Thom nor Burl had any idea of the size of the final geometry of these pairs. They never examined what proves to be the edges of the site, so there may still be remnants of stones which marked the edges, or pits which held wooden posts. Burl makes 'archaeological' comments about the rings in the main source book. At p.359, for the pair of small circles at Shianbank, he says: 'Paired rings such as these are not uncommon in Central Scotland although the Shianbank circles, 43' apart, are more widely separated than most.'

The similarity of the geometry of these pairs to the egg-shaped rings (see next chapter) is overt, and yet consistently different in that the second circle in these pairs is always tangent to the first and both are made from the same geometry either of the same size or differing only in the unit used. In the egg-shaped rings, the narrow end tends to be made from an internal part of the first geometry, or else, when the inner circles are identical, they are so arranged that the second circle 'highlights' parts of the first circle.

9. The Egg-shaped Rings

Basically, the egg-shaped rings are made up of two circles, both containing the same polygram; the second circle being so placed that the polygonal geometry of the first one provides the basis for the same figure within the second one. There is, however, a great variety in the way that the geometers laid out these sites. In some cases, the main circle is enclosed in a hexagon. In others it is enclosed in a polygon of the same number as the main circle, and in still others there is no external extension. (The clue to the presence of polygons in these circles comes from Keith Critchlow (1979), where he shows two examples.)

Thom did not discover the geometry of the eggs. In an attempt to explain their construction, he felt that they were designed with some elaborate Pythagorean or near Pythagorean triangles, and that the curved sides — between the lower and upper circles — were also made from (near) Pythagorean triangles that he placed in certain examples, well outside the main figure.

However, the non-standard egg in Shetland, Stanydale Temple, gives the clue to how the sides were constructed. The main geometry is just about the only standard feature of this egg.

Stanydale Temple, Shetland
(Fig.75, T364)

This is basically an octagram using the 2 GF unit, although the survey measurements given are inadequate.

	Thom's measures	Calculated	Error
Main ring diameter	9 MY = 24.48'	26 GF (25.257')	9.33"
Outer ring diameter	11 MY = 29.92'	30.022 GF (29.164')	9.072"

(i) The main circle cuts the five little walls that form the four small compartments and these walls are finished off with standing stones.

(ii) The whole construction is walled in with an enlarged egg about $4^1/_2$ MY deep, all of which is filled with stones.

115

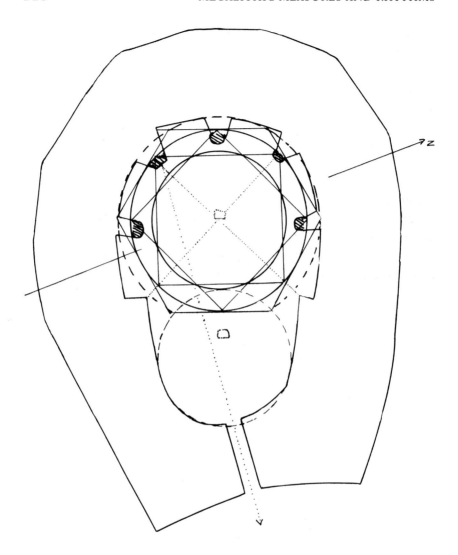

Fig.75

(iii) This site was used as a Midwinter Sunrise observatory: on the first day of spring, sunlight enters through the doorway, on the axis of the passage, striking the face of one of the stones. At that moment the declination is — 8.3°, which is the declination exactly one megalithic month before the equinox; and likewise the last day that the sun shone into the building in the autumn was exactly one megalithic month after the autumn equinox (see Thom 1967, Tables 9.1 & 9.2).

(iv) Unlike any of the other eggs, in this case the outline of the egg is broken by a considerable step on both sides.

This main geometry is formed by an octagram with a diameter of 13 × 2 GF. Every second point is joined to form two squares inside the circle, and the inner circle is formed by the junction points of the squares. The narrow end of the egg is made up of a circle with the same diameter as the inner circle, which it is just touching.

Figure A: the egg-shaped outline is in two parts. The larger end is formed by an elliptical curve based on the triangle A(1) A(2) A(3). The smaller end is formed by an elliptical curve based on the triangle A(1) B(1) B(2). As the elliptical curves do not meet, they are joined by a step at the two points where the diagonals of the square are extended.

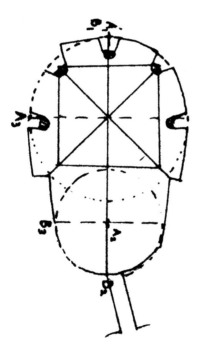

Fig.76

Had it not been for this particular egg-shaped ring, it would have been difficult to determine how the curves joining the two circles were made in all the other eggs. But having said that, it is still not easy to work out exactly how they achieved each of the ellipse-like sides of the eggs.

Their method — example: Choose the point *A* on the small circle where the join has to start,

and the same for *B,* on the large circle.

Join *AB* and define a line *CD* parallel to *AB.*

Join *AC* perpendicular to *AB.*

Join *BD* perpendicular to *AB.*

The points *DCA* (or *DCB*) form the three points for the ellipse-like curve joining the two circles. For a flatter arc, extend *C* and *D* outwards and use the points *C*⁺ and *D*⁺, and either *A* or *B,* as the three points for the half ellipse. For a rounder arc, move *C* and *D* nearer to each other and either A or B as the third point at *C*⁻ and *D*⁻.

At Stanydale, they used the central axis of the figure to form the 'points' for the elliptical curves of the sides. This inevitably led to the 'step' in the outline. In the method (Figure B), the axis is moved to *CD* parallel to the line *AB,* which gives the typical unbroken *(sic!)* egg shape to all the other eggs.

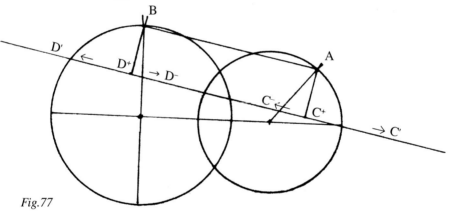

Fig.77

In view of the uncertainties surrounding the analysis of this site, it is worth comparing with Thom's (1978) original interpretation — without the benefit of knowing about the Greek foot yardstick:

We have carefully superimposed two egg-shapes to which we believe the geometry of the site conforms. The inner egg is based on the perfect Pythagorean triangle 25-24-7. The outer egg may be based on a perfect triangle 13¹/₄ - 11¹/₄ - 7, but is much more likely to have been based on the triangle 13-11-7. The two eggs have co-linear major axes and the radius of the small end of each egg is 3¹/₂ MY while the radii of the large ends are $4^1/_2$ and $5^1/_2$ MY. The distance between the centres is 7 MY in both cases.

Loch of Strom, Shetland
(Fig.78, T368)

A 9-pointed star with a small circle marking the 40° division of the circle, using the unit 1 GF. Thom's measurement for the diameter of the main circle was 5 MY, which equals 14 GF. The hatched stones are in their original settings; the outlines mark fallen stones.

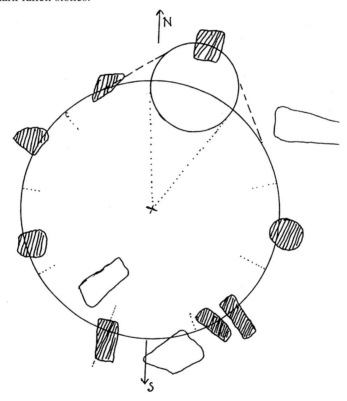

Fig.78

They must have completed the usual method for dividing the circle into nine equal parts. Then they defined a little circle to mark one-ninth of the circumference of the main circle. The diameter of this little circle is 4.788 GF, so presumably no measurements were made — which shows that they knew how to construct this circle without measurements. However, using a value of π as 16/5, then $^1/_9$ of the circumference of the large circle = 4.835: approximating to 5 GF. QED!

East Burra, Shetland
(Fig.79, P169)

A 2 × 14-pointed star, using unit 1 GF — this is a strange site with a single large standing stone and the rest of the markers made from little piles of stones. Thom seemed somewhat doubtful of its authenticity but it proves to be a typical egg. Thom assumed an egg-shaped circle based on a 5-12-13 triangle, having a perimeter of 74.14 MY or nearly 30 MR, but he added that: 'Obviously the site is worthy of much greater attention than we gave it.'

	Thom's measures	Calculated	Error
Main diameter	21 MY	21.03205 MY	1.046"

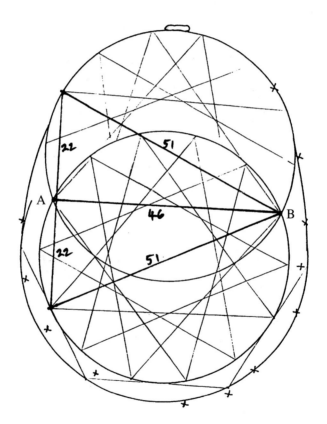

Fig.79

The main circle has a hexagon inscribed internally. A circle of diameter 18.2 MY (= 51 GF) is inscribed within the hexagon. Using the 51-46-22 formula, a 14-pointed star is formed.

The narrow end of the egg is formed by a second identical circle joined at the common horizontal division *AB* (= 46 GF).

Kynoch Plantation, Aberdeenshire
(Fig.80, T212)

A standard octagram in the form of an 8-pointed star, using the unit of 1 GF and the usual 5-12-13 triangle, the central circle being placed tangentially to the main circle to form the narrow end of the egg. Measurements are missing.

(Thom did not recognize this little site for what it is, describing it as boat-shaped.)

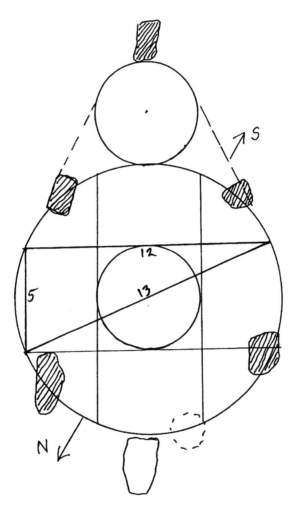

Fig.80

The small circle, as drawn, looks too small. Its size could have been chosen from many other parts of the octagram. However, the two stones on the large ring (beside the small circle) accurately mark the straight tangent from the large to the small circle.

Druid Temple, Inverness
(Figs.81–82, T270)

A 9-pointed star within an egg, built enclosing a passage grave with its entrance due south, which is now indicated by fallen stones in the centre of the figure. It is difficult to measure accurately, and impossible to know how they connected the nine divisions of the circle. However, the second, smaller circle forming the egg (Figure A) depends on the divisions, every pair joined in the area of the small circle which is all that is shown. There is also no clue as to how the enneagon of the smaller circle was defined. As the figure is already cluttered with large stones, I have deliberately left out the possible enneagons.

	Thom's measures	Calculated	Error
Main ring diameter	14 MY	14 MY	exact
Outer ring: hexagram enclosing			
Main ring (Burl)	74'4"	75.7"	1'3"

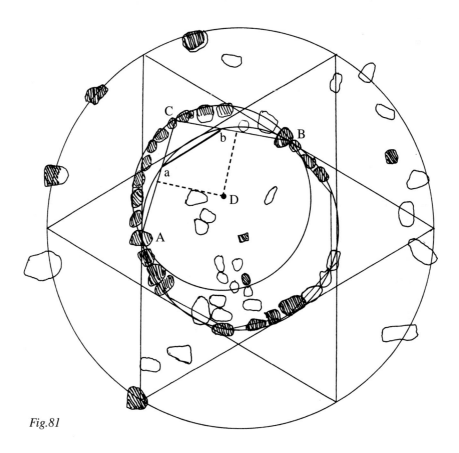

Fig.81

Fig. 82 Druid Temple, Inverness

In the upper, smaller circle, *A* & *B* are the two points formed by three equal divisions (40° × 3 = 120°) on the main circle. The two points on the arc *A — B* are labelled (a) and (b) respectively. *Aa* is extended to *C* where it cuts *Bb* extended. The smaller circle is then created so that *ACB* are all on the circle.

To find the centre of the smaller *ACB* circle, halve the lengths *AC* and *CB* and define perpendiculars at the half-way point; where they join is the centre *D* of the new circle.

AC and *CB* subtend an angle of 80° at the centre *D*.

Esslie the Greater, Kincardineshire
(Figs.83–85, T200)

Two pentagons on 13/21 Fibonacci numbers, using unit 1 MY, the main circle enclosed in a 9-pointed star, and the small circle using unit GF.

The pentagrams are placed so that one side of the upper pentagram coincides with the pentagon side of the lower: A — A(1)

	Thom's measures	Calculated	Error
Pentagram circle diameter	22 MY	22.116 MY	3.82"
Central circle diameteruncertain	17.68'		
Outer circle diameter	28 MY	29 MY	mismeasured

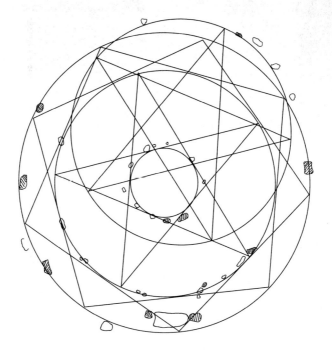

Fig.83

This site is of explicit form. They designed this egg in a mix of styles, both as a Clava cairn type (Inverness area) and as a recumbent stone type (Aberdeen area). In this north-eastern area, the more adventurous geometries appear, so it should be no surprise to find that the outer circle of the main ring is a 9-star, instead of the pentagon or hexagon that is found so commonly elsewhere.

Based on a 13/21 pentagram, the diameter of the outer circle enclosing the 9-pointed star is exactly 29 MY. The small central circle has a diameter of 19 GF.

Figs.84 and 85 Esslie the Greater, Kincardineshire

Twelve Apostles, Dumfriesshire
(Fig.86, T288)

A pentagram based on a 5/8 Fibonacci series and unit 25 GF, surrounded by a pentagon.

	Thom's measures	Calculated	Error
Main circle diameter	94 MY	255.36'	3.9"
Inner circle diameter		212 GF	

The diameter of the inner circle is $8^{1}/_{2} \times 25$ GF

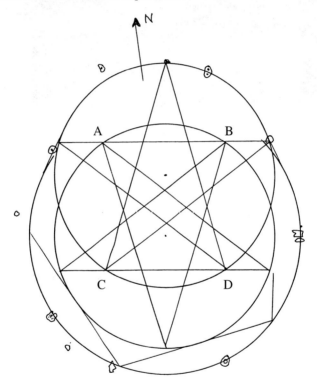

Fig.86

The upper pentagram is placed so that one arm of the upper pentagram lies on the pentagon side of the lower (*A-B*). Hence the lower arm of the pentagram in the lower circle coincides with the pentagon in the upper circle (*C-D*). This arrangement gives the impression of an ellipse with six equally spaced points in it.

The lower inner circle is enclosed by a pentagon which defines the main stone circle, though there is no indication of a preferred orientation of this pentagon.

Fig.87 *Anne Macaulay at Borrowstone Rigg, Berwickshire*

Borrowstone Rigg, Berwickshire
(Fig.87–88, T304)

A circle, based on 2 × 14 star and unit MR / 4, surrounded by a heptagram.

	Thom's measures	Calculated	Error
Diameter of outer circle	50 MY	51.12 MY	1.12 MY / 3' = 1'1"
Diameter of upper circle	31 MY	31.87 MY	2'4.4"

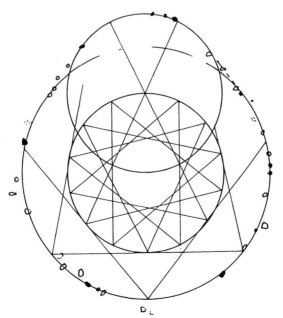

Fig.88

The main inner circle diameter is 51 × MR / 4, and is defined by the enclosing heptagram. The upper circle is the same size and is placed with its centre on the first circle — incidentally creating a *vesica piscis* with the overlap. The outer circle is formed by a heptagram surrounding the main circle.

It would appear that the number 51 was meant to be the common factor, with the outer large circle set at 51 MY and the inner one 51 × MR / 4.

Allan Water, Roxburghshire
(Fig.89, T308)

A hexagon enclosing an egg, based on a 9-pointed star, on the 14 / 9 formula, with a 14 MY diameter.

	Thom's measures	Calculated	Error
Main circle	16 MY = 43.52'	16.166 MY (43.97')	5.4"

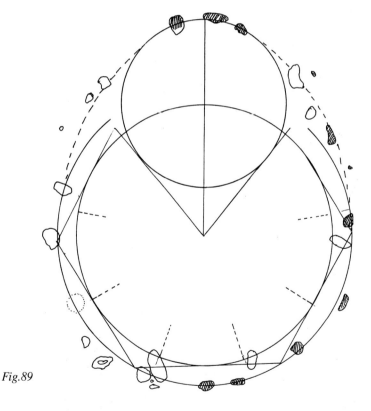

Fig.89

The 14 MY circle has an enclosing hexagon, whose outer points define the stone circle. The small upper circle, which is 9 MY in diameter, has its centre lying on the circumference of the 14 MY circle, and occupies a sector of 80° in the larger circle.

All the nine points of the star would have been marked but there is no indication of how they were joined.

Kerry Pole, Montgomery (Powys)
(Fig.90*, T380)

Thom did not call this site an egg but its shape naturally places it among the other egg-shaped sites.

	Thom's measures	Calculated	Error
Outer circle diameter	32 MY	32 MY	exact
Middle circle		27.7 MY	

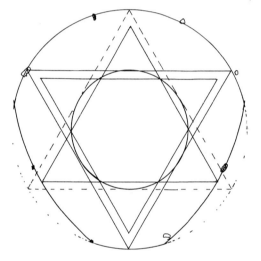

Fig.90

As all the other egg-shaped sites start from the inner geometry, the same order is presumed here.

Define a hexagram with each side of the two triangles being 24 MY. The enclosing circle has a diameter of 27.7 MY. Draw an inner circle which cuts the internal contact points of this hexagram. Now define a second hexagram tangent to this circle. The circle that encloses the larger hexagram has a diameter of 32 MY. The narrowing of the outer circle is achieved by touching two points of the inner hexagram.

* EDS. This drawing is not quite accurate to scale.

Maen Mawr, Powys
(Fig.91, T393)

This is based on a pentagram by 21 / 34 Fibonacci numbers and unit MY / 2, surrounded by a pentagon. The outer circle is defined by the outer points of a pentagon which encloses the first pentagram circle. The narrower end is formed by a second pentagram of exactly the same size, placed so that the centre of the second circle falls on the perimeter of the inner circle of the pentagram of the first circle.

	Thom's measures	Calculated	Error
Diameter of main ring	22 MY	22.08 MY	2.64"
Diameter of long axis	24 MY	12.54 MY	1.5"

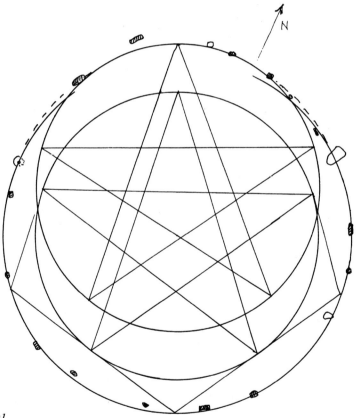

Fig.91

The Hurlers (central site), Cornwall
(Fig.92, T74)

This is a large site made up of three separate rings. The northern ring, with a diameter of 42 MY, is a 9-pointed star, based on unit 3 MY. The southern ring, with a diameter of 39 MY, is an octagram, based on unit 3 MY. The central ring is an egg.

	Thom's measures	Calculated	Error
Long diameter	50 MY	50.26 MY (136.703')	8.48"
	Burl's measure		
Main circle	132'11"	132.78'	1.64"
Long diameter	136.666"		0.43"

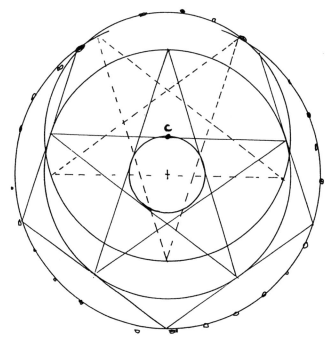

Fig.92

The main stone circle is formed around a pentagon which in turn encloses a circle circumscribing a pentagram based on the Fibonacci numbers 13 / 21 and unit 5 GF.

The narrow end is formed by a second circle identical to the pentagram circle with its centre (c) placed on the internal circle, tangential to the arms of the first pentagon.

Thom surveyed many sites in Brittany (Thom, 1978, chapters 6–9), including the vast stone rows at Le Ménec. At both ends of the rows, there is a large cromlech, to use the local name. Both of them are egg-shaped rings.

Le Ménec (East), Brittany
(Fig.93, P64)

This is a pentagram — P(1) — based on Fibonacci proportions 8 / 13 and unit 7 MY, surrounded by a hexagon. The main circle circumscribes the hexagon (H). The narrow end of the egg is formed by a circle with its centre on the edge of the pentagram circle. This small circle encloses a pentagram — P(2) — based on the Fibonacci pair 13 / 21 and unit 1 MR, whose points are marked by the projection of the main pentagram/ pentagon arms.

	Thom's measure	Calculated	Error
Main circle diameter	44 MR	44.00466 MR	0.38"

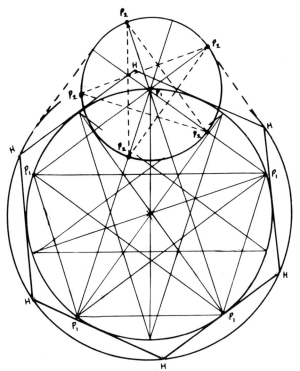

Fig.93

One can't help being amazed by the size of this geometry. The short diameter is almost 300 feet long (299.23') and the long diameter is nearly 355 feet long (354.35').

Le Ménec (West), Brittany
(Fig.94, P63)

	Thom's measures	Calculated	Error
Main circle diameter	34 MR	33.94058 MR	4.85"
Long radius	27 MR		

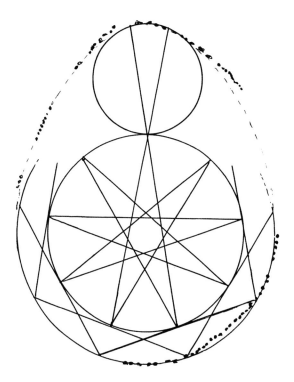

Fig.94

There are two possibilities here:

Main circle — a 9-pointed star with diameter 26 MR and unit 13 GF ×
14, surrounded by a 9-pointed star. Outer diameter — 33.94058 MR, the
diameter of the narrow end of the egg going to the inner circle to give
it the diameter of 14 MR on which there is another 9-pointed star based
on unit 1 MR.

The diameter length of 34 appears elsewhere in Britain and in
Brittany. They were using the series 12-17-24-34 for √2, the relationship
between the side of a square to its diagonal.

If the geometry of this site also involved the side of the square, it would
be approximately 24 MR. The little square forming the narrow end would
have the diagonal of 20 MR and the side 14 (actually 14.142).

The multiple site at Clava, Inverness–shire

This is the site that gave the name 'Clava' to such a type of cairn. There are two 'passage grave' cairns and one plain one with no passage to the central area. In addition, there are two little satellite circles. The site lies near the River Nairn on a small flood plain.

	Thom's measures	Calculated	Error
Outer ring — long radius	23 MY	22.7946 MY	6.7"
short diameter	38 MY	38.27928 MY	9.12"
Main ring	not given	19.1396 MY	
Inner ring	not given	7.31 MY	

About half a mile upstream lies the site of Milton of Clava (p.43). In the River Nairn valley, there are several other sites including Gask (p.138). A Victorian report listed far more sites but most of them have since disappeared.

The egg-shaped ring (T246): details from Thom (1967, p.62). Thom did not realize that this egg-shaped outer ring of the northernmost cairn was integral with the inner double-ring passage-grave that it surrounds.

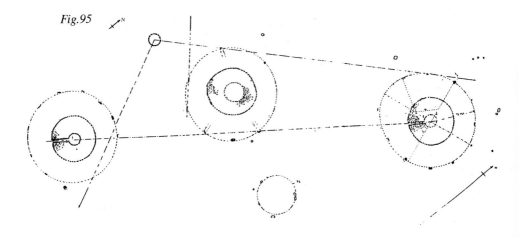

Fig.95

Fig.96 Clava, Inverness-shire

All three main circles contain a pentagram based on the $^3/_5$ ratio and unit 1.5 MR. The inner circle is formed on the junctions of the pentagram arms, and all three are enclosed in a hexagram (tangent). (See p.115 for construction of egg-shaped rings.) The narrow end of the egg is formed by a second identical pentagram with its circumference touching the inner circle of the first pentagram. The northernmost circle is the only egg-shaped ring.

Comment on the egg-shaped rings
There is no new geometry involved in these sites. Thom's theory of these eggs being made on elaborate Pythagorean triangles has turned out to be mistaken. What is shown here is that the geometers must have laid out these figures, presumably with string or cord, so that they could contemplate the design in order to decide how the main geometry should be laid out and thus where the narrow part of the egg was to lie in relation to the main circle. During planning, the sites must have been covered in a web of string markers!

In those sites where the second circle protrudes from the first circle by only a few feet, it cannot be obvious to the visitor that it is an egg; yet others must be instantly recognizable.

As the geometry of the egg-shaped rings emerged on analysis, there was the feeling that they showed the geometers at play, revelling in all the complications of their geometric figures!

Fig.97 Anne Macaulay at Gask, Inverness

10. Unique Designs

Most of the geometries of the various rings clearly fall into categories, each of which contains the same type of geometry but differing only in the unit used at each site. Though proportion by square root was very rarely used, the presumption is that this geometry was probably used by farmers for enlarging fields to prepare for sowing grain. The rare use of the hexagram/hexagon as the main geometry of a site is offset by the common use of these figures for wrapping round the geometry of many other figures.

The first oddity — apparently unique — is the geometry of Gask near Inverness. The symbolism of the circle, the square and the triangle in Gask has survived down the ages. Furthermore, 'squaring the circle' is also present in this site. The explicit sites, using two or three circles to define the geometry, was only practised generally in a small area of north-east Scotland — elsewhere all the detectable features of this geometry disappear, only the outer circle ever being marked.

137

Gask (Mains of Gask Farm), Inverness
(Figs.97–99, T264)

This unique site combines the symbolic geometry of the triangle, circle and square. Polygons and the different types of rings are present all over the British Isles, but there is no other ring with this combination of geometric forms. The unit is 1 MR.

	Thom's measures	Calculated	Error
Diameter of outer circle	119.4'	119.0'	4.8"
Diameter of inner circle	82.45'	82.446'	5.45"
Centres apart	2 MY = 5.44'	2.0305 MY	0.99"

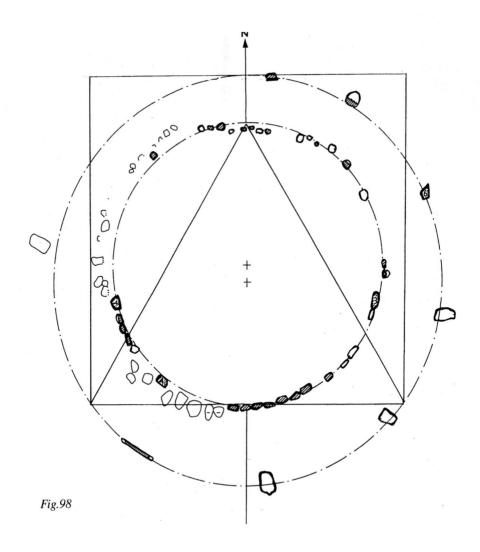

Fig.98

Fig. 99 Gask, Inverness

The inner circle diameter, by calculation, measures 12.1245 MR (82.446'), representing the height of the equilateral triangle, the base of which touches the outer circle at two apices. The side of the triangle measures 14 MR. The square is formed on the base of the triangle. The perimeter of the square = 4 × 14 MR = 56 MR. This just touches the outer circle at its northern tip. There are three known points on the outer circle. Its radius measures $8^3/_4$ MR and diameter $17^1/_2$ MR.

Therefore the circumference of the outer circle, using $\pi = 16/5$, also equals 56 MR.

So here is an example of squaring the circle, not in terms of areas but in terms of perimeters.

The distance between the centres of the circles = 2.0305 MY = 5.52'.

The next oddity emerges from three circles with the same diameter.

Dean Moor (Fig.100), Cumbria (T50), Urquhart, Moray (T240) and Broomend of Crichie, Aberdeenshire (T216):

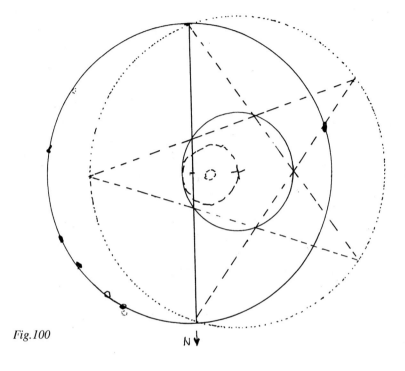

Fig.100

N

These three rings have the same diameter:110 ft = 16.1764 MR within an error of 0.32". This is equivalent to $10 \times phi$ = 16.18034 MR.

The site at Urquhart is very dilapidated and there are no extra details recorded; but, with the identical diameter one can presume that it was made in the same way as the site at Dean Moor.

The site at Broomend of Crichie is of a strange form, the measured diameter being the top of a circular bank.

If Dean Moor had begun by defining a circle enclosing a pentagram, on the Fibonacci pair 5-8 and using the unit of 2 MR (the dotted circle), then the long sides of the pentagram arms are each 16 MR, which approximates to $10 \times phi$ MR (16.18 MR). One arm can then be used as the diameter of the circle — this is the surviving circle marked out with the ring of stones. Over the diameter of the circle (110'), this represents an error of just 1%.

The dotted circle contains a central circle passing through the junctions of the enclosed pentagram's inner arms. This circle has the diameter of 44.189 Imperial feet. The centre of this first circle is on the western edge of the 'squint' central ring and its diameter is half of 44.189 ft (error on 22' = 0.0945' = 1.134").

In order to get the diameter of this circle exactly $10 \times phi$ in MR, they had laid out the circle of a pentagram by Fibonacci 5 / 8 and unit 2 MR completely. The evidence for this is shown by the off-centre inner circle.

But why, in the first place, did they want to make a circle with the diameter $10 \times phi$ in MR? Most of the geometries that have been analysed are formed by a polygram, sometimes enclosed in another polygram or polygon. All the other geometries analysed have been exclusive, in that there has been no question as to the specific geometry by which the site was laid out — because in each case there was no alternative.

So why was this interesting circle laid out with a diameter of 110 ft? Was it planned to represent a statement concerning the Golden Mean?

Woodhenge, Wiltshire
(Fig.101, T130)

This is one of two unique designs. Situated just south of the great earthen enclosure at Durrington Walls, Woodhenge derives its name from the pattern of postholes, first discovered from the air in 1925. Thom accurately surveyed them and then superimposed six egg-shaped rings to fit their outline. All these six rings are based on a 12-35-37 Pythagorean triangle.

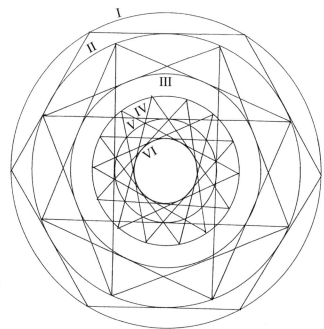

Fig.101

The radius of each ring has been chosen in such a way that successive perimeters are multiples of 20 MR. As Heggie (1981) observed: 'a remarkable mathematical feat.' Archaeologists believe that the rings originally formed the foundations of timber buildings that were roofed over with thatching, implying that they were of no astronomical significance.

The treatment of the geometric plan is unlike any of the other eggs. The geometry of the broader (SW) end is basically made up of an octagram using unit 9 GF and a 14-pointed star using unit $1^1/_4$ GF. Following Thom's numbering, the outer ring is number I, the first inner ring II, and so on, with the small central ring being number VI.

The octagram

Ring number II encloses the octagram, which has a diameter of 117 GF (113.5714') = 13 × 9 GF. Ring I is formed by a hexagon outside number II, with a diameter of 135.0999 GF (131.24') = 15 × 9 GF. Ring III marks the circle lining the two squares formed by joining every second point of the octagram: 74.185' = $8^1/_2$ × 9 GF.

Ring IV is formed from the points of a square made by joining every third point of the octagram: 61.82' = 7 × 9 GF. (This is like the geometry of the station stones at Stonehenge.)

But this ring also comes into the 14 / 7 star — see below.

Ring V forms the circle within the square of number IV: 43.714' = 5 × 9 GF. Hence the five outer rings are derived from the octagram at ring II.

Now Ring IV's diameter, calculated from the octagon measures 63.638 GF; but 51 × $1^1/_4$ GF = 63.75 GF, the difference between them being just 1.29".

This circle encloses a 14-pointed star on the formula 51-46-22, by joining every fifth point (using a chord of 46 units).

The inner circle, number VI (27.06') is formed by the inner chords of the 14-pointed star inside circle IV. But notice that ring V is also confirmed by the 14 star as the outer junctions of the chords fall on circle V. Thus, circles IV, V and VI are all involved with the 14 star geometry. Did they finish off by putting a heptagram in the central circle?

Circle VI has a diameter of 22.2 × $1^1/_4$ GF, close to the 51-46-22 geometry of the 14-star geometry. It is also interesting to note that, using the 9 GF unit, the circles define a series: 15, 13, $8^1/_2$, 7 and 5, the significance of which is not immediately clear. The innermost circle relates to the 14-point star geometry.

The narrower end of the egg

This is where irregular practices come to light! In all the other eggs, the narrower end is formed by a development of the main geometry in a variety of ways. This is not so at Woodhenge. Here they simply repeated the main geometry with a new centre at a point on the north-east perimeter of the smallest circle (VI). To create the 'egg' form, they simply left the north-east section as it was and then 'trimmed' some of the sides inwards from about 30° off centre so that it appeared to be an egg: which also, incidentally, made the lines of wooden pillars more regular in shape.

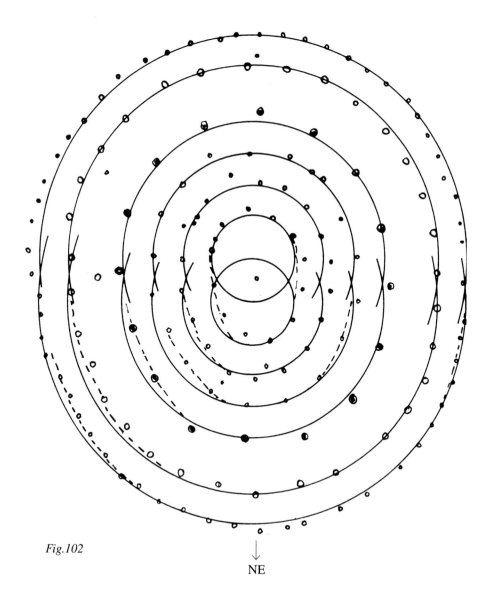

Fig.102

NE

The Sanctuary, Wiltshire
(Fig.103, T124)

This is another unique design. Situated near barrows on the top of Overton Hill, on the south side of the A4 road, the site was largely destroyed in 1724 but rediscovered and excavated in 1930. It was linked by what became known as the West Kennet Avenue which extended $1^1/_2$ miles SE to Avebury. The pattern of six concentric rings of concreted post-holes and two rings of stone are still discernible.

Thom's lettering and measures (MY)		Calculated (MY)	Error
A	47.6	48	1.088'
B	23.8	24	6.53"
C	17.2	17	6.53"
D1	12.6	12.75	4.9"
D2	11.4	11.487	2.85"
E	7.1	6.94	5.22"
F	5.0	4.9074	3.02"
G	4.4	4.25	4.9"

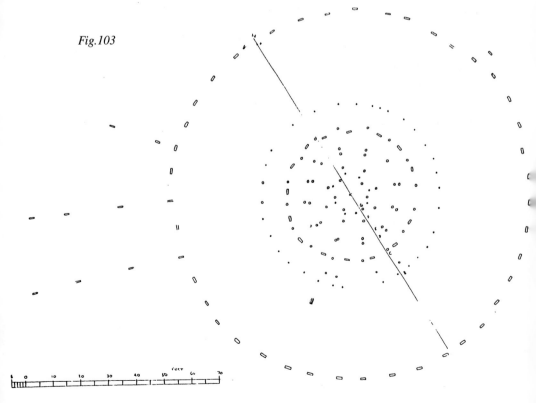

Fig.103

To quote Richard Muir (1981): 'The initial nucleus seems to have been a hut structure of slender posts with a diameter of 14 ft. Then a larger timber house 38 ft in diameter, its roof carried on two rings of posts, was set up on the same centre; a third and even larger building 66 ft across then surrounded the second building and a 45 ft diameter circle of standing stones was erected inside the structure, with a circle 130 ft in diameter enclosing the whole.'

Two centuries of abandonment followed by dubious restoration have inevitably produced inaccuracies, requiring adjustment of Thom's measurements.

Circles A, B, C and G are all from the series for $\sqrt{2}$ that has been used elsewhere, so it presumably represents a series of squares within squares.

Circle C has the diameter of 17 MY = 51 × MY / 3. As 51 is part of a heptagram geometry, I suggest that a heptagram belongs in C; though the next circle D1 has the diameter 12.75 MY which is 51 × MY / 4. However, 12.75 MY is both 3 × 4.25 (circle G) and $^3/_4$ × 17 MY (circle C). Furthermore, if circle D1 is taken as the heptagram, with a heptagon inside it, then this inner haptagon has the diameter 11.487 MY = D2.

For the inner circles, start with G = 4.25 MY. Define two hexagons outside G. This gives circle F the diameter of 4.9074 MY. The double hexagon on circle G gives the division of 12 for the circles of stones between F and D1. Circle E appears to be formed by a square on F. This is the only site bearing the division by 12 marked on the ground. However, this solution is bound to be uncertain.

11. A Summary

The ease of calculating the various geometries with a pocket calculator nowadays has hidden the difficulties that the megalithic builders must have faced in dealing with the incommensurable factors employed in several of their distinct geometries. From Thom's very accurate surveys in Britain and Brittany, it is clear that the yardsticks remained constant, not only along the entire Atlantic seaboard but also throughout the period from early in the fourth millennium until about 1200 BC — longer than from the beginning of the Christian era until today. (The erection of stone circles was also carried out from parts of Scandinavia in the north to southern France and even into Spain — though these have not been surveyed.) The devastation caused by the eruption of Hekla in Iceland in 1159 BC was probably the reason why the whole system in Western Europe collapsed at that point.

It has been suggested by some that pacing could have been used to mark out the sites. But all three of the basic yardsticks — Thom's MY and MR plus my GF — were used as well as fractions of them. Furthermore, an outer ring was often enclosed in another polygon that had an incommensurable diameter. No person could have coped with these demands by pacing.

In any event, pacing could never be as accurate as Thom's meticulous surveys indicate. At sites that are still in good condition, Thom's measurement can come within an inch of the calculated size. This surely demonstrates that accurate yardsticks were generally used in laying out the sites.

There were three important but incommensurable factors that even the earliest megalithic geometers had to cope with:

a) the square root of $2 = \sqrt{2}$

b) the square root of $3 = \sqrt{3}$

c) the Golden Mean (*phi*) $= (\sqrt{5} + 1) / 2 = (2.2360678 + 1) / 2 = 1.618033989$

(see Appendix 9). So $\sqrt{3}$ and the modern English foot might be regarded as two additional or secondary yardsticks, since they clearly emerge from the same mathematical system. However, all the megalithic sites so far analysed have been laid out using the three main yardsticks: the MR (= the Greek fathom), the MY and the Greek foot. It was centu-

146

ries later that the √3 yardstick was used specifically in sacred buildings in ancient Greece, and the modern English foot (in competition with the 'Saxon' foot) reappeared a thousand years ago.

It is tempting, therefore, to speculate that in megalithic times the √3 measure was reserved for sacred areas, leading eventually to its use in sacred Greek buildings; and perhaps the '*phi* foot' that became the imperial foot was originally used for measuring fields that were considered sacred because there the Earth Goddess produced the grain on which the earliest settlers depended, or for measuring sacred spaces such as places of remembrance.

It must be constantly borne in mind that all the megalithic pentagrams were based on the Fibonacci series, and that those using the ³/₅ ratio and the unit of 1 MR produced the measure representing 33 imperial feet or the double imperial rod.

The megalithic system of land and sea measurement must have survived among the traders from the British Isles and northern France who travelled into the Mediterranean. If it had not meanwhile been in use elsewhere altogether, how otherwise did it re-emerge? For it is a fact that the birth of Ancient Greek civilization (*c.* 1200–1000 BC) precisely followed the collapse of our megalithic culture.

The dating, in historical time, of the building of the standing stone sites runs from about 3200 BC till about 1200 BC. Over the whole period of 2 000 years, the yardsticks remained exactly the same over the entire area from Shetland to NW France. It must be emphasized, moreover, that all the stone rings can tell us is when megalithic man had acquired the engineering skills necessary to erect them; for he might have had the mathematical skills to design them much earlier — from pre-literate history we cannot know. What is even more astonishing is that the identical yardsticks reappear later in ancient Greece. Fernie (1981) in his re-examination of the Anatolian Greek carved lintel (or pediment) in the Ashmolean Museum in Oxford, dating from pre-400 BC, rejected the concept of the Greek fathom consisting of seven Greek feet, on the grounds that no other early system of measurement included such an awkward division; but that has proved an erroneous conclusion.

The standing stone sites vary in many respects from one area to another: e.g. the recumbent stone circles of the Aberdeen area and the Clava Cairn type of the Inverness area. This variability has led to theories that the country was made up of isolated tribes that had little connection with one another. Yet, no matter how they may have decided actually to construct their sites, they all used the same yardsticks and the same geometry.

The fact of variations in architectural styles simply points to the existence of different 'schools' from one area to another. Further, the fact that the geometry was so widely identical suggests that there must have been means of communication between the various 'schools.' The ellipses, for instance, are thought to be later than the flattened circles and the circles containing the polygons. But these later designs appear everywhere! According to Burl's assessment, there are around 700 sites still to be surveyed, and until they have all been measured with the same accuracy as that of Professor Thom it will be impossible to say whether the same types of geometry were used universally. But one may be reasonably confident, from the fair sample (including virtually all the most prominent) which have been rigorously analysed, that such would indeed prove to be the case.

The most striking feature of this whole science of geometry is its sheer sophistication. Certain of the flattened circles are among the very earliest sites, yet every pentagram — the basis of the flattened circle — was created on Fibonacci numbers. Stonehenge itself, dating from 3000 BC or earlier, demonstrates knowledge of methods for creating polygons. Almost as amazing is the megalithic builders' familiarity with the Golden Mean and with the use of square roots.

One aspect of the geometrically defined rings that has so far been ignored is the astronomy. Most of Thom's plans show alignments to certain astronomical rising and setting positions of astronomical bodies. My concentration on geometrical analysis and interpretation is perfectly complementary to his initial focus on the astronomical functions. Moreover, his discovery of their astronomical awareness reflects further on the advanced state of their scientific knowledge generally, hence reinforcing the credibility of my own conclusions concerning their skills in geometry and rudimentary trigonometry.

In ancient times there was no means of telling the time except by observing the sun, moon and stars, but an agricultural community needed to know when to sow next season's crops and when the festivals would fall due. By using a single gnomon, be it a tree trunk or a single standing stone, the midday hour and the south-point can be easily defined. With a complete circle of stones and knowledge of the stars, it would be practicable to master the calendar. In today's urbanized environment, the night sky is very seldom clear and mostly invisible, owing to two centuries of increasing pollution and artificial lighting, so people are simply less aware of it. Besides, in today's secular world, the heavens mean no more than outer space, whereas in pre-historic society they ruled people's beliefs too.

It was the early Christian church, after all, which organized the modern calendar, with Christmas at the winter solstice (the sun) and Easter governed by the moon. When clocks were invented, it was the church tower that held the timepiece, and the bells within that tolled the time across the streets and fields. Now I see the function of the megalithic rings as being very much the same as the medieval church in these respects.

Having discovered how precise and sophisticated the megalithic designers were in the erection of their sacred sites, the question may well be asked whether they applied that same diligent standard and precocious brilliance to their astronomical studies? One can only wonder, because of course in that faculty no record could be kept nor any evidence survive.*

---

* In the eight years that have elapsed between Anne's final draft and publication of this book, a number of developments have taken place which support her thesis about the antiquity of knowledge in NW Europe: e.g.
  — Orkney building technology discovered in Egyptian pyramids
  — Hazelnuts, proof of cultivation, found on an archaeological site at Cramond, near Edinburgh, dated at 10 000 BP.
  — Work by Oxford Professor Barry Cunliffe on Atlantic seaboard civilization. EDS.

PART II

Migration to the Mediterranean

At this juncture, let us take stock. As we have already observed, between about 4000 BC and 3000 BC, the British Isles and Northern France saw the creation of large stone monuments that are preserved today as stone circles or alignments, or as dolmens or henges, although severely diminished by several thousand years of weathering and neglect as well as by pillaging for other building and agricultural uses. As we have also shown, the great circles (or 'rings') were built primarily as astronomical observatories or ceremonial temples or both. The designers of these monuments were accomplished mathematicians who used complex geometry to plan the layouts. Moreover, the designs incorporated 'yardsticks' — precise standard units of measurement — which were employed by the Greeks over 2 000 years after their use was well established here.

Again, it must be emphasized that the dates of these structures can only indicate the time by which the necessary engineering knowledge had been gained for their erection, which would have been long after the mathematical knowledge had been acquired for their conception and planning. From all these findings I realized that knowledge of metrology could have diffused from Britain and the Atlantic seaboard to the Eastern Mediterranean.

So I propose first to consider the transition from a hunter-gatherer society to a settled farming community, within which a specialist individual in the form of a shaman or bard developed the astronomical and geometrical skills for forecasting the seasons and measuring boundaries.

We shall then have to explore the journey that took this knowledge to the Eastern Mediterranean. There were several possible routes, some partially on land and rivers. However, the route invoked here involved a sea voyage which tin traders would have made from Cornwall to the Mediterranean. Gibraltar lies at latitude 36° North — the same latitude for which the first known navigational aid, the Eudoxus Star Globe, was designed in *c.* 2100 BC. As the megalithic mathematicians were the most advanced in the world, who else could have created it? That date, moreover, is only about one hundred years after the first known date for extraction of Cornish tin.

Yet another crucial piece of evidence of the Western tin traders comes from Minoan Crete where seal stones appear with geometric figures on them that are similar to those featured on the plans of the stone circles.

Finally, an exploration for remnants of this knowledge in Britain, named here the Apollo Wisdom, produces a remarkable amount of evidence to support the theory that knowledge of music and construction techniques were born in these islands. In turn, this theory — of the diffusion of mathematical knowledge from Britain to the Eastern Mediterranean some 4000 years ago — is reinforced by the legends of Apollo and the Hyperboreans and by Apollo's connections with music.

As discussed more fully below, it was conventionally believed that civilization could not develop without the formation of cities, because of the necessity for a wealthy ruling class that could control the masses and devote its hours of leisure to cultivation of learning and the arts. The Babylonian, Egyptian and Greek civilizations all represented a form of urban society. In contrast, the megalithic epoch in the British Isles was predominantly agricultural, which required the concepts of measure and proportion, essential to land management. In addition, knowledge of astronomy would allow the creation of a farming calendar.

In order to consider how an élite class could have arisen in megalithic times, it is necessary to think back to the very first farmers. By the first farmers, I imply two groups; the very first people who worked out how to sow, gather and store grain, and also the ever-expanding numbers of people who abandoned the lifestyle of the hunter-gatherers for farming. Compared with the standards of today, early farming seems a precarious and hard occupation, but compared with the condition of the hunter-gatherers these first farmers were enviably rich in food resources. Long before the start of agriculture, hunter-gatherers had been highly successful but if the food resource was over-exploited then food became scarce. There are parallels in North America in more recent times. Certain Red Indian tribes depended on the American bison for food and clothing, but when the Europeans came and slaughtered the bison, the native tribes suddenly lost their means of survival. Another example of developed stages of dependence upon wild animals comes from Lapland where these people migrate with the reindeer, and live off them. In both these modern examples, it is obvious that the people whose lives depend on the wild animals have to be very fit and have to be constantly on the move in order to follow animal migrations to their seasonal feeding grounds. There is no question of a settled existence nor, by the very nature of their lifestyle, is there the possibility of the emergence of an élite class who can afford the time to spend on anything other than survival.

The hunter-gatherer has very little need for counting, no need for measuring nor even the concept of measurement, no idea of volumetric measurement or weights, no need for mathematics, however simple, and no idea of proportion. As hunter-gatherers they do have some sense of time; full moons are useful for night celebrations and the seasons are important for knowing when certain food resources will be available. Apart from moon cycles which are relatively easy to observe, the solar seasons need not be very exact for their purposes and the behaviour of animals and plants may have given them better clues than the altitude of the sun or the observation of the stars.

Farmers, however, had to learn to count properly, understand the concept of measure and of proportion using simple mathematics, in order to know how much land to prepare for the quantity of seed to be sown and how much that quantity would yield until the following harvest. They also had to have a much more accurate calendar to know when to prepare the fields and when to sow seed.

Thus for the first time in the long pre-history of humankind, a specialist class developed which no longer needed to spend its time procuring food but which was fed by the farmers for whom it did the calculations. These farming specialists would also have been required to keep the calendar. They were not involved in the labours of farming so they had time to observe the stars and from these observations, they were then able to work out the calendar in more detail.

So at the beginning of farming practices, these specialists must have emerged who were expected to be competent in land measurement and simple mathematics to calculate volume, weight of grain per unit of land measurement, and astronomy for calendrical purposes.

The practice of land measurement is controlled by a yardstick. Both in Mesopotamia and in Egypt, among the symbols of kingship is the measuring crook. This symbol of measurement has been assumed to imply that the Pharaoh was in control of the land and measured out the fields, after inundations of the river Nile, allocating areas to farmers. However,

I believe that this explanation has to be inverted; the Pharaoh could only originally assume power because he could measure the fields. In other words, the position of the Pharoah evolved from the leadership of the farm specialist class. As well as the measuring crook, the Pharaoh also held a flail, a symbol that is not understood. However, it is obvious that it complements the crook, for the flail is the means of procuring the grain from the husks and straw, grown from the land measured by the crook.

According to the Scottish National Dictionary, the shepherd's crook or staff, in the non-Gaelic speaking areas was called a *kent. Kent* is also a form of the verb to know or learn. Kenneth is also both a popular king name in Pictish Scotland and a term for a priest. The association of priest, king, measuring rod and learned knowledge associated with the root *ken* to know, seems significant in this context. This concept also occurs in Latin, where *regula* is a measuring rule and *regulus* means a king or ruler. Whether or not this Scottish etymology is significant, the crook as the symbol of power was conferred on the bishops in the Christian world and still survives today masked under the interpretation of the shepherd who leads his flock.

It is well understood that the Mesopotamian and Egyptian civilizations emerged as the result of farming practices, for without stocks of grain neither a city nor an élite group could emerge. That the crook is the symbol of kingship implies that in these two areas mentioned, kingship grew out of the position of chief of the farm specialists. Farmland can be divided into two distinct areas. First the warm southern flood plains of large rivers and second usually less warm but very much moister lands where there was no dependence on the annual flooding of the rivers for cultivation. Farming in the warm flood plains was highly profitable where larger amounts of grain could be grown in smaller areas. This meant that the farmers could live in villages and still be near enough to their land: these villages had the potential to develop into towns and eventually cities, which was the case in Mesopotamia and other similar areas.

Perhaps the extreme opposite to this form of farming is exemplified in Britain where the first farmers discovered that it was possible to graze their cattle and sheep and goats on the same land all the year round because of the mild damp climate, and that it was also possible to grow grain. So, unlike the Near Eastern situation where grain was grown intensively on the floodplains of the Nile and the stock was taken to the hills for summer pasture, the northern farmers could survive much better by having a much larger acreage on which the stock was kept and the grain sown and reaped. This geographical position in the northern lands meant that, unlike their southern cousins who lived in villages, the northern farmers became isolated; they could not abandon their crops and their stock so they were unable to travel far to meet these fellow farmers.

Human beings cannot live in isolation. If the community became too small, there would be the risk of damaging interbreeding and tiny pockets of idiosyncratic development would have arisen. This however did not happen; the communities flourished as suggested by the many megalithic remains. Something must have occurred which succeeded in alleviating the isolation of the farming family groups.

On the fringes of history, Apollo's lyre is recorded as the instrument of Homer and the Greek bards as well as of the Druids and bards of Britain and France. So it is probable that the farming specialists, who became the priest-kings of Egypt and Mesopotamia, took on the task of being the communicators for the scattered northern farmers as well. The lyre is a very basic instrument and was very widespread, and I suggest that this instrument was first spread by the farming specialists or bards who travelled with the first farmers. The bards would come to the farmers: not to each farm separately but to local centres that were near enough for a community to reach easily. The bard would discuss farming techniques, give advice on how other farmers coped with problems, give calendrical advice and teach the farmers how to calculate dates by certain stars. The bards would also hold some sort of religious festivals, to thank the gods for the harvest, which perhaps included dancing, singing and recitations, entertaining the people with stories sung or chanted accompanied by the lyre. The farmers might pay them with some of their produce.

These northern bards, unlike their southern equivalents, had no prospect of becoming wealthy kings but lived a hard and exacting existence, travelling around the countryside. In these circumstances, there was no means of subjugating the farmers who remained free and independent, unlike the serfdom inflicted on their southern equivalents. This freedom of the farmers also means that should a bard in some way offend, in extreme cases it would be all too easy to dispose of him by means fair or foul. Thus the bards had to make sure that they made themselves indispensable to the farmers, and perfected their music through which they could captivate their audiences. How exciting it must have been long ago to experience the visit of the bard entertainer when there was no alternative form of entertainment! And how easy it would be for the good bard to influence the farmers if he threatened not to return again unless they followed his advice.

It is accepted that Homer and the Greek bards before him were deliberately used to developed standards of behaviour and belief, both by the examples in the heroic tales that they told and in the tales of the gods. This too must have been one of the duties of the early bards both before and during the megalithic period. Presumably these bards congregated among themselves at certain times, perhaps even wintering together when the weather was too rough for travelling. During these bardic congregations, they would communicate all the news from their own areas and discuss problems.

In the evidence which has survived for the early Mediterranean city civilisations, the communication between the ruling élite and the people seems to have been in the form of food control, display of wealth and religious practices. This contrasts dramatically with the direct communication practised by the bards in the megalithic west.

Undoubtedly the bards and farmers had a symbiotic relationship, each dependent on the other to survive. Their contact with the existing hunter-gatherers in central and western Europe with whom they appear to have assimilated must have altered their perspectives. It is assumed that it was during this period that the spectacular burial sites using stones were built, heralding the start of the megalithic period, though this notion must remain unproven due to a lack of contemporary written records.

Once the farmers were established in the British Isles, the bardic system began to flourish as it had never done before in northern lands (Renfrew 1987). It can be assumed that the bards were the same people who performed all the tasks including the measurement of land, the astronomy for calendrical purposes, the observance of religious practices as well as preserving the history and legends with which they entertained the people. It is perhaps a misnomer to use the term 'religious practices,' for there seems no justification to assume that there existed at this early time anything in the way of an organized religion as we think of it today. It has been proposed that the early phases of the megalithic period represent ancestor worship as the monuments are all ceremonial types associated with burials. As well as ancestor worship, there was presumably some sort of recognition of gods or goddesses or spirits of corn and possibly for cattle. Most of the early records which survive from the Middle East indicate that cattle, and particularly the bull were considered sacred. Whatever their beliefs were, elements of shamanism survived both in the Celtic west and in the Orphic and bardic traditions in Greece up until historical times.

Conditions in the British Isles were in some ways very different from those on continental Europe. The first obstacle they had to overcome was the sea. Farmers had to cross the Channel with their stock to get to France, and endured more sea travel to get to Ireland, and even more to reach the Hebrides, Orkney and Shetland. In mountainous areas, sea journeys would have proved easier than trekking across rough terrain. The second difference from continental Europe was the climate of Britain. The northern island climate, particularly around the coasts, would be markedly cooler in summer but also milder in winter, which must have influenced farming practices. The third outstanding difference in this northern area is the impact of astronomy. The sun set early and rose late at midwinter but in summer there was extended daylight. The setting and rising positions of the sun and moon swing over a wider area of the horizon than further south, and the distribution of the stars is very different, the circumpolar area getting larger and larger as you go northwards. Further, the British Isles run north to south, so astronomers in Orkney and Shetland would have a markedly different picture to those at, say, Stonehenge.

So from earliest times, farmers and their bards were challenged by the ocean tides, the northern climate and the northern astronomy. These are the obvious factors, though there may well have been others too. From the very start, the bards had to set to work to understand these circumstances and the farmers may have become even more dependent on them than before. The northern climate also meant that each farmer needed a larger area of land to feed a family than he would in France, hence thrusting him into even greater isolation and making him even more dependent on the bards.

So the bards flourished and this enabled them to set up permanent bardic centres to which they retreated in the fallow season. There a few specialists may have been left in permanent residence who could specialize in astronomy in order to try to understand the unfamiliar northern circumstances. There is no archaeological evidence for these presumed early bardic centres but they must have flourished for a long time before they were in a position to build their own monuments.

After a long period in which only relatively small tombs were constructed, spectacular large tombs appear like Newgrange in Ireland, built c. 3200 BC and Maes Howe in Orkney, c. 2800 BC, which coincide in time with the development of henge sites and the erection of spectacular stone circles and other structures. This change has been interpreted as the centralization of power and the emergence of overlords as well as a change from worshipping ancestors to worshipping gods. Another interpretation, however, could be that it was the bardic centres that were influencing the erection of these monumental sites, perhaps at their established bardic centres, for example, at Stonehenge.

Given its size alone, Stonehenge would have been a major centre of activity, with a sophisticated knowledge system and some kind of numero-geometric alphabet well developed by around 2800 BC or earlier, approximately the time when the first stage of Stonehenge was constructed *c.* 3000 BC. In this case it would appear that the bardic centre pre-existed any major construction or earth work (Mackie 1977). With the emergence of the concept of gods, there must indeed have been something of a revolution in thinking, the quantum leap into the abstract having been achieved. Filled with vigour at this new idea, the bardic centres must have been responsible for creating these spectacular new sites to proclaim to the people the advent of the gods.

Apart from the ceremonial sites themselves, there are other sites that have been tentatively identified by archaeologists as sacred centres: Maes Howe, the Ring of Brogar, the Stones of Stenness and the Scara Brae village complex, all in Orkney, Avebury, Mount Pleasant in Dorset and Kilmartin in Argyll.

The development of thinking of the bards must be examined. They must have developed a basic knowledge of calendrical astronomy, the concept of measure and proportion, hence the yardstick, and some means of measuring grain either by volume or by weight. They also had a basic form of lyre as their musical instrument. Two other items of knowledge may also have been known to them:

(i) the use of the right-angled triangle with sides in the proportions 3, 4 and 5 for creating square corners for fields and buildings, and calculating field areas (Midonick 1965); and

(ii) the method of describing musical relationships by the relative lengths of the strings required to achieve the musical interval (McClain 1976).

I include these two points because there is evidence for this knowledge being widely applied, which only seems explicable if it was spread by the roving farmer specialists or bards.

The importance of music to the early bards as a means of securing their popularity has already been stressed and in this atmosphere of freedom, there was experiment and development with their lyres. They knew that musical intervals could be described in terms of string lengths. In an established system there would be names to identify the familiar notes and strings of the instrument, but with experimentation and development, there would be no language to describe their new notes. So, the desired new notes that their ears defined as desirable, were measured and described in terms of numerical relationships.

What is clear from what emerges later is that they experimented with groups of notes that sounded pleasant to them, not just two notes but three notes together i.e. the major and minor triads. When these were measured they were found to be in the proportions, 3:4:5, the minor triad, and $^1/_3$:$^1/_4$:$^1/_5$ which is the major triad. Pre-empting Pythagoras, they knew that the proportions 3-4-5 produce the right angle, i.e. a truly square corner which they used in the megalithic monuments. The next step was to use this triangle itself to depict the minor chord.

These two items of knowledge, the shape of the minor chord combined with the farmer's mathematics for calculating field areas in terms of circles and squares, formed a link between music, geometry, land areas and mathematics, and the geometric device itself, the actual triangle, could represent them all. From this point, they appreciated the value of geometry and explored it further, establishing some of its basic rules which they then applied to their astronomical observations as a means of recording their findings. Geometric figures seemed to have started from the agricultural basis of the rectangle 3×4. A circle of circumference 16 units could be defined using the diagonal of 5 units as its diameter (using a value of $\pi = 16/5$, as was known in eleventh century BC China). This was crystallized into a numero-geometric system which was the original basis of the system of geometry that emerges nearly three thousand years later in Euclid and it was within this system that an alphabet evolved, allowing them to create names for their geometric figures.

In contrast to the northern bards, the southern farm specialists rose to far greater personal power in the developing cities, where trade became lucrative as it never did at the early stages in the North. In contrast to the north, these southern bards who became the élite class and eventually Pharoahs, the priest kings, developed material wealth and exercised their control of the people as a whole by amassing land rights, and possession of the grain and other food supplies. Though the southern

peoples developed cities and the architecture of elaborate and costly
palaces and luxury goods, they never succeeded in making the leap into
abstract thinking that their materially less well off northern counterparts
achieved. As transpires later, it was not until these northern bards spread
into the eastern Mediterranean, bringing their ideas with them, that the
materialistic Middle Eastern civilisations could learn to take the leap
into the abstract.

The achievement of reaching the abstract concept of the gods must
inevitably have altered the old ideology and the spread of their new
beliefs is therefore exemplified in the spread of construction work at
sites all over the British Isles, and northwest France, which does demonstrate development of ideas and practices (Burl 1979). That the bards
did thrive is strongly supported by the emergence of communal centres,
the henges and circles of megaliths, which archaeologists interpreted as
the emergence of the gods (Clarke *et. al.* 1985).

The migration

Before going on to examine further the hypothetical journey of western
knowledge to Greece and Egypt, the present-day archaeological understanding of civilization must be considered.

Until the development of carbon-14 dating and its calibration, every
form of civilization was assumed to have arrived in the West from the
Near East. Archaeologists have always referred to the emergence of a
wealthy élite who organized the mass of the population into a working
class, freeing themselves to devote time and resources to the cultivation
of 'higher things.' That is indeed similar to what passes for civilization
in many countries in the world today. But it now appears, with the new
carbon-dating technology, that an advanced civilization had developed
much earlier in the British Isles and northwest France in a rural, tribal
society. These were agrarian peoples, living in semi-isolation. Therefore
the hundreds of massive megalithic structures, many of which took a
lifetime to build, must have resulted from collective, local enterprise
rather than armies of slaves. The culture was propagated, not by a rich
ruling class but by a caste of peripatetic shamans, priests-cum-bards (the
forerunners of 'Druids') who, as dedicated intellectuals, proved rather
more effective. Babylon made an immense contribution by inventing
numerals and the alphabet, but in the pre-literate, pre-recorded Neolithic

age, mathematics evidently evolved on the northwest Atlantic seaboard, compounded with music and astronomy. The outrageously heretical conclusion is that the movement of civilization was not, after all, centrifugal — from the centre to the periphery — but centripetal!

That old and still-prevailing perspective arose because it followed the outward spread of Judaic and Arab religions and also because of the many archaeological discoveries in Egypt and the Near East in the nineteenth and early twentieth centuries. Such was the archaeologists' urban mind-set that at one time they even went so far as to argue that an ancient site could not be termed 'civilized' unless a settlement could accommodate a certain minimum number of inhabitants. In megalithic Britain there are no remains that can be interpreted as signs of the development of a ruling class until very late in the megalithic period, in the Wessex culture, where rich grave goods are found in some burials. But the crucial fact is that many megalithic monuments and other remains predate any signs of civilization in the Near East. Pyramid building did not commence in Egypt (at Cheops) until *c.* 2600 BC, well over 1300 years after the earliest megalithic monuments here.

Stonehenge has been accepted as an astronomical temple and so, no doubt, are many others (MacKie 1977). The élite in megalithic Britain were not wealthy in the sense of gold or stores of trade goods, but they must have been very persuasive to muster the labour required for these megalithic structures. MacKie suggests that the Druids were the inheritors of the ancient megalithic wisdom. Certainly, the limited historical information we have about the Druids and their bards gives a picture of a powerful priesthood spread all over Britain, Ireland and France, which has left very little in the way of archaeological records — and what there is can be recognized only because of Roman reports. There were no palaces filled with gold on Anglesey when the Roman forces eliminated the main body of Druids, and there were no wealthy cities — no cities at all, in fact — before the Romans came; yet the education of the novice priests must have taken many years.

If an ancient culture is measured by the practices or items that are still in use today, then the peoples of the British megalithic period come high on the scale. They invented the principles of geometry and trigonometry, which came back to us again much later via Greece. The Apollo tuning is the basis for Western music and survives in the top four strings of the guitar, and their science of music, in turn, still forms the basis of acoustics. They named two constellations that go by the same names today:

Cygnus and Lyra. (How many more star names go back to this era?) Though the god Apollo is not worshipped today, he is still looked upon as the symbol of excellence in the arts and sciences; hence the use of his name for spaceships to the Moon. And hundreds of their great buildings still survive.

So could the British megalithic peoples have been the proto-Greeks. If so, how did this Western wisdom get to the Eastern Mediterranean? In the absence of any conventional archaeological evidence, I have formulated an hypothetical journey.

The journey

There are so many cultural instruments in megalithic Britain that are also found in Greece in the Pythagorean mode that megalithic Western Europe must have had a very strong influence on the proto-Greeks who arrived in the Eastern Mediterranean late in the first half of the second millennium BC. It was just after this period that erection of new megalithic structures in Britain dwindled and then ceased altogether, many of the ancient sites being abandoned. Some elements common to Greece and Britain were:

— The yardstick. The Greek fathom is the same as the megalithic rod. The Greek foot is also found in the West and was used in the construction of the megalithic Rings.
— Symbolic or Sacred Geometry. It is generally assumed that Pythagoras received his mathematical training in the Near East, though nowhere there has geometry of this type been detected. But symbolic geometry, 'Pythagorean' triangles, number symbolism, the Platonic solids, pentagrams and other polygons have all been found throughout megalithic remains in Britain, where they were often laid out using the 'Greek' fathom or a set proportion derived from the 'Greek' measures.
— Music — the use of string length ratios. The music of Apollo and of Lyra is expressed in comparative string lengths in megalithic Britain. Pythagoras was reputed to have invented the same system. However, the Greeks used the term 'high' to describe what we call low notes and 'low' for our high notes. This can be explained as a result of the very long tradition of the use of the monochord. The early Greek

form of Apollo's lyre was made on an ox's skull and is paralleled by ox-skulls in burials in Britain during the Bronze Age and earlier. The ancient tuning, called 4:3:4 tuning, was preserved in Western Europe and survives today.

— A mnemonic 'alphabet.' The profusion of knowledge found in the megalithic sites will have required some proto-alphabet or similar system to enable the priests to remember data in the absence of writing of any sort in a pre-literate society. This sacred system remained secret after its arrival in the Eastern Mediterranean.

— The Titan Deities. Apollo is the outstanding example, particularly as he was the God of the Pythagoreans in historical Greece and is associated with the Hyperboreans.

— Astronomy. The only astronomy mentioned so far here is that of Apollo, but it is clear that the megalithic peoples knew a great deal of astronomy and knew how to record it accurately within geometric theorems in the Neolithic period. All four elements in the Pythagorean Quadrivium are present in mature form in megalithic Britain: number (arithmetic), number in space (geometry), number in time (music), number in space and Time (astronomy).

So how did the British megalithic culture reach Greece? It is safely assumed that early British farmers travelled around Britain and Ireland by boat, carrying their livestock as well as people. But that was some two-and-a-half millennia before the journey in question. Ancient canoes have been found, and it is presumed that both rafts and coracles could also have been used. Whether they had developed any more substantial boats is not known. What is known is that there was a steady traffic across the Channel as well as to Britain's offshore islands including Shetland. Ample sailing expertise was obviously available.

The hypothetical journey of the megalithic British has to be placed long before the proto-Greeks appear in Greece as the Myceneans; this journey would have started around the time of the tin mining in Cornwall. It has long been recognized that tin deposits of Devon and Cornwall were being exploited as long ago as 2100 BC (Penhallurick 1986) which implies that tin would have been traded. How the traders got to the western Mediterranean is not obvious, but there are two possibilities: they either travelled by rivers across France with a comparatively short land porterage, or by sea the whole way via the Straits of Gibraltar into the Mediterranean.

As the trade developed, trading posts would be set up. The traders would have created trade settlements anywhere in the western Mediterranean that would accept foreigners.

Tin is a key component of bronze, which is essentially a mixture of copper and tin. The earliest known bronze artefacts appeared in Mesopotamia *c.* 2900–2700 BC and also in northern Syria *c.* 3000 BC. The problem with these bronzes is that the source of tin in western Asia has not yet been identified. Small deposits of tin in Yemen, Saudi Arabia and Egypt were not exploited until 1 000 to 2 000 years later. Analysis of lead isotopes (atomic variants of lead) in bronzes failed to identify the tin source, although a potential source in Afghanistan was considered (Weekes 1999).

It appears that the ancient bronze in western Asia may have been imported as ready-made bronze ingots rather than the alloy being made locally. Weekes *(op. cit.)* concludes that 'the definitive determination of Bronze Age tin sources is a challenge which still faces the archaeologist.'*

There are a number of archaeological clues for the journey to the Eastern Mediterranean:

Dentated bone
Dentated bone, that is bone cut in a toothed zigzag, was used as decoration for wooden handles in megalithic Britain and in early Greece. In a small archaeological museum in Alicante in south-east Spain, there is an unfinished piece of dentated bone in the Bronze Age display case. It has no label and no information was available.

Stone circles
There are at least two stone circles in northwest Africa, which could have been on a shipping route.

Seal stones
In Crete there are a large number of small engraved seal stones from the Minoan period as well as some clay sealings with the impressions of seal stones. Many of these seals are recognizably Minoan; there are also for-

---

* Could it be that Cornish tin has never been considered as a source for 5 000 year old bronze because of an inbuilt reluctance to accept that the British Isles may have had an advanced civilization so long ago? [RAB].

eign types whose country of origin can be identified. But there are also quite a number of seal stones with purely geometric designs upon them. Within this group are the two which bear the Apollo geometry.

Building techniques

Similarities in building technology between British megaliths and the Egyptian pyramids have recently come to the attention of British archaeologists. Building techniques found in some Egyptian pyramids were first seen at Maes Howe in Orkney, which is a far older monument.

Eudoxus star globe

There is an ancient artifact called Eudoxus' star globe, which was created about 2000 BC specifically for latitude 36°N. Eudoxus, a Greek who lived from 409 to 356 BC, travelled in Egypt where it is reputed that he obtained an old star globe showing the constellations which he described in detail in two books, the *Phaenomena* and the *Enoptron* (Roy 1948). These works have not survived but Aratus (315–250 BC), a poet, was commissioned to write a poem containing the material of Eudoxus' work and this poem is extant. In it he states that Eudoxus had recorded that this star globe came from an earlier age (Penhallurick 1986) though whether Eudoxus realized the significance of this situation is not recorded. It was not until the second century BC that the astronomer Hipparchus discovered that the account of the old star globe by Aratus was wrong and did not describe the constellations as observed in his time; he must have realized why this ancient astronomy was wrong, as he subsequently studied older surviving, astronomical accounts and discovered the precession of the equinoxes.

The estimated date of the star globe is close to the earliest known date for Cornish tin extraction (about 2100 BC). The only habitable land at this latitude in the Mediterranean is Gibraltar, so it is possible that Eudoxus' star globe was made at Gibraltar by the Cornish tin traders. Having sailed so far south, there would be a band of stars that would be unfamiliar to them; if they were to venture in this unknown sea, the Mediterranean, they would need to become familiar with this new astronomy.

There is a strange twist to this story. If the astronomical interpretation of Apollo's killing of the Python or Dragon (Draco) when he arrived at Delphi is accepted, the early Greek astronomers of that period must have understood the Precession of the Equinoxes which would imply that the science of astronomy in the intervening period had been partly forgotten.

Other modem astronomers before Roy (1948) have examined the Aratus poem and all have come to the conclusion that the astronomy was apparently correct for a much earlier date. Roy used for his calculations the many references to the position of the equator and the tropics of Cancer and Capricorn that were described on the ancient sphere. With this method, he has deduced the date of 2000 BC ± 200 years for the production of this star globe. The latitude of the observations is also evident by the limit of the southern stars which are recorded, and is about 36° north. As well as the equator and the tropics of Cancer and Capricorn, there is in Aratus' poem a revealing comment on their attitude to the stars which shows a 'sophisticated degree of astronomical knowledge in its easy acceptance of the earth poised in space, the heavens revolving about it, with two poles one of which is not visible. Believing as we do that the *Phaenomena* enshrines knowledge from a much earlier epoch, it cannot but support the hypothesis that the constellation-makers themselves had achieved this insight into the nature of the world as far back as 2300 BC.' By all the associations of this information contained within the poem by Aratus, Roy and all who have examined it in the past have no doubt that this star globe was created for navigational purposes by some seagoing peoples.

According to Roy, the contenders for devising this star globe are:

— the Phoenicians: they are at the correct latitude, but 'they lived too recently to meet the requirement of date';
— the Egyptians: a civilization that was flourishing at the right time but 'Egypt lies entirely south of latitude 32° north, too far south for the locality of the constellation makers or the navigator peoples';
— the Babylonians, whose constellations are virtually the same as those described by Eudoxus; records of Babylonian astronomy reach back to 2100 BC though the names used for the constellations are different. Babylonian sailors, however, sailed down the Persian Gulf to India which is very far south of the limits of the star sphere described by Eudoxus. 'And so a certain reservation should perhaps be attached to the Sumero-Akkadian solution...';
— the Minoans from Crete whom Roy suggests took the Sumero-Akkadian constellations which they adapted for navigation in Mediterranean waters and superimposed their mythological characters on the Babylonian constellations.

There is a flaw in the conclusion that the star globe came from Crete because the Greek language and their mythology of the stars had not yet arrived in Crete at the time that this sphere was made. This error is in fact most intriguing. If the star globe described by Eudoxus showed the Greek mythology upon it, then the Greeks must have been in the Mediterranean at this period, because the latitude 36°N at which the scheme was devised, passes through the Straits of Gibraltar, North Algiers and Tunisia. However, the Greeks with their mythology had not yet arrived in Minoan Crete by 2000 BC and the Greek language on the Linear B tablets is only attested after about 1400 BC. If the star globe had been created in Crete for navigational purposes, where there is known contact between Crete and Egypt, the stars at the latitude between Crete and the north coast of Egypt would have been known. I suggest that the limit of 36°N, the latitude of Gibraltar, indicates that the proto-Greek sailors were in the western Mediterranean at this date, where the land mass of north-west Africa forms the barrier to the exploration south of latitude 36°. Thus they must have been in the western Mediterranean about 2000 BC and the context identifies them as astronomer-navigators. However, as the constellation Lyra was named in Britain in associa-tion with the creation of Apollo and the constellation Cygnus was also known, this is confirmation that both the proto-Greeks and their mythol-ogy which was used to name the constellations had reached Gibraltar at this time.

If the constellations Cygnus and Lyra were known in Britain pre-2100 BC then the conventional Greek constellations would also have been known and the similarity of the Aratus star globe with Babylonian constellations simply demonstrates that the use of the constellations for calendrical purposes was a common feature of the agricultural world derived from the first farmers who spread from the fertile crescent in all directions thousands of years before Sumer and Babylonia ever came into being. The very first farmers' constellations, therefore, formed the common source for both Babylonian and megalithic British astronomy. The fact that Taurus was at the start of the year, does not prove that the whole system needs to be dated to the Age of Taurus. The Babylonians may well have reorganized their mythology in this age.

This ancient star globe perhaps gives the clue for another reason why the proto-Greeks spread into the whole Mediterranean, namely that they were highly proficient astronomer-navigators, inevitably a highly prized accomplishment when sea trade was expanding in the Mediterranean and starting to develop in the Atlantic too. As proficient navigators, they would be welcomed on foreign ships which would inevitably take them to the Eastern Mediterranean and the ports of all the flourishing civilizations.

The art of navigating by the stars must have developed in megalithic Britain as the result of the accurate astronomy that was observed and defined in the early stages of the monumental standing stone temples. The ancient Greek globe described by Eudoxus thus reflects something of the quality of the astronomy that was practised at Stonehenge and the other British megalithic sites.

The sophisticated application of astronomy to navigation is stated in Greek mythology, for Apollo in his aspect as the dolphin has generally been accepted to represent this god as navigator. In view of the ancient Greek star globe it is clear that Apollo's navigating abilities were based on astronomy. Apollo's battle with the dragon pole star in Draco on arrival at Delphi, marks the astronomical period when the Heavens had moved sufficiently to render this ancient pole of the Heavens, the dragon pole as useless.

The Pythagoreans were reputed to be astronomers, but nothing of their astronomical activities is known. It would appear that this early brilliance in the art of astronomy had been allowed to fall into disuse at some time after the Apollo Wisdom had been established in Greece.

Gibraltar to the eastern Mediterranean

The bronze age in the Eastern Mediterranean was at its height in the period when the Cornish tin traders arrived at Gibraltar. There was another land in the Eastern Mediterranean that was at this period developing extensive trade links with the West; this was Minoan Crete. From what emerges a little later, it is evident that the Cretans met the Cornish tin traders and encouraged them to carry on their tin trade in Crete.

The first signs of the Cornish traders come from seal stones. It was common practice in the Levantine areas for each trader to mark his wares with a seal on wax or soft clay. A large number of seal stones have emerged from excavations in ancient Minoan palaces. As the 'calligraphy' of each country was very individual, it is quite easy to identify the country of origin of many of the seals. There are also many seals of Minoan origin. But there are other seal stones that have not been identified with any specific culture. This group of unidentified seals from

Heraklion Museum shows geometric figures of various polygons including the method of defining the nine-pointed star (Nos.773 and 2498).
There are also some that are reminiscent of the cup and ring marks found
in Britain. Of particular note is seal stone No.2498 which bears a strong
resemblance to the geometry behind the stone circle at Loch Buie, Isle
of Mull (see Part I, p.55).

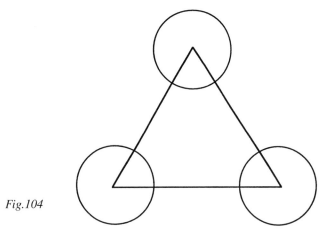

Fig.104

The site in Crete where these two seals were excavated is Phaestos
which is about half way along the southern coast of Crete. It was built
on higher ground with a port by the sea. Nearby Phaestos is another
small palace called Hagia Triada. It was from this site that the Hagia
Triada sargophagus came, now in the Museum at Heraklion. The
funeral procession painted on the sides include a priest playing the
lyre, with swans head terminals. It is dated at *c.* 1400 BC. Homer in
the *Iliad* lists all the places that sent troops at the siege of Troy. Of
all the cities on Crete, Phaestos is the only one with a Greek name in
Homeric times.

Emergence of the Apollo Wisdom in the Eastern Mediterranean

The Apollo Wisdom in Egypt
The first identifiable evidence of the arrival of the Apollo Wisdom in
Egypt *c.* 2600 BC can be found in the Pyramid of Cheops which was built
on the design of the Apollo geometry. This period in Egypt was one of
rejuvenation and immense development.

One of the outstanding features of megalithic Britain at the point of development from ancestor worship to that of the gods, was the construction of carefully planned immense burial monuments that must have served functions other than as a tomb alone. Two outstanding examples of these tombs are Newgrange in Ireland *c.* 3100 BC and Maes Howe in Orkney. Maes Howe is dated to *c.* 2800 BC and it was built with immense stone slabs to form a large central chamber with further side rooms off it and a long low narrow entrance passageway.

The Pyramid of Cheops was not designed on a circular base like Maes Howe but on a square, but otherwise there is a basic similarity of concept and construction. In all the ancient world there is nothing comparable with Cheops' pyramid except Maes Howe.

Pyramid building continued after Cheops until the end of the fourth dynasty, *c.* 2180 BC, when there appears to have been a breakdown in social organization and anarchy prevailed. On recovery of the social structure more pyramids were then erected but on a much smaller scale than in the first period. Pyramid building continued later for non-royal burials for a long time.

The concept of geometrical proportion, which seems to have been devised in megalithic Britain, is the factor which survived in Egypt and attests to the survival of some of the Apollo Wisdom that was introduced *c.* 2600 BC (Schwaller de Lubicz 1977).

There seems to be evidence of the use of sacred geometry in the layout of Egyptian temples (Lawlor 1982). Apart from architectural layouts, there was another application of sacred geometry and proportion which is well known and that is the canonical proportions within which the human form is depicted in Egypt (Harris 1971). The use of systems of canonical proportions was also prevalent in the Greek and later Roman worlds and continued well up to the Renaissance after which they were gradually abandoned.

There are many records preserved in Egypt of invasions from both east and west in the coastal areas and delta region. There are records of people from the west who were sometimes welcomed as helpful innovators, and others as enemies that had to be repelled; it was not till about the fifteenth century BC that the western peoples were named as Libyans. It is thus possible that there were several points in time when influences from the megalithic west arrived in ancient Egypt.

Another line of evidence for migration from NW Europe to Egypt is the physiognomy of the Ancient Egyptians. Some early Egyptian paintings clearly represent some important persons with white skin, blond hair and blue eyes. In particular, there is a painting on the Tomb of Menna at Thebes, which shows a blond haired man (Amon's superintendent in the fields) and his assistants involved in surveying a field using a knotted rope. This strongly implies that the blond people had brought mensuration skills which had been developed much earlier in northern Europe.*

There are many facets of Egyptian culture from the first dynasty *c.* 3100 BC onwards that have direct parallels in earlier Euphrates cultures. That neither are slavish copies of the other prompts Emery (1961) to say that: 'modern scholars have tended to ignore the possibility of conquest and immigration to both regions from some hypothetical and as yet undiscovered area.' The type of artefact that he is here discussing is the 'architectural concept of the panelled facade.' But this perspective arises after discussion of the idea that the first dynasty in Egypt marked the arrival of outside peoples of the dynastic race, a theory that many support. Architectural features of the type being described have no parallels in megalithic Britain yet it was the megalithic west that introduced the design of the Pyramid of Cheops, that is, the concept of geometrically controlled structures. If megalithic Britain influenced Egypt, is this the unidentified hypothetical source that also affected the Euphrates area? Babylonian astronomy is traced back to 2100 BC but the naming of the constellation Lyra was made in Britain in 2800 BC. If the formation of constellations is not accepted as a part of the knowledge of the very first farmers, then was it the megalithic British who first defined the constellations and influenced both Egypt and the land of two rivers?

The idea of the presence of a dynastic race gives a strange slant to the emergence of the early rich civilizations. Outsiders who for some reason or other had developed a better system of social organization, had the opportunity to enter the rich areas and take them over to the benefit of the persons involved as well as to the people that they had invaded.

---

* Recent research into the size and proportions of skulls of Egyptian Pharaohs show an uncanny similarity to those of people from northern France and the Nordic countries. The skull of Rameses II is described as pelasgic ellipsoidal, which is a Nordic trait. He also had reddish-yellow hair. Another study of Egyptian mummies showed that 50% were Caucasian, 40% Cro-Magnon and 10% Negroid. All this evidence points to an influx of 'northern' peoples into Egypt at that time. [RAB]

The arrival in Greece

Mainland Greece, which was not called by that name in those days, was populated by Luvian-speaking peoples in the first half of the second millennium BC. Crete, which seems to have had various linguistic groups at this period, had a thriving advanced civilization based on sea trade. The Cretan Minoan culture was already influencing mainland Greece at this early period.

It is in this early stage that the first Apollo seal dated to before 1700 BC emerges in Crete. Was the owner of this seal an expert navigator or a missionary of the Apollo Wisdom or both? Exactly what damage was done by the devastating eruption of the island of Thera in *c.* 1470 BC is not certain but soon after this event the old language of the Linear A tablets in Crete, which has not been deciphered, changes to Greek Linear B, and similar tablets are also found in mainland Mycenaean palaces. This suggests that the emergence of the Greek-speaking Apollo people was a consequence of a natural disaster and not war.

Why did the proto-Greeks come in force to the eastern Mediterranean at this point and become the rulers of the land? They could have come as navigators or they could have been invited in by the existing people to fill the gaps in the management and bureaucratic infrastructure caused by the eruption of Thera. Alternatively, they could have come as opportunists in the wake of the natural disaster, or they could have come for a combination of all these reasons.

I have the suspicion that it was Minoan Crete itself that was first taken over by the Greek-speaking peoples of the Apollo Wisdom. It was from Crete that the Apollo centre of Delphi was set up, an event recorded in Greek legend. Minoan pottery shards have been discovered at Delphi strengthening this mythical account of the setting up of the Apollo site.

Another very early site was founded on Delos, a small island off eastern Greece, and associated with legends which describe how Zeus approached Leto in the disguise of a swan and Leto became pregnant. Hera, the wife of Zeus was furious and chased Leto from place to place and, when hidden, she gave birth on Delos to twins, Apollo and Artemis. Zeus seems to have been the pre-Greek father god in Luvian Greece and so has no relationship with Apollo in any sense. However if Apollo was to be accepted into the old Pantheon, then it would seem much more credible if he were the son of Zeus. Why did Zeus take the form of the swan? The swan Cygnus is the constellation beside and almost intertwined with Lyra and therefore becomes significant in this respect. In addition the swan was also one of Apollo's main attributes, so this swan attribute was re-translated to signify the fatherhood of Zeus. That Hera chased the pregnant Leto suggests that an existing mother cult, of which Hera was the goddess, resisted the introduction of the god Apollo into the Greek world. On the central hill on Delos there is an ancient trilithon which is highly reminiscent of British megalithic constructions.

The swan symbolism that is associated with Apollo has a strange quirk about it. Aratos, the first Greek to record the names of the constellations used for navigation, names the constellation Cygnus as the hen and not a swan. For some reason the Latin peoples named the same constellation 'the Swan.' So although the Latin peoples were using the term swan for the constellation which is adjacent to Lyra, the Greeks themselves were not. However Italy, where the Latin speaking peoples came from, is slightly closer to Britain and there is no reason why they should not have adopted the swan name direct from Britain. Why it did not survive in Greece is not known. The fact that Apollo was associated with the swan from the time of his arrival in Minoan Crete would suggest the relation-ship with the constellation of Cygnus originated in Britain.

A third possible Apollo site is Phaestos in Crete. This was a most beautiful palace in southern Crete built on high ground overlooking the great fertile plains behind which Mount Ida rises. To the south there are sandy beaches and the open sea. It is from this site that the first evidence of the cithara is found as an image on a sarcophagus from Hagia Triada; this is also where one of the Apollo seals was found. It was a Minoan palace but acquired its Greek name in antiquity.

The names of these three very early Apollo sites are interesting. Phaestos means the place of light. The root of the name Delos is *del* which in Greek means deep or profound, so Delos means 'the profound place.' Delphoi then can be interpreted in terms of *del* and *phos* which means 'fire' or 'light.' So three of the earliest Apollo sites have profound names indicative of the intentions of the Apollo Wisdom and its estab-lishment in the eastern Mediterranean.

For a variety of reasons, not fully understood, the Cretan site at Phaestos did not thrive though it did not sink into total oblivion as did the great palaces of Knossos, Malia and Zacros. The reason for the posi-tion of Phaestos in relation to Miletus is discussed later.

Apart from the sacred centres, the incoming Greeks set themselves up as the ruling class in various palaces around mainland Greece and in Crete, some of which have been excavated by archaeologists. Homer, in the Iliad, names many of the Greek princes who contributed to the pan-Hellenic force that besieged Troy at about 1250 BC. In some cases he describes their ancestry, which in each case is short, indicating only a small number of generations. This suggests that the timespan between the siege of Troy and the first arrival of the Greeks was short.

Pythagoras

Pythagoras was a Greek philosopher (most active around 540–510 BC) who was born in Samos and moved to Croton. He set up a school that was as much concerned with religion as with arithmetic and music. His death may have been due to his unpopularity with the local ruling faction because he was also trying to get his followers to enter politics. In spite of the sketchy details of his life and teachings he became a legend in his lifetime and when future Pythagoreans mentioned 'new' information, they tended to ascribe it to Pythagoras. This included certain theorems and the proportional string lengths in use in the theory of music. It was believed that he was the reincarnation of Hyperborean Apollo.

At first sight, the whole position of Pythagoras seems bizarre. There seems to be no direct link with Pythagoras' students and the later Pythagoreans in Athens or elsewhere. This position is in keeping with the idea that the ancient Apollo Wisdom from megalithic Britain had been maintained in an oral form since the Greeks arrived in the Eastern Mediterranean. But what circumstances existed in Greece prior to the emergence of Pythagoras?

There were no kings any longer in Greece but the Apollo establishments were supported by the Greek aristocracy and, though no records remain, they presumably had their children educated by learned people from the Apollo centres. Over 300 years later, Alexander the Great was educated by Aristotle. This old political order came to an end as the result of the invention of coinage, possibly in Lydia or at Aegina. The aristocracy did not undertake trade but there were lesser Greeks who did, as well as a number of foreign traders who settled in Athens and, with ever expanding trade, they became very wealthy. These traders were not educated in the Apollo tradition but instead had adopted Hermes who was the god of travellers. The result was that the aristocracy became impoverished and could no longer support the Apollo centres. The wealthy traders demanded and eventually achieved the right to have their say in the running of Athens, because it was they that filled the city's coffers through the trade dues. So in the sixth century BC, the old aristocracy as well as the Apollo centres were impoverished and the new wealthy class knew nothing of Apollo or the traditional wisdom that it disseminated. There was thus an acute crisis within the Apollo establishments.

This is the point at which Pythagoras emerges. Was he commissioned by the Apollo priests to go out and teach the Apollo Wisdom openly for the first time, and try to establish an Apollonian education directed at the new rich section of the population?

No direct evidence survives from this period as to whether or not the new rich traders were considered 'uneducated' yet one aspect of the lack of an Apollonian education in the new rich society was described fully. In order to incorporate the newcomers into society, they were invited to feasts or dinner parties. Traditionally, after the feasting, they amused themselves by singing and making music on the lyre. One man would start by singing a spontaneous verse, accompanying himself on the lyre, and then he would pass the instrument on to someone else, who had in turn to respond with a new verse which was sung to the lyre accompaniment, then pass it to a third person and so on round the guests. This practice presumes that aristocratic boys were 'schooled' in the arts of lyre playing and spontaneously inventing verses. The new traders, however, had not been taught these arts, which led to riots at dinner parties and comments on the 'terrible situation' appear in plays. This musical situation informs us of only one aspect of aristocratic education but it shows that there was an Apollonian (musical) education system in existence of which the traders knew nothing.

Though various schools of philosophy emerged later, it was not until Plato (429–347 BC) set up the Academy in Athens that the Apollo Wisdom was re-established on a sound footing, and it became fashionable for the sons of the wealthy merchants to attend the school.

Returning to Pythagoras, though his name is believed to have been given to him while young, it was a very apt one for one who espoused the Apollo Wisdom. *Agora* means the market place but primarily meant 'the speaking place.' The Agora was where you could meet and talk to the public. At the time of Pythagoras, Delphi was the most prominent Apollo centre and was commonly known as 'the Pythia.' Hence by combining *pythia* and *agora, pythagoras* could be interpreted as 'the spokesperson for Apollo.' This was never recorded but it would explain why the subsequent philosophers and geometers were known as Pythagoreans. They, too, were the spokesmen of the ancient Apollo Wisdom.

As early as the time of Plato, there was scepticism about the old gods. By the time the Romans had conquered the known world and the various Caesars deified themselves, many new religious movements sprang up and there were several new 'saviours.' For the neo-Platonists or neo-Pythagoreans, to label their way of thinking under the name of Apollo would be useless, so instead they 'deified' Pythagoras and embroidered the fame of the man himself. They were trying to revive the ancient Apollo Wisdom in the name of Pythagoras and also trying to compete with the new forms of belief that were current at that time.

Though none of this is to be found in ancient texts, there is one recorded aspect of Pythagoras that sums up this whole argument. Pythagoras was described as being the reincarnation of the ancient Hyperborean Apollo, or in other words, the renaissance of the ancient Apollo Wisdom. Perhaps the activities of Pythagoras, the man, records some of the factors involved in the ancient Apollo establishments both in Greece and megalithic Britain. These activities were the quadrivium, that is the sciences of arithmetic, geometry, music and astronomy/astrology; religious beliefs and practices; control of political activities.

Finally, to find further support for this thesis, it is now necessary to look for the remnants of the Apollo Wisdom in Britain, from whence I believe it came.

Memories of the origins of Apollo in Britain

We would expect any memories of ancient events in Britain to be incorporated in legendary material. In pre-literate societies the 'history' of the people was preserved by the bards within the oral tradition. It is surprising therefore to find that it is early Greek travellers' tales, as well as the Celtic myths, that give the clearest evidence for the British Isles being the seat of the 'Greek' gods.

Hyperborea was a word used by the Greeks to describe any land lying to the north of Greece and means 'beyond the north wind.' The Greeks set up trading stations in the Black Sea and as they became acquainted with the peoples, the name Hyperborea was replaced by Scithia, and the Celts' lands became Keltica. By about 320 BC, the term Hyperborea ceased to be used. Many of the travellers' tales come from before this date so Hyperborea remained in use and the true names of these old discovered lands still have to be deduced by other means. Before examining the legends, a brief historical outline of the British Isles needs to be given.

Bronze Age society continued to flourish after *c.* 1500 BC when many of the megalithic sites were abandoned but in 1159 BC there was a very large-scale eruption at Mount Hekla in Iceland. The ash from Hekla has been found by archaeologists at many sites in northern Scotland. From dendrochronological studies it is believed that there was a prolonged period of climatic instability which lasted for nineteen years. This event has been studied also by scientists working on ice cores from Greenland and thus it has been possible to date this event precisely. The climatic irregularities caused by this huge eruption appears to have effected the entire northern hemisphere including China. Many upland sites were abandoned although life gradually returned to normal after this devastating natural catastrophe.

It is only in the Roman period that we learn that Britain was mainly inhabited by Celtic-speaking peoples. Apart from brief Roman reports, the only written sources for the Celtic culture come from Ireland and Wales. The legends, however, were not recorded until after Christianity became established and literacy increased among the population. Though these are the only sources of Celtic literature to survive, a predominantly Gallic culture existed from north-west Spain (Galicia) across the centre of Europe to Anatolia (the Galatians of the New Testament). Nothing of the legends of the mainland European Celts survive so it is impossible to know how the insular traditions differed from the mainland Celts as a whole.

According to Irish legends, when these latest Celtic invaders took political control in Ireland, some of the previous deities were retained and the memory of the burial mounds, such as Newgrange, was also retained. Any surviving ancient legends in the West had three points of fracture: the crisis of the Hekla eruption; the influence of the Celtic overlords; the influence of the Christian Church which turned the ancient gods into mere mortals, or converted them into their own deities.*

---

* There is new evidence that the pagan god Dionysius was used as a model for the Christian Jesus (Freke & Gandy 1999). [RAB]

Ireland and northern Scotland were the only parts of western Europe
not conquered by the Romans. Elsewhere the rule of Rome system-
atically renamed the conquered gods, giving them the names of Roman
Gods that seemed to have the same attributes. This was soon followed
by the deification of the Roman Emperors themselves! A Gaulish god
of both war and healing sometimes got the title of Mars and sometimes
Apollo. This is but one example of the many anomalies caused by the
Roman system.

Before the Romans moved into the West, a few Greek geographers
had explored the oceanic coasts and Britain. A few of their reports survive mainly as brief extracts in later authors' work, but for the most part
they are rather uninformative. However, there is one example which is of
great interest. It comes from Diodorus Siculus who is possibly quoting
Pytheas who was active *c.* 330 BC.

> ... it will not be foreign to our purpose to discuss the legen-
> dary accounts of the Hyperboreans.
>
> ... Hecataeus and certain others say that in the regions
> beyond the land of the Celts there lies in the ocean an island
> no smaller than Sicily. This island, the account continues, is
> situated in the north and is inhabited by the Hyperboreans,
> who are called by that name because their home is beyond
> the point whence the north wind (Boreas) blows;
>
> ... Leto was born on this island, and for that reason
> Apollo is honoured among them above all other gods; and
> the inhabitants are looked upon as priests of Apollo, after
> a manner, since daily they praise this god continuously in
> song and honour him exceedingly. And there is also on the
> island both a magnificent sacred precinct of Apollo and a
> notable temple which is adorned with many votive offer-
> ings and is spherical in shape. Furthermore, a city is there
> which is sacred to this god, and the majority of its inhabit-
> ants are players on the cithara; and these continually play
> on this instrument in the temple and sing hymns of praise
> to the god, glorifying his deeds.
>
> ... They say also that the moon, as viewed from this
> island, appears to be but a little distance from the earth and
> to have upon it prominences, like those of the earth, which
> are visible to the eye. The account is also given that the god

visits the island every nineteen years, the period in which the return of the stars to the same place in the heavens is accomplished; and for this reason the nineteen-year period is called by the Greeks the 'year of Meton.' At the time of this appearance of the god he both plays on the cithara and dances continuously the night through from the vernal equinox until the rising of the Pleiades, expressing in this manner his delight in his successes.

There are many items in this quotation that need comment:

Hyperboreans. This is a mythical name for all unknown peoples in the North. As this term went out of fashion about 320 BC, presumably this report is from Pytheas or an earlier source.

Hecataeus is believed never to have explored outside the Mediterranean.

... an island in the ocean beyond the land of the Kelts, no smaller than Sicily. By this description, the land could have been Britain or Ireland.

Leto and Apollo. The Greeks interpreted all foreign gods in terms of their own deities. The name Apollo, however, may have been known in Britain in the form Avalon.

Notable temple ... which is spherical. The temple is assumed to be Stonehenge in this translation. The description 'spherical' is given in Greek as σφαιροειδη (*sphairoeidé*) which means sphere shaped. Was the original word   σφαιρικος (*sphairikos*) spherical, implying the doctrine of the spheres, which is astronomy? The other references to the moon and the return of the stars to their same place, imply that the temple is an astronomical observatory. This would be highly appropriate to Stonehenge.

A city sacred to this God. Could this be Glastonbury?

... and the majority of its inhabitants are players on the cithara. The Greek geographers were highly educated people and would know the difference between a cithara, Apollo's lyre and any other type of lyre. Hence the instrument being played is clearly identified.

The moon. The description of the moon having prominences like on earth demonstrate that astronomical knowledge in Britain was in an advanced state for they knew that the moon was 'like' the earth and spherical.

Every nineteen years. The comment on this nineteen year cycle is that it is called the 'Year of Meton' in Greece. The Metonic year was well known in Greece. The cycles of the moon come on exactly the same calendar dates every nineteen years, that is, new and full moon. However, the description of the festivities which were celebrated from the spring equinox till the rising of the Pleiades (autumn) hardly fits in with a purely calendrical dating system.

I believe that the Apollo geometry defines the astronomy at the latitude of Stonehenge of the solar year represented by the circumpolar stars including Cygnus and Lyra, and the extreme southerly rising position of the moon which occurs every 18.62 years, or nearly 19 years as quoted in this description. At the time of the extreme southerly rising and setting of the moon, there is only one date at which the lowest point is reached but this period is known as the major standstill, for the moon nearly reaches its extreme positions over a period of some months. Further, the musical ladder, which is the tuning of Apollo's cithara, is not in the arrangement of the stars until the time of the standstill, appropriately described as 'this appearance of the God' (Apollo) when 'he both plays on the cithara and dances continuously the night through.'

The return of the stars to the same place in the heavens. The moon at the 19-year metonic cycle is not in the same position in the sky in relation to the sun and the stars, from one period to the next. As the description of the Moon is quoted and highlighted in this context, it is thus the moon that denotes the festival of the return of Apollo whose geometry cannot be completed till the Moon has returned to its same position at the Lunar standstill. This festival fits exactly with the Apollo geometry. The duration of the Lunar standstill explains why the Apollo festival lasted from the spring equinox till the rising of the Pleiades. The next similar festival would fall earlier in the autumn, that is, 18.62 years later. It would appear that the astronomy of Apollo was indeed remembered and celebrated in Britain at the edges of history.

Who kept this festival alive? The bards in the West went on playing the cithara and by Roman times there is much more detail to be gleaned.

But the bards were an integral part of the Druid culture at the beginning of the British and Gaulish historical period. Whether the priests/astronomers were called Druids at the time of this report is quite irrelevant. What is clear is that the later Druids were the inheritors of these earlier Apollo priests. Mackie (1977) also believes that the Druids, the Iron Age British priests, were the inheritors of the megalithic wisdom.

Hesperides
Diodorus relates more legends about the West but whether these later ones were influenced by some Western tradition or not is unclear. Book IV, 27 states:

> but we must not fail to mention what the myths relate about Atlas and about the race of the Hesperides. (p.429 Loeb edition)

Here, Atlas is clearly associated with the Hesperides, the Islands in the West. Towards the end of this section, Diodorus continues:

> For Atlas had worked out the science of astrology to a degree surpassing others and had ingeniously discovered the spherical nature of the stars.

The phrase 'the spherical nature of the stars' has generally been accepted to imply that the stars were understood to be on a sphere. Here then in legend is the assignment of the Star Globe to Atlas, who is associated with the Western Isles, or Hesperides. The earliest star globe, described earlier, was dated to around 2000 BC with latitude 36°N, which is the latitude of Gibraltar and North Africa. As neither North Africa nor Spain can be described as islands, it is tempting here to associate the Hesperides with the British Isles.

Avalon — or Apollon
In some of the Celtic tales and myths that have survived, the word *Affalon,* pronounced Avalon, is used to refer to a wondrous mythical site. It was also the burial place of the legendary Arthur. The usual translation of Avalon is apple orchard, which is questioned by some scholars.

In the type of Celtic spoken in the west of Britain in Roman times, the letter P was pronounced V. Hence Apollo, Apollon becomes Avollo,

Avollon. As these peoples were preliterate there was no question of the
niceties of correct spelling

Glastonbury is only about forty miles from Stonehenge. The 'ton'
and 'bury' are post-Roman additions denoting settlement. The 'Glas'
element is thought to come from the fact that glassmaking was carried out there in the Dark Ages. William of Malmesbury in *The
Antiquity of the Church at Glastonbury* associated Glastonbury with
Avallon, while Geraldus of Wales, writing a little later, describes two
names for the town, Inis Avallon, and Inis Gutrin, the Isle of Glass.
Glastonbury was built on a piece of higher ground that was cut off
from the mainland by marshes, but one could sail from the open sea
of the Bristol Channel the whole way to the town. Geraldus also says
that Avallon derives from a person called Vallo who lived there in
the distant past. So, here, the island of 'glass' and Avallon/Vallo are
connected.

This double sense appears much earlier. Pliny, quoting Pytheas refers
to an island called Abalus (Abalwn) where amber was washed up from
the sea. The Germanic name for amber was Glaesum, used also by the
Greeks and Romans. It is generally believed that the Wessex culture
(Stonehenge) traded with northern Europe for amber, among other
things, and Glastonbury is at the western edge of the Wessex culture. But
amber is associated very strongly with Apollo; it was described as the
'Tears of Apollo' in Greek and Roman myth. The West of England had
the tin, Glastonbury the amber, both tin and amber being highly prized
goods in the eastern Mediterranean.

So the two names of Glastonbury, Glaesum and Apollo would appear
to be linked and were indeed remembered in the Celtic areas, though by
the time of William of Malmesbury and Geraldus, their original meaning
was forgotten (Ahl 1982).

The dream of Aengus (Õengus)

Before discussing this Irish myth, a little background explanation is
necessary. The mythologies of several ancient lands have survived in
part, from which it emerges that the sun was considered feminine and
the moon masculine in many early sources (McKrickard 1990). The rise
of patriarchy in the Bronze Age altered the previous system and con-
demned women to be looked on as the source of evil; hence the position

of Eve in the Old Testament. The goddess of the sun was demoted and replaced by a male god. With the emergence of Christianity, the feminine element was retained as Sophia, one of the Trinity, but was soon replaced by the Holy Ghost. Within this perspective, the sun could be feminine and the moon masculine in Irish legends. In Scotland the word Loun, or Loon, denotes a lad or youth (and lasses had the name Quean, Quine or Quinie). The connection between the moon (loon) and the male of the human species is overt.

In the legend of 'The Dream of Aengus,' Aengus appears to be the moon and the object of his love is Caer, the swan maiden. Swan maidens represented the sun, or sunbeams or daughters of the sun and they were closely interwoven with Apollo, whose symbol is persistently the swan. By the time that this legend was written down, Christianity had eradicated the pre-Christian deities and saw the sun as masculine.

The story goes that Aengus was a youthful princeling who one night saw the most beautiful young woman in Erin, but when he tried to take her she disappeared. Aengus promptly developed 'love sickness' and didn't eat. The next night she came again, this time with a timpan on which she played beautiful music which made him sleep. Aengus grew sicker and she continued to visit him at night for a year. Aengus was now really sick. He sees a magical doctor who realizes what is wrong with him and summons his mother to search all Ireland for Aengus' beautiful love. She searches for a year unsuccessfully. Then the doctor recommends that they send for the Dagdae, the father of Aengus, who is King of the Side (pronounced shee) of Erin. Dagdae can't help but can contact Bodh, King of the Side of Mumu whose knowledge spread throughout Erin. Both makes a search of all Ireland and reports back that the girl has been found at Loch Bél Dracon in Cruitt Cliach (Loch Bél Dracon means loch of the dragon's mouth). So Aengus goes to Bodh who takes him to the Loch Bél Dracon where he sees his visitor, Caer, the Swan Maiden, among three fifties (150) of girls, each pair linked with a silver chain. Bodh tells Angus that this girl is Caer Ibormeath, daughter of yet another King of the Side.

Bodh has no power to give Caer to Aengus because she is in bird form for one year and human form the next year and 'her power is greater than mine.' Later Aengus goes at Samhain to Loch Bél Dracon again, sees Caer and one hundred and fifty other swan maidens. Aengus calls her and she comes. They sleep in the form of swans till they have circled the lake three times. They eventually leave as two white birds, flying to Bruig ind Maicc Oic where they sing to all the people who then fall asleep for three days and three nights.

This is a complicated story perhaps describing a hierarchy of ancient deities, fairy people who lived in ancient tumuli of the Newgrange type. Every 18.62 years, when the moon is at the lunar standstill, the moon can hardly rise very far, that is, the moon is too ill to get up, then at other times it goes 'all over the sky.' The lunar standstill forms part of the Apollo astronomy, and the 'beautiful music' only emerges in the geometry at this point.

The time covered between Aengus first seeing Caer (at the moon standstill) and the eventual marriage seems to be over three years, approximately. Is the 'marriage' of the Sun Maiden and the youthful moon an eclipse? The eclipse is described in other mythologies either as the marriage of the sun (female) and moon, or the rape of the sun by the moon.

Here then, the Apollo astronomy has been described by an early Greek traveller and in an Irish myth. The memory of the name Apollo in the form Avalon is overt. By the time that the Romans eventually arrived in Britain, memories of the megalithic wisdom still survived. Though the Irish had tales of sea voyages, some literal and some purely symbolic of inner journeys, there seems no trace of any recollection of their peoples settling in another land, Greece.

Carved stone balls

Over 400 carved stone balls have been described from various locations in Scotland, North England, and Norway (Marshall 1976). Eleven types have been identified with variable number of knobs, from 3 to 55. They have mostly been located as stray finds, but those found at Skara Brae (Orkney) were manufactured in the late Neolithic period. How long afterwards they went on being made is not known. They have not been found in graves so they are not considered as personal objects.

The distribution of the localities in which they were found is revealing. Most came from the East of Scotland between the Moray Firth and the River Tay, though several have been found in Fife and

Fig.105 Carved tetrahedral Neolithic stone ball

north of the Moray Firth. Thirteen have been found in Orkney. A few came from the West of Scotland and the Hebrides, the South-West of Scotland, four in the North of England, one from Ireland and there is one in the Trondheim Museum which was found at Lindas in Norway.

Five of the types of carved stone balls, those that form a symmetrical division of the surface, have the same form as the five Platonic solids (Critchlow 1979). Plato, who gave the first written account of them, considered these objects to be sacred, and represented Fire, Air, Earth, Water, and the Ether or heaven. To the Pythagoreans, these were not just mathematically perfect forms but sacred objects. To them, the geometry of these forms, like all their geometric studies, were sacred, the creations of the One or the creator god. In megalithic Britain the Clava type burial cairns and the recumbent stone circles, like all the other rings and circles, were sacred spaces and the ceremonies within them were to enable the people to find a link with the heavens, the dwelling place of the gods. One must conclude that the carved stone balls were also sacred objects. *

Conclusion

This new theory of the nature of the British megalithic culture hinges on the Greek god Apollo (and his Titan ancestors) as well as the yardsticks of the 'Greek' foot (and its related 'Greek' fathom), both of which are present in the megalithic remains in Britain. The Greeks themselves in pre-Christian times believed that Apollo came from the North and Pythagoras was described as the reincarnation of the Hyperborean Apollo. Not only is the Greek mythology associated with these islands but the actual 'Greek' yardsticks were also used in megalithic Britain for the plans of their sacred sites and the geometry that many of them contain.

All the four elements of the Pythagorean quadrivium, (1) number (arithmetic), (2) number in space (geometry), (3) number in time (music) and (4) number in space and time (astronomy/astrology) have been identified in megalithic Britain.

---

* Intriguingly, a book entitled *The Riddle of Prehistoric Britain* by Comyns Beaumont (1945), contains much in common with Anne Macaulay's thesis, namely that the Ancient Egyptians and Greeks originated from Britain. It is known that Anne's father, Sir David Russell, owned a copy of this book but nowhere does Anne refer to it.

Beaumont claims that parts of the western seaboard of Scotland actually represent the land of Greek legends. For example, Mull becomes Euboea, Iona was Delos, Appin was Achaia and Ardgour was Thessaliotis. Ben Cruachan he ascribes to Parnassus and Ben Nevis becomes Mount Olympus. The Hesperides are naturally related to the Hebrides. He goes on to claim that the Phoenecians, who are believed to have traded with Britain for tin, actually belonged to these islands and exported the metal to other lands. He believes that the people who colonized the eastern Mediterranean left Britain in *c.* 1322 BC when a catastrophe befell these islands. This date is not far removed from the date 1159 BC for the Hekla-induced evacuation.

Finally, Beaumont believes that Apollo, the deity beloved of the Ionians, originated from Iona, once the seat of pagan learning. Certainly there is historical evidence for Druid activity on the island, which is one reason why the early Celtic Christian missionaries such as Columba made their base there. I have reason to believe that the island of Iona contains elements of sacred geometry within its landscape, which will become clear one day.

Whatever one thinks about Beaumont's sometimes fanciful linguistic links between Britain and the ancient world, Anne has brought a more rigorous mathematical approach to this intriguing interpretation of ancient British history. [RAB]

If this theory proves to be acceptable, then much light is thrown on both megalithic Britain and the proto-Greeks' arrival in the eastern Mediterranean. However many questions also emerge.

— Where did the tin trading British sailors set up staging posts? If so how can they be traced?
— If they were trading in bigger centres, could they be traced by the presence of their geometric seal stones, or tin products similar to those found in Crete?
— Were the stone circles in North West Africa built by the British tin traders?

I propose that the whole British megalithic way of thought be called the Apollo Wisdom. Did this Apollo Wisdom spread throughout Europe at the start of the Bronze Age? Alexander Thom did not find the megalithic yard in all megalithic sites in Britain because the circles were all defined by geometric constructions which used both implicit and explicit geometry based on one or more of the three yardsticks: the megalithic yard, the megalithic rod and the 'Greek' foot. Professor Thom calculated that some of these megalithic structures were built for astronomical observations. So what were these astronomical observations carried out by the megalithic astronomers for?

Caesar writes of the Druids in Britain:

> They [the Druids] hold long discussions about the heavenly bodies and their movements, about the size of the universe and the earth, about the nature of the physical world, and about the power and properties of the immortal gods [the planets], subjects in which they also give instruction to their pupils. (Wiseman 1980)

Were they trying to discover the size of the earth, the distance and size of the moon, or were they aware of the precession of the equinoxes and trying to understand what was happening? By 1700 BC, the date that Thom gives to later astronomical sites, the earlier pole star in Draco was no longer usable as true North. And this is the same event that is the basis for the legend that Apollo 'killed' the Dragon or Pytho when he arrived at Delphi.

Perhaps it is time to examine the later megalithic astronomical alignments to see if they might have been used for more subtle measurements than has previously been thought possible.

In some sense, the activities of these megalithic specialists appear to be approaching pure science. Their observation of the sun, moon and stars was remarkably accurate, as was their approach to music which defined the basic acoustic laws. They obviously made immense strides in their understanding of their world and the emergence of the gods indicates that they had achieved a degree of freedom from the superstitious ideas associated with all powerful spirits which exist in so many early communities. From their accurate observations, the idea of natural law must have emerged but unlike the materialistic attitudes of today, these natural laws were themselves respected as sacred. The geometry of the gods is the pattern of the stars, moon and sun in relation to the earth; it is also the pattern of acoustic laws, land measurement, the ingredients for squaring the circle, hence basic mathematics. But the gods were sacred just as the arts involved in their creation were also sacred, This perception of the unity of design behind all manifestation in heaven and earth, time and space, music and matter must represent the belief that all things were sacred to them. It is hardly surprising then that in the Greek world, Apollo is the god of music and harmony associated with the idea that the goal is to keep everything in harmony, or in accordance with the natural laws. The name of Apollo's musical harmony in Greek is *kithara* (cithara) and the word for purging disease in mankind is *katharsis*.

Perhaps the most intriguing aspect of this work is the rise throughout all western Europe of a man-made god, Apollo. Though he was man-made, Apollo also implied fundamental proportion in everything. Did these ancient events determine the ways and thinking of western Europe? One aspect of the megalithic Apollonian culture clearly survives today. The musical triangles of Apollo and Lyra bear the tuning of the major chord (D, G, B) combined with its relative minor chord (G, B, E). This tuning survives on the classical guitar today and it was this tuning that created the development of harmonic music, the great wonder of the western world.

With the feeling that I have only scratched the surface of the British megalithic enigma, it should be pointed out that there are still vast fields for further research. Work on the microgeometry of the megalithic monuments was started by Thom but needs further attention. The so-called 'cup and ring' petroglyphs, which appear engraved on seal stones in Minoan Crete, must have been sufficiently meaningful for them to be used as identity marks. Was this a form of script? And the largest megalithic phenomena, the stone rows and avenues of which there are over a thousand spread over Brittany, Ireland and Britain (Burl 1993) demand closer investigation.

It appears that in this little corner of north-west Europe, partly isolated by the ocean, something very important emerged that is still fundamental to the way of thinking in the West despite the many Eastern influences.

The people of the megalithic West of Europe developed highly advanced mathematical skills prior to 4000 BC which they eventually translated into engineering skills; the transport of huge stones; the erection of stone structures preserving their superb geometries and their highly refined astronomical skills, which showed that the earth was round.

After *c.* 2800 BC, there was a long period of great development culminating in the period between 2400–1800 BC when the greatest number of standing stone sites was constructed. After this time there was a marked tailing off in building activity and by 1400 BC Stonehenge and other sites had been mostly abandoned. Thus this period of 1400 years reflects the creative activities of the bards.

The late Professor Alexander Thom applied his engineering and scientific skills to the British megalithic remains and surveyed many sites with great accuracy and identified the yardsticks that they used. His approach to astronomy led to the understanding of the ancient calendar with the quarter days that still exist today! Without the accurate and pioneering work of Professor Thom and his ability to approach the megalithic remains without the limitations of the standard theories, my research would have been impossible.*

---

* During the editing of this book, news appeared about the discovery of a skull of a Caucasian female in New Mexico, USA, dated at 13000 years old. It is believed that she must have migrated from central Europe through Asia to Alaska then New Mexico. Another explanation for this discovery is that people from northern Europe could have migrated directly to America, which in turn implies that a civilization could have existed in northern Europe capable of navigating the Atlantic Ocean. This new evidence offers further support to Anne Macaulay's thesis that an advanced civilization existed in the British Isles. [RAB]

Appendix 1

Anne Macaulay — A Biographical Note

On March 11, 1924, in Aithernie, Fife, near the Lundin Standing Stones, David and Alison Russell celebrated the safe arrival of their youngest child Anne. The family lived here only for a short while and on the death of Anne's grandmother, they moved to Silverburn a few miles away from Lundin Links.

Silverburn was ideal for raising children. The house, surrounded by a sea of lawns and pillowed around by mature woods, overlooked Largo Bay. Her father, Sir David Russell, was a remarkable man whose interests ranged from industry to religion, combined with a great love of home and family.* As head of the family papermaking business, Sir David suffered many worries through the 'Twenties,' and being a spiritual man his resolution was shared in part with his children, in whose development he always took a strong interest. Thus Anne was already learning much that was to give her the overview that proved so effective in later life. She was also influenced by Annie, chief cook and factotum for the family. Annie used to tell the most wonderful stories, revealing much ancient earth knowledge and Druidic magic, disguised as folklore and fable.

When she was no more than eighteen months old, Anne had her first intimation of what was to become a life-long quest. As she later told a friend, while in her pram in the garden at Aithernie, she had heard the sound of a guitar being played quite beautifully. There were no guitarists in the family, yet that music haunted her down the years, and she was past 30 before she heard it again — the famous classical guitarist Segovia playing Francisco Tarrega's 'Alhambra.' Her music! It was to weave through the tapestry of her life, giving it purpose and meaning to the end.

Those early years at Silverburn, under her father's influence, nurtured her questing spirit. Her years at St Leonard's School, St Andrews, during

* See Bibliography for L. Macintyre's biography of Sir David Russell.

the Second World War, were not so happy. She did not fit in, feeling trapped within its conventional attitudes. The emphasis on games, including cricket, was the last straw. Anne left early but not before meeting her lifelong friend Ludi How who was later to become a foil and sounding board for many of Anne's ideas, both 'sublime and ridiculous' as her family describe them. On leaving St Leonard's, Anne had a brief taste of academia at Edinburgh University, found it wanting at that time and then departed to South Africa where she learnt to pilot a plane and to meditate. She informed Ludi that she now had access to both outer and inner worlds.

The end of the War brought sadness to life at Silverburn. Those who had not returned left a void, although Anne's parents found consolation in the arrival of grandchildren. The loss of her brother Patrick, and another great friend Alexis, hit Anne hard. It brought questions of survival after death and the possibility of the existence of another greater reality beyond the perception of our five senses. Much later, when her own time came, Anne found that she could face death with humour and calm acceptance.

Meanwhile, accompanying her father on an excavation which he had funded in Istanbul, she met with her future husband Bill Macaulay, a scholar in Byzantine art, whose expertise in mosaics her father greatly valued. They subsequently married, living first in Glasgow where Bill was Curator of the Glasgow Museum of Art. In 1953 Bill became a partner in Aitken Dott, art dealers in Edinburgh, and the family moved to Johnsburn House in Balerno on the edge of the Pentland Hills.

Just before the birth of her fifth child in 1957, came a turning point in Anne's life. Her creative energy was rekindled by an intense interest in classical guitar music. She learnt to play the instrument, attaining a proficiency close to that of a virtuoso.

Something was still missing, however; it was unclear where music and the guitar were leading. She confided to a friend that they seemed to form a bridge with inner orbiting satellites, rich in influences and experiences. Like many people in the 1960s Anne found herself questioning established values and dogmas and found them wanting. This emptiness of spiritual values left Anne and others disillusioned and despairing of answers. Anne felt herself more and more drawn by the healing powers of music into exploring the Pythagorean School which revealed to her a deeper connection between mathematics and music.

Then something strange happened. A frozen thumb put paid to Anne playing the guitar. Despite this setback nothing halted her obsession with the instrument's early history and its uses. Her mind was also obsessed with Apollo, the god of music and healing, and why he, too, was associated with the lyre. Inspired, she married numbers to the letters in the Greek alphabet for the name Apollo. The result was the discovery of the elegant geometric figure whose proportions are found in many megalithic stone circles and from which a guitar may be tuned as well as other uses.

Looking for support for her discovery, Anne's attention was drawn to the work of Professor Alexander Thom, as yet in its infancy. An early survey of his drawings convinced her of her own findings and over several years she resurveyed much of his work and drew her own conclusions from her research. This task dominated the rest of her life. She travelled widely in search of further proof of her ideas, to Greece, Turkey, Malta, Egypt and throughout the British Isles.

1971 was an auspicious year in Anne's life. It brought together several influential people who supported and confirmed her work. But it also brought the break-up of her marriage. She met Andrew Glazewski, a Polish priest, musicologist, cosmologist, a serious student of quantum physics and music in relation to healing and, like Anne, he too was a skilled practitioner with the dowsing rods which they used for survey and measurement. Anne always maintained that he was the one person who understood the full potential of her Apollonian geometry. She also learnt much from members of the Sufi tradition — the Chisti Order is particularly associated with music. In 1971 she met Pir Vilayal Iniat Khan, the head of the Chisti Order, and she also met the guitarist Paul Segovia.

The next seventeen years, until her early death in 1998, were filled with trying to bring her work to some kind or order and to record the huge mass of material which she had collected and written. Her work became well known and she was invited to speak at conferences and symposia in the United States and in Britain. In 1994 she was awarded an Honorary Fellowship by the University of Edinburgh.

It is hard to say with any certainty where Anne got her genius from, but it is clear that the people she knew and the life style which she had enjoyed as a child had more than a passing effect on her, from restoration work on Iona Abbey, partly financed by her father, to exciting excavation finds in Turkey, or international politics over esparto grass used in the paper industry and discussions round the dinner table at Silverburn on subjects too numerous to mention. She was fortunate to walk with many who knew the ancient ways, and she uncovered the truth as easily as drinking a cup of tea.

The above biographical note was contributed by Anne Macaulay's family.

Appendix 2

In Memory of Anne Macaulay

An appreciation contributed by Jay Kappraff, Associate Professor of Mathematics, New Jersey Institute of Technology

I met Anne Macaulay for the first time at the Nexus conference in Edinburgh in March 1995. She knew that I was coming and telephoned ahead to express her wish to meet me. After the conference she was my guide for a ride to the Scottish countryside. She escorted me to my first stone circle at Kilmartin and I in turn took her to visit Lawrence Edwards in Strontian near Fort William to learn about his work on the influence of the moon and planets on the shape of plant buds.

This trip gave me an opportunity to learn about Anne's scholarly endeavours and her strong will. She has been a determined presence pitting her will against the established order of academicians unprepared to consider and evaluate the intertwined threads of geometry, archaeology, anthropology, mythology, history, astronomy and music that make up the core of her studies. She was bedevilled with the problem of finding someone in the academic world that could comprehend the many areas of knowledge required to properly evaluate her work. On the one hand she appeared to gather her inspiration and even some leads from another dimension: dreams, meditation and quiet contemplation. Yet she never left an idea in a half-baked stage. In fact, she loathed sloppy or incomplete thoughts. She continually tested her revelations and discoveries against all that was known. She never hesitated to discard an idea that did not square with the data. In her more energetic years she would travel great distances to make a 'find.' She could discover great significance in nuances that less fertile minds would overlook.

As a mathematician, perhaps what impressed me most was her ability to get the mathematics correct. Often she carried out difficult geometric constructions with involved trigonometric computations, all with an almost total lack of training ... Her notations were often faulty but never her end results. I have yet to find a flaw in her math. In fact, she would generally solve her problems with much simpler and more elegant computations than the ones that I used to check them.

I asked her how she gets her ideas. She said, 'I think hard on them and the answers come in dreams.' I am sure that she is somewhere in the universe looking down on our absurd comedy and having a chuckle.

Excerpts from Anne Macaulay's letters to Jay Kappraff

The following extracts from letters written by Anne Macaulay, and reproduced here with permission from Professor Jay Kappraff, may help further to illuminate Anne's personality and methods of research.

(date uncertain)

I am very intrigued with the chapter that you sent me and your lecture. I have done a great deal of thinking about my own ancient research and am still to publish it, but I'm waiting till after the Apollo and other megalithic geometry is published. Before getting down to details, the prehistory of corn growing and domestication of animals is of importance and relevant. The peoples of the 'Fertile Crescent' — i.e. where the wild grains grew naturally — were the first to develop farming. The Fertile Crescent ran from Greece through Anatolia to the head waters of the Euphrates. In Anatolia, they were gathering grains and using querns by 12 000 BC, also developing villages. By 8000–6000 BC they were building towns. The farming communities grew in numbers because this new life-style could support many more people than the hunter-gatherers. Colin Renfrew believes that the first farmers were Indo-European speaking, who sped into Europe westwards and eastwards into Persia and India. There are even remnants of an Indo-European farming group in western China.

These first farmers who came into Britain *c.* 4700 BC brought the farming 'package' with them. This of course included grain growing and domestic animals. But what else? They have been described as 'rude farmers' but they were not so 'rude.' I have identified a few items that seem to be present both in the East and in Britain that must have come originally as part of the farming package.

1) The idea of measurement: they needed to know how much grain to sow (volume) and how much land (measuring rods). But also, I think, the 3:4:5 triangle was a part of this package to make a 'square' field. It is easy to think up the ritual of square fields and culling the first seed.
2) They already had a type of Lyre at this early stage made on a horned ox-skull.
3) As farmers, they required a suitable farmers' calendar, hence the zodiac.
4) Whether they had the idea of a 360 degree circle, I don't know. I cannot find any lead in the British material about degrees in a circle. However, if they counted the days in the year, 360 is a close approximation, and leaves 5 days holiday to celebrate the New Year — whether it was held at the Winter Solstice or in the Spring makes no difference. You say that the sexagesimal system grew out of musical scales: it could have grown out of the days in a year just as well.
5) The use of pottery. This feature is well known and taken by the archaeologists as a sign that farming had arrived in Europe.

From this package it can be seen that the various elements of culture went both east and west with the ever-spreading farming revolution. The most easily confirmed point is the constellations. The megalithic British constellations were the same as the Babylonian ones, but with different names. This does not reflect a physical contact at 3000 BC between the west of Europe and the Euphrates, but it does reflect the common source — probably in Anatolia — already several millennia before we can detect it in the archaeological/historical record.

(date uncertain)

... Of the more senior archaeologists, there is only one, Euan Mackie, who has taken Thom seriously — and he is labelled by the others 'a bit queer with mad ideas!' The basic geometry by Thom is simply 'beyond taking seriously.' The younger generation of archaeologists who meantime have no voice can, however, take it in their stride. My battle to get my ideas over is even greater than you think.

The megalithic British culture came to an end about 1400 BC when Stonehenge etc. were abandoned — this same date is when the

Proto-Greeks are believed to have taken control in Greece, or later. The two cultures did not run parallel in time. (Brain drain from Britain?)

Thom was a very eminent engineer and Oxford Professor. British archaeologists look on him as a very good and accurate surveyor but beyond the Pale in his ideas. It is unwise to call him an archaeologist — maybe 'amateur archaeologist' would be safer!

[Colin Renfrew] says nothing about measure in *Archaeology and Language*. The farming package so far as he is concerned includes grain, domesticated animals, goats, sheep, pigs and cattle, and ceramics — i.e. crude pottery, which the hunter gatherers did *not* have. Because the 3:4:5 'Pythagorean' triangle appears in Mesopotamia, Egypt and Britain before 3000 BC, I have assumed this was also part of the farming package. And I believe it was the very first farmers who worked this out before they left Anatolia.... The 'proof' concerning the triangle comes from *Geometry and Algebra in Ancient Civilizations* by B.L. Van der Waerden — see also *Science and Civilization vol.3* by Joseph Needham.

The standard interpretation of the flail is that it was for beating slaves. But no civilization could exists without farming [Osiris was the god of grain; his symbols were the measuring rod for laying out the fields and the flail for separating grain from chaff], so farming came first with the God and his symbols, and civilization only came afterwards, perhaps involving slaves.

The Proto-Greeks were in Minoan Crete before 1700 BC. See the picture of two Minoan seal stones of the Apollo geometry. The date 2100 BC — a carbon-dating of a wooden spade found deep in the earth — is the first surviving evidence of large-scale tin production from Cornwall. The European Bronze Age starts much earlier than 1500 BC. Even Britain, which was late using bronze, is now known to be much earlier — and if they were exporting tin from 2100 BC they must have known what it was for.

(24 April 1995)

When Thom claimed to have found geometry defining the egg-shaped and flattened circles as well as the yardsticks, the archaeologists were unbelievably stupid and derided the whole idea completely. The much respected journal *Antiquity* published two key articles after

Thom died. One commended him for making such accurate surveys of so many sites but totally discarded both his geometry and his yardsticks. The other was an account of an experiment by a college of further education (not a university) which involved students laying out big circles without the use of a rope and then surveying the results. Hey Presto — they were flattened circles! Therefore Thom's flattened circles were merely badly laid out circles. As most archaeologists in Britain are innumerate, I have an uphill task producing both yardsticks and geometry! It is not a rash generalization to say they are virtually all innumerate: when school-leavers say they want to go into a science but they have no maths, they all get directed into archaeology.

After finding that Thom's yardstick was basically the ancient Greek fathom — and that the Greek foot was also used — the mass of archaeologists will feel a bit bruised and embarrassed at what they have said in the past. However, they will not understand the geometry. (It's horrifying how few people can comprehend simple geometry!) So I have tried in every figure to find where the first step in the construction was; i.e. where the exact number of units comes. To this end, the first thing I did was to convert all the lengths in the given figure into megalithic rods and megalithic yards and megalithic feet. From this, with the exception of one site, I could immediately recognize if the 'unit' was in quarters or thirds of a unit, etc. This method may make Thom's figures have slightly larger 'errors' than appear from using his figures alone, but the errors are so slight when one considers that the sites were built between 5 000 plus and 3 800 years ago.

I am very grateful to you for keeping me straight on the proper terminology ... Yes, it is I that have found the various polygons and geometrical relationships in sites; it is also I that re-analysed Thom's flattened circles to reveal the possible links in all four forms with the Golden Mean.

(23 June 1995)

There is no doubt that I should have put in a chronological table. The dating is crucial and needs to be right. The appearance of the geometry on seal stones in Crete before 1700 BC puts their presence in the Levant sufficiently early to coincide with the Sinaitic alphabet, though I don't say anything about it in the text. I enclose a copy of your geometric instructions, and the chapter on Thom's measuring rods from *Megalithic Science* by Douglas C. Heggie (Thames & Hudson 1981) which is now out of print. He is rather too negative though he does accept that the megalithic yard of 2.72 ft does seem to be genuine. No wonder there was doubt, as Thom believed all the diameters of circles were made in MY. From my analysis it becomes obvious that the MY as such was not necessarily the final diameter. This is why I try to find the one standard measure in each of the geometries, which indicates the starting point of the layout. Perhaps I should publish an article on the measuring rods myself to get the position aired. You ask about the yardsticks: in the Mid Clyth example, the measure is exactly the same as 8 Greek feet. Because it is such a good example, with least possible error, I use this one alone. Aquorthies, Kingussie, is also in Greek feet. Thom published many lists of diameters in his books (all out of print) which I have had a superficial look at: most of those that are not in exact MY can be found to be multiples of the square root of 3 or in Greek feet or a division of one or other of the basic standard measures. (2.5 MY = 1 MR / Greek fathom = 7 Greek ft)

The measuring rod is an artefact. Though most rods have long since rotted away, their presence can still be detected in measurements on the ground. It is therefore an *artefact* when assessed as Thom did. Heggie, I feel, listened too much to the archaeologists when they said that a standard unit was quite out of the question. The best evidence for the standard measures comes from Scotland, where most of the concentric circles and Platonic circles are found. So should I claim that the Greeks and Proto-Pythagoreanism come from my back yard? Perhaps I should, but I have carefully avoided doing so. 'NIMBY' has become current in English lately: perhaps we should also coin 'YIMBY' — 'Yes in My Back Yard'!

(26 July 1995)

I am somewhat relieved that you are now thinking of writing up the yardsticks only. There is so much that I still have to publish in order to support the earlier material, that it makes it all a little frail. I enclose as requested: (a) Zerox of Mid Clyth: this is from *Stone Rows and Standing Stones, Part ii* by A & AS Thom, collated with archaeological notes by

A Burl (BAR International Series 560 (ii) 1990); (b) the address to get a photograph of the so-called Arundel Stone or Metrological Relief is The Ashmolean Museum, Beaumont Street, Oxford, OX1 2PH; (c) a copy of Eric Fernie's article on the Metrological Relief; (d) The book by Colin Renfrew about the 'farming revolution' is *Archaeology and Language* (Jonathan Cape 1987). Renfrew started as a scientist and went over to archaeology. He is the Disney Professor in Oxford and now has a title which I always forget. He is accused by most other archaeologists of changing horses mid-stream: as they see it, he is prepared to change his ideas when new evidence emerges — i.e. he is not a stick-in-the-mud like them.

(27 August 1995)

Thom seemed more interested in the astronomy of the megalithic sites than the geometry. Virtually every plan of the circles has one or more astronomically defined date marked on them by Thom. There are how- ever also a large number of rows of standing stones which seem to be purely astronomical. I enclose some chunks out of his books. What I find fascinating is that the Four 'Quarter Days' in the year come out most strongly, and they are the same Quarter Days still used today — and the basic date for Income Tax (the beginning of the financial year) falls on one of them! And all the traditional Celtic Festivals are the same as Thom's peak days. It was because Thom found so much astronomy in the megalithic remains that the Archaeo-astronomical Society was formed and started a journal.

I enclose the analysis and picture of one of the egg-shaped rings. This one is from southern Scotland. All the 'eggs' are similar in that they have two circles, usually with one smaller than the other but both containing the same polygon. Their choice of five units for the base of each arm of the pentagram is very clear. 125 cannot be divided by anything but 5. Usually these 'hidden' numbers were chosen with only one factor which makes it clear, but in one case the pentagram base was 40: is it to be taken as 5 or 8? I find the egg-shaped rings very satisfying to analyse. The upper circle is never just stuck on the top; there is always some rea- son for placing it where it is. In the case of 'Twelve Apostles,' the two identical pentagrams have lost the typical pentagonal shape and appear to be an ellipse with six points!

Enclosed are bits of Thom's books on astronomy. There is far more elsewhere but I hope this will give you enough to be assured that the astronomy is not fictional!

(17 September 1996)

Enclosed are all the slides that I can get; very sorry I can't get more. I've left in the info. from English Heritage, i.e. that you have got to acknowledge where they came from — what arrogant rot!

New book: *Stonehenge* by John Nash (Harper Collins). It is all about astronomy, and has very good reviews from astronomers. 'John Nash moved in 1977 from Oxford to the University of Groningen (Netherlands) where he is Professor of the History of Philosophy and Exact Sciences' (from the blurb on the jacket). I intend to write to him as he could be very helpful about Apollo and the Titans. Can I mention that you have checked some of my geometry? No-one else knowledgeable has so far looked at my figures! So many academics seem *terrified* of amateurs — and it only takes the time to read the three pages on the Greek yardsticks to know whether I am daft or not. You suggest I write an article for *Nature.* Should I simply rewrite these three pages, or do I put in some of the analyses of the megalithic rings? Putting in some geometry seems to require some explanation of the ancient builders' methods — so it becomes a huge article! I am very grateful to you for disseminating information on my research. You too seem to have come under the fascination of seeing the design principles on exact 'science' from over 5 millennia ago!

(16 January 1997)

Knowing what academics do, I have been careful to use academic and reputable sources! Curt Sasch was the first academic to open up the field of organology; i.e. the study of the development of the shape of musical instruments. But he was a wind player and knew nothing of how string instruments worked. He came to some awful conclusions about Greek lyres. 'They could not have used harmonics on the lyre because they did not know anything of the harmonics of wind instruments.' Neither is correct! But all Greek scholars who have looked at the musical possibilities of the lyre have repeated Curt Sasch! All the musical research is from the organological perspective ...

My academic credentials: NIL! I did one year at Edinburgh in Science but failed all but one exam — I passed in physics. But, looking back, I think there are sufficient excuses. We moved temporarily to a flat in Edinburgh as there was neither enough coal to heat the house in the country nor enough petrol to get anywhere, with war-time rationing. I hated moving into town — my mother was in the middle of a nervous breakdown — my younger brother was killed in the war and my only remaining brother was badly injured in France and my boyfriend was also killed. It was a very black time. Anyway, I should have gone to Art College instead of sciences, but I felt it would have been unpatriotic in the war. Further, I am mildly dislexic to the extent that I can't spell! I had been given such a bad time about that through my school days, I swore that I would never write again (apart from letters). So I have NO academic background. After having my family, I took up the classical guitar which I had always wanted to play. It had a strange effect on me. I went into a 7 year long period of strange happenings and revelations. I would wake up in the morning *knowing* things about the history of the guitar and being able to *recognize* ancient depictions of instruments. Books would fall into my lap, and in the library, I put my fingers on information at random.

So eventually, I joined the Galpin Society (all about old instruments and music) and worked very part-time in that for many years and learnt a lot. But perhaps the most significant thing is that from childhood I rejected all the silly literature offered to girls in my days and demanded *real* books and the *truth*. And before my teens I had started reading about Eastern philosophies, lives of great people and much else of that calibre. This attitude has never left me: I want the hard facts and not stupid romancing by ill-informed authors. And I have found my hard facts in the megalithic geometry to support the series of 'coincidences' about Apollo!

But hard facts is one thing — I also go in for dowsing. The other day an architect showed me a map of a site he is working on. They did not know where the main drain was and it could have cost them a lot of money to find out. But I found it, dowsing on a map. But this ability had more to do with our ideas on space and time than anything *material*.

I am sending you a list of all the sites I have analysed. Sorry it is not yet typed and is still needing certain small additions which are not crucial to what you asked for — i.e. the Fibonacci proportions. As you will see, all the pentagrams are on Fibonacci numbers. There are 30 flattened circles and 23 other circles enclosing pentagrams. I also enclose a copy of Archie Roy's article. He is Professor of Astronomy at Glasgow University and, unlike many academics, he is deeply interested in psychic things — though he manages to keep these two aspects well separated!

(22 July 1997)

... I have been working solidly at the analysis of Thom's measures and finished it and sent it to a statistician at Glasgow University. He had done the same for some others and is himself interested in Thom's work and standing stones. I am waiting to hear what he makes of it. Ben Tawney, the statistician, was taken aback by the size of the analysis; but he, like everyone else, had no idea that there were so many different types, all of which have to be explained in detail with one or two examples. Once they are all analysed, it is clear that:

1) Their geometry was already in a mature state before they started building the circles *c.* 3200 BC.
2) The yardsticks were constant throughout the whole period.
3) The dates are from *c.* 3200 to 1200 BC.
4) The Fibonacci series was used for their pentagrams from the start.
5) Over a third of the sites analysed include pentagrams.

So the analysis has turned out to give an accurate description of the most ancient 'maths' in the world! Thom himself used statistical methods as well as other statisticians to try to prove the two yardsticks that he had discovered; and the archaeologists are prepared to accept this method as proof. But without the third yardstick, the Greek foot, and without the incommensurable factors that come into the geometry (square root of 3, the cosine of 30 degrees, etc), no conclusive proofs have emerged so far. It is for these reasons that I have turned to Ben Tawney. Further, an archaeological friend of mine surprised me when I rang to tell her that I had completed the analyses and it was going to a statistician. It emerges that she has always felt that there must have been something more than 'rude farmers' in megalithic Britain, and she says she will get in touch with Colin Renfrew if the statistician agrees that I have proved it! Colin Renfrew is the top archaeologist in Britain and probably the only one who is capable of understanding what it means.

Now that my work is completed, I am beginning to realize how extra-ordinary it all is! It's as if I had got a keyhole in which to view this ancient world ... This raises a whole lot of questions about how the English King in the mediaeval period adopted the 'imperial' foot as the standard measure. The Masons used the Greek fathom/megalithic rod in the building of Chartres (before AD 1200), and St George's, Windsor (very late Gothic) also used the Greek fathom/MR *and* the 'imperial' foot. Both these plans include pentagrams which produce (Golden mean × MR), hence imperial feet.

So, though it was never recorded, the Masons kept the secret ancient yardsticks. But by the time of the Italian Renaissance, it had been forgotten that there were 7 Greek/Roman feet in the fathom; hence the difficult task of fitting a man into a six feet square! Vitruvius says man's height is 6 ft (Greek/Roman) and he fits into a square 'at the bottom of his arms': he does *not* say to his fingertips! This passage was badly misread in the Renaissance. Hence 'Vitruvian Man' by da Vinci, etc. So back to the mediaeval English adoption of the 'imperial' foot: who persuaded the King to use this unit?

(17 August 1997)

 I want to get on with it, but between being a bit poorly and with an awful lot of people about, it has not got far. (I seem to have a duodenal ulcer.) [This was the first sign of her fatal illness. EDS.]

I have deliberately kept a low profile concerning the sacred beliefs about numbers and forms. This would probably put a lot of people off! But if the yardsticks and the geometry are accepted as a 'proof,' then in the rewrite of *The Gods and Science in Megalithic Britain* the sacred aspect can be overtly stated.

I have not got round to looking for any book about yardsticks in the early world. But there is a book with several references to ancient measures: *Science and Society in Prehistoric Britain* by Euan W. Mackie

(Paul Elek 1977). He is a trained archaeologist but has been blackballed by virtually all the others because he supported Thom. He identifies sites that must have been used by the elite class who saw to the astronomy and building of circles and yardsticks. I look on his book as another aspect of what I am doing — if you can get hold of it it's worth reading. One book of many that he quotes is *Historical Metrology* by A.E. Berriman (J.M. Dent 1953) — a chaotic jumble that takes a lot of time to find anything you want to pursue.

(15 March 1998)

You seem to be worried at the presence of so many pentagrams, all of which are made on Fibonacci pairs. How I proceed with the initial measure of the diameter of a circle. Let us call it d (in imperial feet, Thom's usage). Then: $d / 6.8 = y$ MR; and $y \times 2.5 = z$ MY; and $z \times 2.8 = w$ GF (Greek feet). Also, y, z & w are each divided by:

		to discover if the circle is	
i.	51	to discover if the circle is	7 / 14 star
ii.	37		11
iii.	14		9
iv.	13		8

Having examined the sites with concentric circles (the first approach), it has been seen that they chose 'units' in order to produce a site of a 'chosen' size; so by this stage one has already eliminated the four main polygrams. The ellipses and flattened circles obviously do not come into this scheme.

Squares were only rarely used. But it was found in one of the large sites in Brittany that they were using the series 12-17-24-34-48 for the square root of 2. These figures only appear rarely, both in ellipses and squares.

If the circle encloses a hexagram as the main geometry, the calculation is: $d \times$ square root of 3 divided by 2 which also equals the cosine of 30 degrees. Note that they started the hexagon by laying out the desired equilateral triangle and then the circle and then the last triangle.

If nothing has emerged by this time, then the calculations for the pentagram start. Because this is the longest calculation, I always left it to the end! As the result of going through all the sites, I can now see that I would have saved myself a lot of time if I had started with the pentagram calculations.

From Greek sources, it is known that they were using a larger foot too for sacred buildings. But 1 MR = 6.8 imperial ft, so half a MR = 3.4 or 34/10 ft, and 34 × the Golden mean (1.618034) = 55.01315, so we have the 34-55 Fibonacci pair. Hence the imperial foot as known today was originally created, presumably in the megalithic period, for the purpose of a ready method for laying out the angle of 36 degrees for pentagrams [36 + 36 + 36/2 = 90]. Why was the imperial foot established in mediaeval England? Who still knew of its existence? Presumably it was the guild of Masons; or was there a secret society still in existence in England, that knew of ancient yardsticks?

There are three circles in Britain with the diameter of 110 ft; i.e. 10 × the Golden mean in MR [10 × 1.618034 × 6.8 = 110.026]. This suggests that the megalithic builders had two more yardsticks; the first for square root of 3 [1.73204], the second the imperial foot.

Furthermore, I place the creation of the ancient Star Globe of Eudoxos at Gibraltar by British tin merchants at *c.* 2000 BC (the astronomical date of the Globe). This implies that they knew the earth was round. How could they know this? From Harris in the Western Hebrides, you can see the very steep isle of St Kilda, 40 miles out to sea, on clear days. You can't see it from sea level at low tide but you can at high tide or by climbing up any of the hills on Harris. Knowing that they were using a simple form of geometry for their circles — e.g. 51/46/22 triangles — and other triangles for creating 7/14 stars or 8, 9, or 11 stars, they could not only realize that the earth is round but even make a rough stab at working out the earth's size. And the carved stone balls (including the Platonic solids) demonstrate an interest in spherical geometry.

Now, does use of the Fibonacci series really seem out of place in this extraordinary flourish in Western Europe? But why this extraordinary flourish? The geometry started in Brittany and N France soon after 4000 BC and arrived in Britain about 3200 BC. Shetland, where there are many megalithic remains, is over latitude 60 degrees: from there they could sail into the Arctic. Around latitude 47 covers the best of the early French material. The behaviour of the Sun and Moon don't change much between the Tropics of Capricorn and Cancer, but the changes become increasingly dramatic travelling northwards in line with the English Channel and even more so beyond Scotland, into the land of the midnight Sun. So the megalithic Britons must have realized what happened to the Sun at night, and their view of astronomy must have changed radically from that of the Egyptians, who thought the Sun went on a 'dangerous journey' to the dawn. Perhaps it was the variations of the Sun and Moon in Orkney and Shetland compared with the astronomy of Brittany that forced megalithic Britons to rethink their notions of the world and astronomy. And perhaps this was what gave them the energy and excitement to pursue their new discoveries.

(17–20 July 1998)

I'm not certain of what you mean by 'my tolerances.' I presume you mean the 'error' between Thom's measure and the calculated measure. If the difference turns out to be say 5 inches and the site is in good condition, then I would look further to find a better fit. But if the difference is 5 inches on a dilapidated and broken site, I am prepared to accept it. So the tolerance depends on the condition of the site, Thom marked all his plans carefully, distinguishing stones in their original settings from those in dubious settings.

A newly discovered burial tomb, *c.* 3000 BC has been found near Kirkwall on Orkney. This date is among the earliest for anything in Britain. Orkney stone happens to split with square edges, which is why so many ancient sites have survived here.

I got a very kind letter from Keith [Critchlow]. Their checking of the geometric workings is just at the start, but he seems to be impressed. After Keith has had them checked, all my possible blunders will come to light!

I feel that you sometimes doubt my analysis of the geometries! I could have put in the workings for each type — but then I would have to teach the basics of trigonometry too. So there is room for someone else to write the basics of the mathematics required to analyse these sites ... I have to admit that geometry was my best subject at school — it all seems so obvious to me! Perhaps this is inherited: my mother's family for generations were civil engineers and my father's brother was a brilliant mechanical engineer who made many patented devices for the paper mills.

I still feel it is strange to know that death is near. Stomach cancer is not painful but, like all forms, is terribly debilitating from day to day. The only part of me that is working normally is my head.

Back to the geometry. Professor Fernie doesn't believe that geometric plans were ever used for Gothic and many other churches. I have done a little of this (for Gordon Strachan) and, yes, the ground plan is usually a very exact geometry. As there were no available side views, I could make no estimate of that geometry. It is very good to see a revival of interest in ancient geometry.

Appendix 3

The Great Antiquity and Scientific Origin of Feet and Inches

Adapted from an article by Robin Heath, *Journal of the British Weights & Measures Association (The Yardstick)* April 2001

In my book, *Sun, Moon & Stonehenge,* I show that if one assumes that the MY represents a lunar period — the time between two new moons — then the length of one foot (12.0") marks the required calendrical period between the end of the lunar year (12 lunations — taking 354.367 days) and the end of the solar year of 365.242 days: i.e. diagrammatically, if a bar is divided into 13 equal sections, each measuring 1 MY and assumed to represent the length of one lunation, then the length of the first twelve sections will constitute the lunar year and the portion extending into the thirteenth section to represent the additional 10.875 days from the end of the lunar year to the end of the solar year will measure exactly one imperial foot.

Furthermore, the final portion, between the end of the solar year and the end of the 13th lunation — an additional 383.898-365.242 = 18.656 days — corresponds precisely with another basic unit of length from antiquity, the Royal cubit of 20.63" or 1.72 ft. The Royal cubit was used by Newton, who deduced that a value of 20.63" would make the size of the Kings Chamber within the Great Pyramid measure exactly 10 × 20 of this measure. In the 1880s, Sir William Flinders Petrie accurately measured the Great Pyramid, identifying 20.63" as a primary linear unit throughout the Egyptian dynastic buildings. Hence the astounding fact that 1 MY = 1 imperial ft + 1 RC.

Now, assuming that the MY was the primary unit (bearing in mind that our Stonehenge was built almost 1 000 years before the great Pyramid), then the derivative foot and cubit would appear to have formed a logical and essential part of the astronomical and calendrical studies of our neolithic ancestors. If, however, the foot *preceded* the MY (considering that 1 000th of 1 degree of arc of the equatorial circumference equals

210

365.244 ft — the same number as days in the solar year), then knowledge of the roundness of the earth must have predated use of the MY ... nobody can say how long ago!

My story doesn't end there, for there are 12.368 lunations in a year, of which the fractional part (0.368 as a decimal fraction) is almost exactly seven-nineteenths. But decimal fractions totally obscure the astronomic wisdom hidden in 12 and $^7/_{19}$; for as a vulgar fraction 12.368 = 235 / 19, immediately informing any astute astronomer of a nineteen year synchronicity between solar and lunar cycles. For after 235 lunations there will have elapsed exactly 19 years! The correspondence is astonishing — a margin of just 2 hours in 19 years. This is known as the Metonic cycle.

Now, 0.368 of 1 MY = 1 ft. Is that not another astounding fact? Do these facts not prove conclusively that the whole cosmic order stands upon the imperial foot?

Again, assuming that 1 MY represents 1 lunation, then totting up the exact number of lunations in the year, all one has to do is add 1 inch to 1 MY at each new moon to discover that, after 12 lunations at the end of the lunar year, these extra inches add up to 0.368 lunations, the required overrun. (This could, of course, have been deduced from the foregoing.) When demonstrating accurate calendrical predictions with my student groups over the years, I use a simple foot ruler, marked in inches, to predict lunations and eclipses to the day, years in advance... Highly accurate, and apparently using those same measures of antiquity now rendered illegal by the government of the same lands that built those stone circles!

Many of the greatest metrologists of our age have suggested that the primary units of length were derived from units of time. I can do little better here than quote that great metrologist Stecchini, who died in 1999 and who wrote: '... all serious scholars of ancient and mediaeval measures have always known that measures of volume and weight are derived from units of length.' During the late nineteenth century, Sir William Flinders Petrie and the equally eminent Carl Friedrich Lehmann-Haupt both concluded that such measures were so strictly defined and so rigorously organized that they must have a basis on some absolute natural measure. I suggest that this 'natural measure' was the lunation period: nothing could have been clearer or more constant to the eyes and mind of megalithic man.

Both also confirmed that, whatever length a system of weights and measures was based upon, there was a coordinating link to units of time.

Thus, an effective system of weights and measures begins with time measurement (for observing the seasons of the year and for gauging age, absences, gestation, etc.), leads to length (for measuring wood for timber and stone for monuments, territorial boundaries and distances for journeys), then to areas (for fields at the beginning of agriculture), and on to volumes and weights (at the beginning of commerce).

So the MY may be considered a calendrical analogue of the lunation period. It is equally clear that the foot and cubit are proportioned within it to reveal the length of the solar year, beyond the twelfth lunation or lunar year. (To make it absolutely exact, the imperial foot would require to be extended by $1/50$ of an inch.) Moreover, as we have seen, any work to predict lunations or eclipses, using ropes or rods, must invoke the inch.

The implications of this research for archaeology and human pre-history are immense. For a start they confirm the primary connection between mensuration and the moon. They also offer a basis for the origins — not merely the human but the natural, scientific origins — of the duodecimal foot.

Appendix 4

The Phaistos Disc

The Minoan civilization on Crete, some 4 000 years ago, devised a system of mathematics, corresponding very closely to the megalithic mathematics of NW Europe about 1 000 years earlier, based on a 366° circle, each degree divided into 60 minutes and each minute divided into 6 seconds. They also appeared to use a calendar of 366 days. This theory derives principally from study of the Phaistos Disc, a plate-like artefact whose two sides are both heavily engraved with pictograms. Now the 'Minoan foot,' equal to just under 11.95", has long been familiar to scholars; it was first identified independently by Professor Thom and the archaeological Professor Graham.

But Alan Butler, in his book *The Bronze Age Computer Disc,* realized that 1 000 Minoan feet exactly equal 366 MY. Furthermore, 366 MY = 1 megalithic second of arc on the Earth's surface. Therefore, 1 megalithic minute of arc = 6×366 MY = 2 196 MY, which Butler called '1 megalithic mile.' So 60 megalithic minutes of arc = 1 megalithic degree of arc = 60 megalithic miles. Accordingly, the polar circumference of the Earth should measure 60×366 = 21 960 megalithic miles, which is extremely close to the official estimate of 24 860 imperial miles.

Thus, the beauty of the Minoan system, presumably inherited from the megalithic people on the Atlantic sea-board, was that 1 megalithic second of arc coincided with 1 megalithic second of time and was represented as a distance of 366 MY on the Earth's surface. So it reconciled time and distance into one system of measurement. To quote from Knight & Lomas' *Uriel's Machine:*

> From his studies of the Phaistos Disc, Alan Butler had rediscovered a verbal system of mathematics which integrated Thom's MY with an incredibly accurate Minoan calendar. The whole system was a logical way of linking the speed of rotation of the Earth on its own axis with the rate of movement of the seasons.

The purpose of the Phaistos Disc was to enable the user to predict the position of the sun against the background stars to an accuracy of one part in 366. But as Alan's expertise developed in the use of this ancient system, he realized that it was subtler than he had at first thought. The geometry of the measuring system also had a latitudinal correction built into it. Because the Earth is almost a sphere, trigonometry can be used to work out its circumference at any latitude, using the angle of latitude. This can be easily measured by sighting on the apparent height of either the pole star or any other convenient circumpolar stars, using a navigator's cross staff.

The system of megalithic geometry had a built-in means of carrying out this calculation with ease because one of its trigonometric ratios of the angle of latitude (the cosine) is exactly the same numerical value as the number of mega-lithic miles across one megalithic degree of arc at any given latitude. The observed cosine of latitude can be turned into $1/366$ part of the polar circumference in MY, by multiply-ing by 6 and then 366. This relationship greatly simplifies calculations, and if the megalithic people had a means of measuring time, then this was the basis of a complete navi-gation system.

[VTL]

Appendix 5

Structural Skills of Megalithic Man

To demonstrate that Stone Rings were not an isolated or peculiar manifestation of mathematical or engineering skills among our ancestors of four to six thousand years or more ago — and to help provide a wider archaeological and historical context for the present specialist study — it may be useful to look at what other forms of monumental structure were being built around then in north-western Europe. The broader the foundations for Anne Macaulay's work, the more readily will the sceptics be convinced of her conclusions. For this purpose, one cannot do better than quote from Evan Hadingham's *Circles and Standing Stones,* a work that is so much more valuable precisely because it treats megalithic mathematics, not as some esoteric marvel, but as the outstanding feature of a general cultural landscape that is everywhere characterized by an advanced understanding and application of the physical sciences:

> To sum up the situation in simple terms: ancient Europeans were more clever and more original than archaeologists had ever suspected before. And nowhere is this more apparent than in the case of one on the most important factors of European prehistory ... the growth of religious and funerary ideas. The picture we hold of our ancestors may again be shaken when we see that the origins of an impressive style of tomb-building apparently goes back thousands of years to a region as far removed from the Near East as could possibly be imagined. On a thickly forested hill, not far from the sea at Carnac in Brittany, there rises an impressive grassy mound, with a rough slab of stone placed upright on its summit. A short distance away on the ground is another upright monolith, standing opposite an entrance façade leading into the middle of the mound ... In prehistoric times this structure was probably used as a tomb by successive

generations for collective interment, and it has been dated by the radiocarbon method as far back as 5700 BC ...

Gavrinis, Newgrange and Maes Howe are awe-inspiring evidence of a long tradition of religious construction using large stones, many centuries before anyone raised the first monoliths at Stonehenge. They were part of a growth of ideas and art of primary importance in the European past, yet a development so imperfectly understood that the research of recent years has completely overthrown many years of scholarly conjecture about the origins and influences of its various styles. No longer can we think in terms of the old diffusion model, of the 'Mother Goddess' and her simple path across the Mediterranean and up the Atlantic coasts. Instead we must recognize at least one strong cultural centre, Brittany, probably linked with Ireland, and accept the individual claims of the independently minded communities such as in Malta, Spain and Orkney.

The new knowledge that the architectural masterpiece of Newgrange was assembled at the same time that [or a while earlier than] the pyramids were rising in Egypt, should dispense forever with the notion of 'barbarians' living under the shadow of innovation from the east. Our barbarians had brains, and startlingly original ideas. By about 3500 BC a strong and distinctive culture was flourishing throughout Britain.

Clearly, this religious and funerary building had close affinities with the concurrent stone circle building, as manifestations of the same high culture. Would these affinities extend to the use of the same mathematics? If only another Thom could explore and survey, and another Macaulay analyse, the measurements of these great covered tombs and passages!

To return to Hadingham's splendid commentary, this time concerning earthen barrows and rings, likewise contemporary with and closely related to our subject of stone rings.

Archaeologists are beginning to unravel a complex pattern of interaction between the round megalithic tombs — the tradition that was ultimately to inspire Newgrange and

Maes Howe — and the long barrows of the western coastal regions. The exact origins of both great styles of tomb construction, and their influence upon one another, is still the subject of intense controversy. Recent aerial photography has revealed the extent of another type of monument built on an even more grand and astonishing scale than the long barrows. In 1723 the famous antiquary William Stukeley was exploring Salisbury Plain a few hundred yards north of Stonehenge when he came across a huge earthwork that he called a *cursus,* because to him it resembled a racecourse. It consisted of parallel twin banks and ditches cut in chalk, over 300 feet apart, running for a full $1^3/_4$ miles across the plain. A long barrow formed the eastern end.

Now much less conspicuous because of ploughing damage, these remarkable ritual enclosures must once have been spectacular undertakings for the prehistoric engineers. They have come to light at locations as widespread as Yorkshire and Suffolk, from Bangor in Wales to Twyford in the Thames valley. The cursus monuments often seem to be sited close to rivers and fresh water ... They vary in size from the shortest example at Northampton — a mere 200 yards across — to the massive Dorset cursus, which runs for no less than 6 miles across two stretches of downland. The ditches and banks are some 300 feet apart and enclose about 220 acres. The staggering figures of $6^1/_2$ million cubic feet of chalk must have been excavated from the two parallel ditches and piled alongside to form the banks. Four long barrows were incorporated into the earthworks.

Men and women were gathering on prominent hilltops in southern England as far back as 4200 BC, the approximate date of the Hembury camp [a causewayed enclosure $3^1/_2$ miles NW of Honiton in Devon] ... The roughly circular enclosures where they met consisted of two or three concentric ditches with frequent gaps and entrances interrupting their course. The excavated earth from these ditches was piled up alongside to form banks enclosing the area inside the camp. The classic site, which first identified the early farmers' phase of settlement in England, was at Windmill Hill, not far from the West Kennet long barrow.

Here a triple ring of ditches was found, the outer examples being eight feet deep....

The causewayed camps show us that as early as 4000 BC there must have been some unifying social interest that drew people together at certain times of the year. The cursus monuments and many of the larger long barrows imply the efficient organization of manpower and its direction towards a preconceived idea or plan ... As the scale of the circular enclosures increases through the third millennium, calling for ever greater resources of labour, we inevitably think in terms of larger communities and a more hierarchical organization of society...

Yet, on the strength of the evidence already exposed, it is abundantly clear that the same genius and energy went into these colossal earthworks as into the funerary architecture and likewise into the stone circles. Once again, one must wonder whether mathematical survey and analysis of the circular earthworks would reveal the same geometry — at however rudimentary a level — as for the stone circles?

[VTL]

Appendix 6

Geographical Distribution of the Yardsticks

In order to make some sense out of the wealth of data presented in this re-analysis of megalithic structures, one approach is to consider the geographical distribution of the three yardsticks; the megalithic yard, the megalithic rod and the Greek foot.

Chart 1   **ENGLAND**

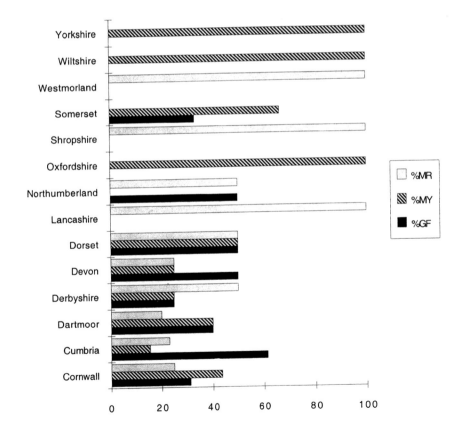

Chart 2   **SCOTLAND**

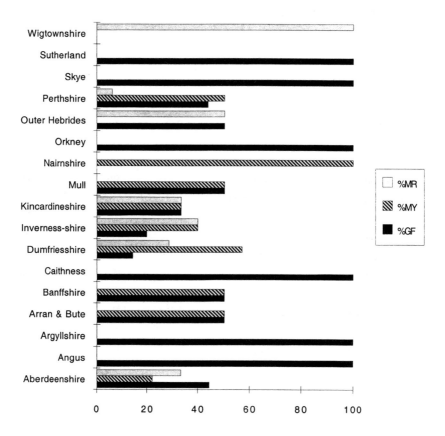

Chart 3   **WALES**

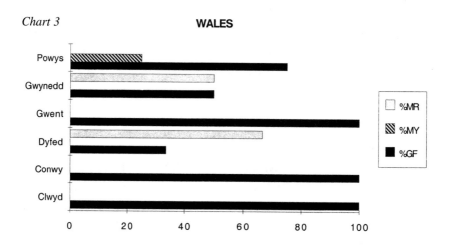

Megalithic sites by county

Thom Ref.	Name	County	Fibonacci	Unit	Y'dstick	Style
T206	Cullerig	Aberdeenshire	5, 8	4	GF	5m
T208	Tarland	Aberdeenshire	8, 13	2	MY	5m
T190	Loanhead of Daviot	Aberdeenshire	3, 5	11	GF	5m, 5on
T198	West Mains	Aberdeenshire	5, 8	1	MR	5m, 6on
T160	Auchnagorth	Aberdeenshire		40	GF	6m
T170	Fountain Hill	Aberdeenshire		15	GF	6m
T198	West Mains	Aberdeenshire		$8\frac{1}{2}$	MR	6m
T158	White Cow Wood	Aberdeenshire		$\frac{1}{3}$	MY	7m
T176	Old Rayne	Aberdeenshire		$\frac{1}{4}$	MR	7m
T180	Westerton	Aberdeenshire		1	GF	7m
T190	Loanhead of Daviot	Aberdeenshire		$\frac{1}{3}$	GF	7m
T210	Tomnaveric	Aberdeenshire		$\frac{1}{3}$	MY	7m
T220	Tomnagorm	Aberdeenshire		$\frac{1}{3}$	MY	7m
T166	Sheldon of Bourtie	Aberdeenshire		$1\frac{1}{2}$	MY	8m
T182	Holywell	Aberdeenshire		3	GF	8m
T184	Yonder Bognit	Aberdeenshire		$\frac{2}{3}$	MR	8m
T172	Balqujain	Aberdeenshire		5	GF	9
T194	Tyrebagger (Dyce)	Aberdeenshire		1	MY	9
T218	Ley Lodge	Aberdeenshire		4	GF	9
T162	Aquhorthies Manor	Aberdeenshire		$\frac{1}{4}$	MR	11
T196	Sunhoney	Aberdeenshire		$\frac{1}{3}$	MR	11
T224	Tullyfourie Hill	Aberdeenshire		2	GF	11
T168	South Ythsie	Aberdeenshire		3	GF	ellip-pyth
T190	Loanhead of Daviot	Aberdeenshire		$1\frac{1}{2}$	GF	ellip-pyth
T192	Sands of Forvie	Aberdeenshire		$\frac{1}{4}$	MR	ellip-pyth
T206	Cullerlie	Aberdeenshire		$\frac{1}{10}$	MR	ellip-pyth
T186	Blackhill of Drachlaw	Aberdeenshire		$\frac{1}{6}$	MR	ellip-nonpy
T346	Blackgate	Angus		$1\frac{1}{2}$	GF	11
T140	Loch Nell	Argyllshire		$1\frac{1}{3}$	GF	7m
T152	Machrie Moor II	Arran		4	GF	9
T306	Nine Stone Rig	Banffshire	13, 21	1	GF	5m
T238	Milltown	Banffshire		$\frac{2}{3}$	MY	7m
T154	Ettrick Bay	Bute		$\frac{1}{4}$	MY	ellip-nonpy
T322	Force	Caithness		10	GF	9
T324	Latheron Wheel Burn	Caithness		12	GF	9
T374	Penbedw Hall	Clwyd	8, 13	6	GF	5m, 5on

T372	Penmaen Mawr	Conwy		1	GF	ellip-nonpy
T78	Duloo	Cornwall	5, 8	$^2/_3$	MR	Fl A 5
T88	Dinnenver Hill	Cornwall	13, 21	$6^1/_2$	GF	Fl A 5
T100	Botallack	Cornwall	3, 5	2	MR	Fl A 5
T96	Boscawen-Un	Cornwall	3, 5	2	MR	Fl B 5, 6
T94	Porthmeor	Cornwall	21, 34	1	MY	B Mod
T86	Rough Tor	Cornwall	8, 13	4	MY	Fl D
T98	Merry Maidens	Cornwall	8, 13	2	MY	5m, 10on
T76	Nine Stones	Cornwall		1	GF	7m
T90	Nine Maidens	Cornwall		$^1/_3$	MY	7m
T74	The Hurlers C	Cornwall		3	MY	8m
T80	Stripple Stones	Cornwall		$1^1/_3$	MR	8m
T102	Trezibbet (Goodaver)	Cornwall		3	MY	8m
T74	The Hurlers	Cornwall		3	MY	9
T84	Leaze	Cornwall		6	GF	9
T82	Treswigger	Cornwall		3	GF	11
T92	Nine Maidens, Ding Dong	Cornwall		2	GF	11
T28	Castle Rigg	Cumbria	13, 21	5	GF	Fl A 5
T40	Burn Moor	Cumbria	21, 34	3	GF	Fl A 5
T42	Long Meg	Cumbria	21, 34	9	GF	Fl B 5, 6
T46	Seascale	Cumbria	5, 8	$1^1/_2$	MR	Fl D
T34	Sunken Kirk	Cumbria	8, 13	1	MR	5m
T38	Burnmoor D	Cumbria	8, 13	4	GF	5m
T32	Elva Plain	Cumbria	8, 13	1	MR	5m, 5on
T36	Burnmoor	Cumbria		1	GF	7m
T48	Lacra	Cumbria		1	GF	7m
T36	Burnmoor A	Cumbria		2	MY	8m
T48	Lacra A	Cumbria		$1^1/_2$	MY	8m
T38	Burnmoor C	Cumbria		4	GF	9
T52	Blakely Moss	Cumbria		4	GF	9
T112	Lee Moor	Dartmoor		5	MY	6m
T104	Grey Withers	Dartmoor		$^3/_4$	MY	7m
T112	Trowlesworthy	Dartmoor		$^1/_4$	MR	8m
T104	Grey Withers	Dartmoor		8	GF	9
T108	Brisworthy	Dartmoor		6	GF	9
T22	Moscar Moor,	Derbyshire	3, 5	$1^1/_2$	MR	Fl A 5
T18	Bar Brook	Derbyshire	5, 8	5	GF	Fl B 5, 6
T20	Owlerbar	Derbyshire	13, 21	$^1/_2$	MR	Fl B 5, 6
T16	Nine Ladies	Derbyshire		1	MY	8m
T106	Merryvale	Devon	5, 8	1	MR	Fl B 5, 6

T118	Kingston Russell	Devon	34, 55	$^1/_2$	MY	Fl B 5, 6
T110	Ringmoor e, w	Devon		37	GF	6m
T114	Postbridge	Devon		$^1/_3$	GF	ellip-nonpy
T118	Winterbourne Abbas	Dorset	8, 13	2	GF	B Mod
	Stonehenge	Dorset		8	MY	2 geom
T292	Seven Brethren	Dumfries-shire		$1^3/_4$	MY	9
T292	Seven Bretheren	Dumfriesshire	8, 13	5	GF	Fl A 5
T296	Loupin Stones	Dumfriesshire	13, 21	$^1/_4$	MR	Fl A 5
T300	Whitcastles	Dumfriesshire	34, 55	1	MY	B Mod
T294	Whamphrey	Dumfriesshire	8, 13	1	MY	5m
T298	Girdle Stones	Dumfriesshire		$^1/_3$	MR	7m
T290	Audgirth	Dumfriesshire		1	MY	11
T384	St Nicholas	Dyfed	13, 21	2	GF	5m
T386	Gors Fawr	Dyfed	3, 5	2	MR	5m, 10on
T388	Castell Garw	Dyfed		$^1/_2$	MR	8m
T398	Gray Hill	Gwent	34, 55	$^1/_2$	GF	5m, 6on
T376	Moel ty Ucha	Gwynedd	13, 21	$^1/_4$	MR	5m
T378	Tyfos	Gwynedd		4	GF	9
T258	Aviemore	Inverness	13, 21	2	GF	Fl A 5
T266	Farr West	Inverness	5, 8	1	MR	Fl B 5, 6
T260	Loch nan Carraigean	Inverness	13, 21	1	MY	Fl D
T246	Clava	Inverness	5, 8	1	MR	5m, 6m
T254	Castle Dalcross	Inverness	8, 13	3	GF	5m, 6m
T272	River Ness	Inverness		$^1/_2$	MY	7m
T246	Clava Cairns	Inverness-shire		$^1/_2$	MR	8m
T256	Easter Delfour	Inverness-shire		$^2/_3$	MR	8m
T250	Boat of Garten	Inverness-shire		$^2/_3$	MY	ellip-pyth
T252	Daviot	Inverness-shire		$^1/_4$	MY	ellip-pyth
T214	Cairnfield	Kincardine	13, 21	$^1/_2$	MR	Fl A 5
T204	Garrol Wood RSC	Kincardine	13, 21	$^1/_3$	MR	Fl B 5, 6
T230	Raedykes north	Kincardine	5, 8	4	GF	5m
T232	Clune Wood RSC	Kincardine	34, 55	1	GF	5m
T226	Aquhorthies	Kincardineshire		1	GF	7m
T230	Raedykes S	Kincardineshire		1	GF	7m
T202	Esslie the Less	Kincardineshire		$^1/_2$	MR	8m
T278	Thieves	Kirkcudbright	3, 5	2	MY	Fl B 5, 6
T284	Cambret Moor West	Kirkcudbright	8, 13	4	GF	Fl D
T282	Loch Mannoch	Kirkcudbright	3, 5	$1^1/_2$	MY	5m
T280	Drannandow	Kirkcudbright	5, 8	$1^1/_4$	MR	5m, 5on
T286	Cambert Moor	Kirkcudbrightshire		6	GF	9

T276	Carsphairn	Kirkcudbrightshire		$1/2$	MR	ellip-nonpy
T70	Birk Rig Common	Lancashire	5, 8	$1^1/_5$	MR	5m
T320	Loch Buie - larger	Mull		1	MY	9
T320	Loch Buie - small	Mull		$1^1/_2$	GF	9
T242	LIttle Urchavy	Nairnshire	3, 5	1	MR	5m, 6m
T242	Little Urchany	Nairnshire		1	MY	8m
T244	Moyness	Nairnshire		$1^2/_3$	MY	9
T316	Pobull Fhinn	North Uist	8, 13	8	GF	B Mod
T312	Sornach coir Fhinn	North Uist		9	GF	9
T68	Lilburn	Northumberland	5, 8	$1^1/_2$	MR	Fl B 5, 6
T66	Felkington	Northumberland		$2^1/_2$	GF	8m
T323	Ring of Brogar	Orkney	89, 144	2	GF	5m, 6on
	Brogar	Orkney		25	GF	2 geom
T323	Brogar	Orkney		25	GF	9
T314	North Ford, Gramisdale	Outer Hebrides		$1/4$	MR	7m
T316	Suidheachadh Sealg	Outer hebrides		1	MR	8m
T136	Rollright Stones	Oxforshire		$3/4$	MY	7m
T330	Killin	Perthshire	3, 5	2	MY	Fl B 5, 6
T360	Scone	Perthshire	13, 21	1	GF	Fl B 5, 6
T332	Weem	Perthshire	5, 8	$2/3$	MY	5m
T338	Lundie Farm	Perthshire		6	MY	6m
T354	Blind Wells	Perthshire		25	GF	6m
T330	Leys of Marley	Perthshire		1	GF	7m
T340	Monzie	Perthshire		$1/3$	GF	7m
T352	Court Hill	Perthshire		$1/4$	MR	8m
T362	Spittal of Glenshee	Perthshire		1	GF	8m
T334	Weem	Perthshire		2	MY	9
T338	Aberfeldy	Perthshire		$1/2$	MY	9
T356	Hill of Drimmie	Perthshire		$1/2$	MY	9
T344	Mickle Findowie	Perthshire		1	GF	ellip-nonpy
T352	Ballinluig	Perthshire		1	GF	ellip-nonpy
T348	Croftmoraig	Perthshire		$1/3$	MY	ellip-root2
T360	Guildtown	Perthshire		$1/4$	MY	ellip-root2
T382	Rhos y Beddau	Powys	13, 21	2	GF	5m
T384	Four Stones	Powys	21, 34	$1/2$	GF	5m
T394	Usk Water	Powys	34, 55	1	GF	5m, 6on
T390	Y-Pigwn Trecastle	Powys		2	MY	9
T24	Mitchells Fold	Shropshire	8, 13	1	MR	Fl A 5

T26	Black Marsh	Shropshire	13, 21	$^1/_2$	MR	Fl A 5
T318	Strathaird	Skye	13, 21	1	GF	5m
T116	Stanton Drew	Somerset	13, 21	10	GF	5m, 6m
T116	Stanton Drew - I	Somerset		$1^1/_2$	MY	ellip-pyth
T116	Stanton Drew - II	Somerset		1	MY	ellip-pyth
T326	The Mound	Sutherland	5, 8	3	GF	5m
T64	Orton	Westmorland	5, 8	$2^1/_2$	MR	Fl A 5
T62	Oddendale	Westmorland		11	MR	6m
T56	Gunnerkeld	Westmorland		$^1/_3$	MR	7m
T54	Tarn Moor	Westmorland		13	MR	8m
T274	Torhouse	Wigtownshire	3, 5	2	MR	Fl A 5
T132	Winterbourne Basset	Wiltshire		4	MY	9
T72	Howtallon	Yorkshire		$1^3/_4$	MY	ellip-pyth
T298	Girdle Stones		8, 13	3	MY	5m, 6on

KEY	STYLE
5m	Pentagram
5on	Pentagon
6m	Hexagram
6on	Hexagon
7m	Heptagram
8m	Octagram
9	Nine-pointed star
10on	Decagon
11	Eleven-pointed star
ellip-pyth	Pythagorean ellipse
ellip-nonpy	non-Pythagorean ellipse
ellip-root2	Ellipse based on $\sqrt{2}$
Fl A 5	Flattened circle type A, pentagram
Fl B 5, 6	Flattened circle type B, pentagram/hexagon
B Mod	Modified circle type B
Fl D	Flattened circle type D
2 geom	Two geometries

It has long been considered that Neolithic populations were very parochial and that social inter-action would have been very limited. Indeed, Atkinson (1982) declared that mainstream archaeology believes that customary measures showed a marked parochialism into mediaeval times. Analysis of the geographical distribution of the three yardsticks indicates otherwise (see Charts 1–3).

From Inverness-shire to Cornwall, there is evidence that all three yardsticks were used. Within the limitations of the data-set, there is a bias in favour of the Greek foot in Orkney, Sutherland, Caithness, Skye, Argyllshire and Angus in Scotland, and in Clwyd, Conwy and Gwent in Wales. Elsewhere, two or all three yardsticks were in use in most counties throughout the British Isles. This argues against any pre-mediaeval parochialism in the use of customary measures.

What cannot be assessed at present is the chronology of the use of the yardsticks. Since very few sites have yet been dated using radiocarbon techniques, no analysis of the evolution of the yardsticks' use can be undertaken. A rare example of a dated structure is the main phase of building at Stonehenge, which has been dated at about 2500 BC and incorporates the megalithic yard as the yardstick. However, judging from the general distribution of yardsticks, it is reasonable to assume that the knowledge required for designing and building the megalithic structures was fairly well disseminated in these islands (see *Atkinson (1982)*

[RAB]

Appendix 7

Seahenge 1999 — A New Site Analysed

During 1999 a wooden henge on the foreshore near Holme-next-the-Sea in Norfolk became exposed on the beach. As this was a new discovery, it was decided to subject it to Macaulay's calculations [RAB].

Description
This is an ellipse made up of 55 wooden (oak) posts, with one large oak trunk in the centre. The major diameter is 7 m (22.967') and the minor diameter is 6.5 m (21.326') measured to the outside of the posts. The structure has been dated at ~4000 BP.

Each post varies in diameter from 260 mm (10") to 540 mm (21"), the average being about 390 mm (15").

Construction
In common with other megalithic ellipses, the design is based upon a Pythagorean triangle. An ellipse based on the 5–12–13 Pythagorean triangle (identified as a template for other ellipses in Britain) can be constructed using three posts and a long rope, as described in Chapter 6 (p.100).

Interpretation
Sea Henge is based on a 5-12-13 Pythagorean triangle. This assumption is based on the fact that the ratio of major: minor diameters of Sea Henge (7:6.5 = 1.076) is very close to the ratio of an ellipse with major radius 13 and minor radius 12 (13:12 = 1.083); in fact no other commonly-used Pythagorean triangles give such a close ratio of axes.

Major axis diameter = $13 \times 2 = 26$ units
Minor axis diameter = $12 \times 2 = 24$ units

If the unit is $\frac{1}{3}$ megalithic yard (MY) = 0.9066'
then

	Calculated	Actual	Error
Major diameter = 26 × 0.9066' =	23.57'	22.967'	7.2"
Minor diameter = 24 × 0.9066' =	21.76'	21.326'	5.2"

The use of a 5-12-13 triangle has been documented in other megalithic ellipses in Britain, the best known being at Stanton Drew in Somerset, in which the unit $1\frac{1}{2}$ MY was used. The use of $\frac{1}{3}$ MY has been recorded in Aberdeenshire (3 sites), Perthshire (1) and Cornwall (1). It is therefore quite reasonable to assume that the designers of Norfolk were also aware of these various units and yardsticks.

Conclusions
This analysis of the Seahenge ellipse could not have been possible without the pioneering work of Anne Macaulay, who re-interpreted Alexander Thom's analysis of stone circles and his discovery of the megalithic yard and megalithic rod yardsticks. She discovered a third yardstick, the Greek foot, and showed that all three yardsticks were in common use throughout the British Isles during the stone ring building period. The designers of the day were therefore aware of customary measures and their application to building stone or wooden structures.

The construction of Seahenge is based on the 5-12-13 Pythagorean triangle using a unit of $\frac{1}{3}$ megalithic yard. It is a smaller version of the stone ellipse at Stanton Drew in Somerset.

[RAB]

Appendix 8

Summary Table of the Site Calculations in Part I

I. Flattened circles Type A: Pentagrams in rings

Ref.	Name	Fibonacci	Unit	Thom's Mean	Calculated	Error	District
T22(a)	Moscar Moor	3 / 5	1.5 MR	54.2'	53.62'	7"	Derbyshire
T54	Mitchell's Fold	8 / 13	1 MR	93.3'	92.95'	4.21"	Shropshire
T26(b)	Black Marsh	13 / 21	0.5 MR	76'	75.2'	9.64"	Shropshire
T28	Castle Rigg	13 / 21	5 GF	104.5'	104.12'	4.56"	Cumbria
T40	Burn Moor	21 / 34	3 GF	104.5'	104.12'	4.56"	Cumbria
T64	Orton	5 / 8	2.5 MR	143'	142.998'	Exact	Westmorland
T78	Duloo	5 / 8	0.66 MR	38.2'	38.56'	4.32"	Cornwall
T88	Dinnenver Hill	13 / 2	16.5 GF	139.7'	139.65'	0.57"	Cornwall
T100(c)	Botallack	3 / 5	2 MR	71.5'	71.499'	Exact	Cornwall
T214	Cairnfield	13 / 2	10.5 MR	*c.* 75'	75.198'	2.37"	Kincardine
T258(d) Aviemore — surrounded by hexagram:							
CC, D outer circle		13 / 21	2 GF	43'	42.97'	0.36"	Inverness
Outer circle				76'	74.93'	1.57'	
T274 Torhouse		3 / 5	2 MR	69'	69.413'	4.96"	Wigtonshire
T292 Seven Brethren		8 / 13	5 GF	66'	66.108'	1.3"	Dumfriesshire
T296(e) Loupin Stanes		13 / 2	10.25 MR	37.7'	37.598'	1.22"	Dumfriesshire

(a) There are a few sites where the higher number of the Fibonacci pair has been taken first, with the base of the triangle, in this case being 7.5 MR / *phi* .

(b) This site is covered in blanket peat, covering the position of the stones.

(c) Compare with T96, Type B flattened circle. The pentagrams are identical and both have the higher number — 10 MR — exact.

(d) There has been earth slippage at the outer ring. Only one outer ring is exact!

(e) This is one of a pair. The second circle, nearby, has the diameter 37.598' / *c.* 30°: i.e. a split Type B flattened ring!

II. Flattened circles Type B: Pentagrams enclosed in hexagons

Ref.	Name	Fibonacci	Unit	Thom's Mean	Calculated	Error	District
T18	Bar Brook	5/8	5 GF	47.7'	47.709'	0.11"	Derbyshire
T20	Owler Bar	13/21	0.5 MR	86.6'	86.83'	2.76"	Derbyshire
T42	Long Meg	21/34	9 GF	359'	360.68'	1.68'	Cumbria
T68	Lilburn	5/8	1.5 MR	100 ± 3	100.189'	2.27"	N'umberland
T96(f)	Boscawen-Un	3/5	2 MR	82.6'	82.56'	0.47"	Cornwall
T106	Merryvale	5/8	1 MR	67.4'	66.79'	7.32"	Devon
T118	Kingston Russell	34/55	0.5 MY	91.1'	90.84'	3.14"	Devon
T204	Garrol Wood RSC	13/21	0.33 MR	58.5'	57.89'	7.35"	Kincardine
T266	Farr West — surrounded by an outer decagon (g)						
		5/8	1 MR	66.8'	66.79'	0.12"	Inverness
T278	Thieves(h)	3/5	2 MY	32.4'	32.06'	4.07"	Kirk'bright
T330	Killin	3/5	2 MY	32.2'	32.06'	1.68"	Perthshire
T360	Scone	13/21	1 GF	24.48'(?)	24.808'		Perthshire

(f) This is a rare example of the large proportion '5 × 2 MR' (taken as exact), so the lower measure is
10 MR / *phi*. Compare T100 above.
(g) Thom thought this was a Type A flattened circle, but he was misled by the fallen stones.
(h) There are no stones at this site; it is marked by very precise banks.

III. Type B modified: the correct construction for defining *phi* and the accurate angle of 36°

Ref.	Name	Fibonacci	Unit	Thom's Mean	Calculated	Error	District
T94(j)	Porthmeor	21/34	1 MY	Long diameter 41.5 MY	42 MY		Cornwall
				Short diameter 33.98 MY			
T118(k)	Winterbourne Abbas	8/13	2 GF	11 MY = 29.92'	32 GF = 31.085'		Dorset
				Short diam. 9.5 MY = 25.84'	25.15'		
T300	Whitcastles	34/55	1 MY	68 MY	2 × 34	Exact	Dumfriesshire
				55 MY	34 × *phi*	0.43"	
T316	Pobull Fhinn	8/13	8 GF	125'	128 GF	7.87"	North Uist

(j) Thom broke his own rules at this site! There is one key stone marked by Thom as in its original
     setting but he measured to the displaced stones instead.
(k) Thom describes this site as an ellipse but draws it as a sort of flattened circle.

IV. Flattened circles Type D

Ref.	Name	Fibonacci	Unit	Thom's Mean	Calculated	Error	District
T46	Seascale	5 / 8	1.5 MR	88.9	88.33'	6.78"	Cumbria
T86	Rough Tor	8 / 13	4 MY	150.7'	150.757'	0.68"	Cornwall
T260	Loch nan Carraigean (irregular)						
		13 / 21	1 MY	22.5 MY	22.5166 MY	0.54"	Inverness
T284	Cambret Moor West						
		8 / 13	4 GF	54.3'	53.84'	5.48"	Kirkcudbright

PENTAGRAMS

Ref.	Name	Fibonacci	Unit	Thom's Mean	Calculated	Error	District
T34	Sunken Kirk	8 / 13	1 MR	92'	92.55'	6.6"	Cumbria
T38(1)	Burn Moor Circle D	8 / 13	4 GF	52'	52.89'	10.68"	Cumbria
T70	Birk Rig Common	5 / 8	1.5 MR	Outer circle 87.3'	86.77'	6.41"	Lancashire
				Inner circle 27.7'	26.82'	10.56"	
T206(m)	Cullerlig	5 / 8	4 GF	33.3'	33.054'	2.95"	Aberdeenshire
T208	Tarland	8 / 13	2 MY	74.1'	74.0406'	0.71"	Aberdeenshire
T230(n)	Raedykes North	5 / 8	4 GF	32.6'	33.05'	5.4"	Kincardine
T232	Clune Wood RSC	34 / 55	1 GF	56'	56.19'	2.28"	Kincardine
T282	Loch Mannoch	3 / 5	1.5 MY	21'	20.824'	2.11"	Kirkcudbright
T294	Whamphrey	8 / 13	1 MY	37'	37.0203'	0.24"	Dumfriesshire
T306	Nine Stone Rig	13 / 21	1 GF	21.76'	21.485'	3.3"	Banffshire
T318	Strathaird	13 / 21	1 GF	21'	21.48'	5.82"	Skye
T326	The Mound	5 / 8	3 GF	24.5'	24.79'	3.48"	Sutherland
T332	Ween	5 / 8	2 / 3 MY	15.4'(?)	15.425'	c. 0.3"	Perthshire

Ref.	Name	Fibonacci	Unit		Thom's Mean	Calculated	Error	District
T376(p)	Moel ty Ucha	13 / 21	0.25 MR	14 MY = 38.08'	37.597'		5.8"	Gwynedd
T382	Rhos y Beddau	13 / 21	2 GF	16 MY = 43.52'	42.97'		6.6"	Powys
T384 (?)	Four Stones	21 / 34	0.5 GF	17.3'		17.353'	0.64"	Powys
T(?)	St Nicholas	13 / 21	2 GF	43'		42.97'	0.36"	Dyfed

(l) The main figure at this site is a large Type A flattened circle. There are four smaller circles too.

(m) This circle is marked with eight stones. There are two later ellipses placed off-centre; one marked with seven heaps of earth, the other marked in stone (see section on ellipses).

(n) Thom marks in the inner circle but gives no measure! It is the circle in the central pentagon of the pentagram. There is a second circle at this site with a 7 / 14 star.

(p) Two of the divisions by 5 were slightly flattened.

PENTAGRAMS IN PENTAGONS

Ref.	Name	Fibonacci	Unit	Thom's Mean	Calculated	Error	District
T32	Elva Plain	8 / 13	1 MR	113'	114.4'	1.4"	Cumbria
T190(q)	Loanhead of Daviot RSC						
	Inner Circle	3 / 5	11 GF	54.4'	54.538'	1.66"	Aberdeenshire
	Outer circle	2 pentagons		68'	67.414'	7.03"	
T280	Drannandow	5 / 8	1.25 MR	89.1'	89.374'	3.29"	Kirkcudbright
T374	Penbedw Hall	8 / 13	6 GF	98'	98.056'	0.67"	Clwyd

(q) The outer circle is made of two pentagons marking the ten stones of the outer ring.

PENTAGRAMS IN DECAGONS

Ref.	Name	Fibonacci	Unit	Thom's Mean	Calculated	Error	District
T98	Merry Maidens	8 / 13	2 MY	77.8'	77.85'	0.61"	Cornwall
T386	Gors Fawr	3 / 5	2 MR	73.2'	72.985'	2.58"	Dyfed

PENTAGRAMS IN HEXAGONS

Ref.	Name	Fibonacci	Unit	Thom's Mean	Calculated	Error	District
T198	West Mains (Castle Fraser) RSC						
		5 / 8	1 MR	66.8'	66.793'	Exact	Aberdeenshire
T298	Girdle Stanes	8 / 13	3 MY	128'	128.24'	2.91"	(?)

T323	Ring of Brogar	89 / 144	2 GF	340'	339.689'	3.73"	Orkney
T394(r)	Usk Water	34 / 55	1 GF	65'	64.88'	1.39"	Powys
T398	Gray Hill	34 / 55	0.5 GF	32.6'	32.44'	1.89"	Gwent

(r) This is one of a pair.

PENTAGRAMS IN HEXAGRAMS

Ref.	Name	Fibonacci	Unit	Thom's Mean	Calculated	Error	District
T116	Stanton Drew	13 / 21	10 GF	372.4'	372.13'	3.22"	Somerset
T242	Little Urchany						
	Inner circle	3 / 5	1 MR	c. 13 MY = 35.36'	34.7'		Nairn
	Outer circle			c. 25 MY=68'	69.4'		
T246	Clava CCC	5 / 8	1 MR		57.84	0.53"	Inverness
	Central circle		22'	22.095'	1.14"		
	Main circle		8.5 MR = 57.8'	57.84'	0.53"		
	Outer circle			c. 100'	100.19'	c. 2.28"	
T248	Milton of Clava (identical geometry to the above)						
T254	Castle Dalcross	8 / 13	3 GF				Inverness
	Outer circle			c. 70'	68.69'	c. 1 31"	
	Main circle			39.2'	39.66'	5.52"	

Inner circle (drawn but no measure)   12.26'

CIRCLES CONTAINING HEXAGRAMS AS MAIN GEOMETRY

Ref	Name	Length of hexagram arm	Thom's measures	Calculated	Error	Distric
T62	Oddendale					
	(Outer circle)	11 MR	c. 86'	86.37'	4.44"	Westmorland
	(Inner circle)	c. 24–25' (Burl)	24.93'			
T110	Ringmoor (East)	37 GF	41.4'	41.503'	1.24"	Devon
	(West — small circle)	37 / 3 = 12.333 GF	12'	11.981'	0.23"	
T112	Lee Moor	5 MY	16'	15.704'	3.55"	Dartmoor
T160	Auchnagorth	40 GF	44.9'	44.87'	0.38"	Aberdeenshire
T170	Fountain Hill	15 GF	16.9'	16.825'	0.89"	Aberdeenshire

T198	West Mains (Castle Fraser) 8.5 MR		66.8'	66.74'	0.72"	Aberdeenshire
T296	Loupin Stanes Ring 1: Type A flattened circle Ring 2: Circle with hexagon		*c.* 44'	43.415'	Dumfriesshire
T338	Lundie Farm	6 MY	18.8'	18.84'	0.54"	Perthshire
T354	Blind Wells	25 GF	28'	28.043'	0.51"	Perthshire

CIRCLES CONTAINING HEPTAGRAMS OR 14 STAR (formula 22-46-51)

Ref	Name	Unit	Thom's measures	Calculated	Error	District
T36	Burn Moor (B)	1 GF	49.7 ± 0.7'	49.543'		Cumbria
T48	Lacra (B)	1 GF	49.7'	49.543'	1.88"	
T56	Gunnerkeld, 14 stars(s) 0.333 GF		Outer circle Inner circle	17 MR 17.333 MR		Westmorland
T76	Nine Stones	1 GF	49.6'	49.543'	0.68"	Cornwall
T90	Nine Maidens (surrounded by ahexagon) 0.333 MY		53.6'	53.3933'	2.48"	Cornwall
T104	Grey Withers (smaller of two circles)	0.75 MY	104.5'	104.04'	5.52"	Dartmoor
T136	Rollright Stones	0.75 MY	103.6'	104.04'	5.28"	Oxfordshire
T140	Loch Neil, 7 star Argyllshire Circle A Circle B	1.333 GF	65' 14'	66.087' 14.7'	12.68" 8.4"	
T158	White Cow Wood	0.333 MY	46.666'	46.24'	5.12"	Aberdeenshire
T176	Old Rayne	0.25 MR	86.6'	86.7'	1.2"	Aberdeenshire
T180	Westerton	1 GF	49.5'	49.543'	0.52"	Aberdeenshire
T190	Loanhead of Daviot 0.333 GF (small circle added later)		6 MY = 16.32'	16.51'	2.28"	Aberdeenshire
T210	Tomnaveric (very dilapidated) Inner Outer 56'(?)	0.333 MY (Burl 59')?	46'	46.24'	2.88"	Aberdeenshire

T220	Tomnagorn					
	Outer	0.333 MY	27 MY = 73.44'	74.16'	8.64"	Aberdeenshire
	Inner		16 or 17 MY	17 MY	Exact	
T226	Aquhorthies					
	Inner	1 GF	49.7	49.543'	1.88"	Kincardineshire
	Outer (26 star)		75.1'			
T230	Raedykes South	1 GF	(no measure given)	49.543'		Kincardineshire
	Outer circle (hexagon)		57'	57.21'	2.48"	
T238	Milltown	0.666 MY	91.7'	92.48'	9.36"	Banff
T272	River Ness					
	Main	0.5 MY	29.5'	29.92'	5.04"	Inverness
	Outer		69.1'	69.36'	3.12"	
T298	Girdle Stanes	0.333 MR	128'	128.306'	3.68"	Dumfriesshire
	(surrounded by heptagon?)					
T314	North Ford	0.25 MR	87' (Burl)	86.7'	3.6"	Benbecula
T330	Leys of Marley	1 GF	49.4'	49.543'	1.71"	Perthshire
T340	Monzie	0.333 GF	16.4'	17 GF = 16.514'	1.37"	Perthshire

(s) Thom marked the very few stones still in their original setting but took the measures from the fallen stones. The measures used here refer to the original stones.

CIRCLES CONTAINING TWO GEOMETRIES

Many of the circles are 'wrapped' in a second geometry, most often with a hexagon or hexagram. The two cases here are unique because both the geometries are on the same centre.

Ref	Name	Unit	Thom's measures	Calculated Error	District
Stonehenge(t) Octagram	8 MY		104 MY		Wiltshire
Heptagram (using 56 Aubrey holes)			104 MY		
Brogar(u) 9 star	25 GF		50 MR = 350 GF		Orkney
Pentagram (89 / 144)	2 GF				
Enclosed in hexagon			349.68 GF	0.32 GF = 3.73"	

(t) Details from *Megalithic Remains in Britain and Brittany,* p.138 onwards.
(u) The double geometry here is confirmed by the broad ditch, formed by an *enneogon* for the inner edge, and a pentagon for the outer edge.

CIRCLES CONTAINING OCTAGRAMS (5-12-13)

Ref	Name	Unit	Thom's measures	Calculated	Error	District
T16	Nine Ladies	1 MY	35.5'	13 MY = 35.36'	4.32"	Derbyshire
T36	Burn Moor (A)	2 MY	70'+/-2'	70.72'		Cumbria
T48	Lacra (A)	1.5 MY	19.5 MY	19.5 MY	Exact	Cumbria
T54	Tam Moor Ring cairn, inner	13 MR	89'	88.4'	7.2"	Westmorland
	Octagram with outer octagon, outer		96'	95.68'	3.84"	
T66	Felkington	2.5 GF	c. 31.5'	31.57'	0.84"	N'umberland
T74	The Hurlers (C) (1 of 3)	3 MY	c. 39 MY	39 MY		Cornwall
T80	Stripple Stones	1.666 MY	147'	147.333'	4"	Cornwall
T102	Trezibbet (Goodaver)	3 MY	39 MY	39 MY	Exact	Cornwall
T112	Trowlesworthy	0.25 MR	22.3'	22.1'	2.4"	Dartmoor
T166 Sheldon of Bourtie (8 star tangent to outer hexagram, or 2 squares developed from octagon)						
	Inner	1.5 MY	53'	53.04'	0.48"	Aberdeenshire
	Outer		108.4'	106.08'	2.32'	
T182	Holywell RSC	3 GF	37'	37.88'	10.63"	Aberdeenshire
T184	Yonder Bognit RSC	0.666 MR	c. 58.48'	58.933'	5.44"	Aberdeenshire
T202	Esslie the Less RSC(v) Kincardineshire					
	Outer	0.5 MR	43.5'	44.2'	8.4"	
	Inner (not given)			31.25'		
T242	Little Urchany(w) Inner	1 MY	13 MY	13 MY	Exact	Nairnshire
	Outer		c. 25 MY	25.129 MY		
T246	Clava Cairns (small circle) Inverness					
	East of middle ring	0.5 MR	16 MY (?)	6.5 MR = 16.25 MY	8 .16"	
T316	Suidheachadh Sealg	1 MR	88'	88.4'	4.8"	Benbecula
T352	Court Hill	0.25 MR	22 or 23'	3.25 MR = 22.1'		Perthshire
T362	Spittal of Glenshee	1 GF	12.5'	12.63'	1.56"	Perthshire
T388	Castell-Garw	0.5 MR	43.8'	44.2'	4.8"	Dyfed

(v) Circle inside square formed by joining every second of the 8 points.
(w) Every second of the 8 points in central circle are joined and extended to form an 8 star.

CIRCLES CONTAINING 9 STARS (formula 9-10.72-14)

Ref	Name	Unit	Thom's measures	Calculated	Error	District
T38	Burn Moor (C)	4 GF	54.6'	54.4'	2.44"	Cumbria
T52	Blakely Moss	4 GF	54.8'	54.4'	4.8"	Cumbria
T74	The Hurlers (1 of 3)	3 MY	42 MY	42 MY	Exact	Cornwall
T84	Leaze	6 GF	81.5'	81.6'	1.2"	Cornwall
T104	Grey Withers Dartmoor (large circle)	8 GF	108.7'	112 GF = 108.8'	1.2"	
T108	Brisworthy	6 GF	81.4'	81.6'	2.4"	Dartmoor
T132	Winterbourne Basset (x) Wiltshire					
	Inner ring	4 MY	156'	152.32' (?)		
	Outer ring(?)			198.84'		
T152	Machrie Moor II	4 GF	54'	54.4'	4.8"	Isle of Arran
T172	Balquhain	5 GF	68'	68'	Exact	Aberdeenshire
T194	Tyrebagger Outer		59.3'	59.292'	0.69"	Aberdeenshire
	Inner	1 MY	c. 38'	38.08'	0.96"	
T218	Ley Lodge (extremely dilapidated) Aberdeenshire					
	Inner	4 GF	c. 54'	54.4'	4.8"	
	Outer	c. 97'	(?)			
T244	Moyness(y) (very dilapidated) Nairn					
	Main circle	1.666 MY	23 MY	23.333 MY	10.88"	
	Central space		20'	18.916'		
	Outer circle		98.42'	98.74'	3.85"	
	(only 1 stone left) (Burl)					
T286	Cambert Moor (circle with many astronomical lines) Kirkcudbrightshire					
		6 GF	82.1'	81.6'	6"	
T292	Seven Brethren (very dilapidated) Dumfriesshire					
		1.75 MY	66'	66.64'	7.68"	
T312	Sornoch coir Fhinn					North Uist
	(enclosed in hexagon)	9 GF	c. 141'	141.335'	4.03"	

T320	Loch Buie (2 circles, the larger contained in hexagon)					Isle of Mull
	Larger	1 MY	44.1'	43.97'	1.44"	
	Smaller	1.5 GF	c. 21'	2.04'	7.2"	

T322	Force (within a hexagon) 10 GF 157.5'		157.039'	5.53"	Caithness

T324	Latheron Wheel Burn (likewise contained within a hexagon)				Caithness
	12 GF	188.3'	188.447'	1.765"	

T323	Brogar (pentagram in hexagon) 50 MR		Orkney
	25 GF	350 GF	
		340'	

T334	Weem (no hexagon) 2 MY	76'	76.16'	1.92"	Perthshire

T338	Aberfeldy(z)	0.5 MY	18.8'	19.04'	2.88"	Perthshire

T356	Hill of Drimmie	0.5 MY	19.04'	19.04'	Exact	Perthshire

T378	Tyfos (no hexagon)	4 GF	c. 55'	54.4'	7.2"	Gwynedd

T390	Y-Pigwn Trecastle (one of a pair; the other is an octagram)				
	2 MY	76.3'	76.16'	1.68"	Powys

T38 and T356 are identical

(x) There is no outer ring now and the inner ring is suspect. Stukely in 1724 gave circle diameter as 208'; Lukis in 1883 gave inner circle as 165' and outer circle as 240'.

(y) Excavation of this site in 1850 reported the central space. Outer circle formed from tangents to the nine divisions, the second crossing.

CIRCLES CONTAINING 11 STARS (formula 20 - 31.128 - 37)

Ref	Name	Unit	Thom's measures	Calculated	Error	District
T82	Treswigger	3 GF	108.3'	107.83'	5.66"	Cornwall
T92	Nine Maidens, Ding Dong 2 GF		71.6'	71.88'	3.36"	Cornwall
T162	Aquhorthies Manor RSC					Aberdeenshire
	(11 stones in a circle) 0.25 MR		63'	62.9'	1.2"	
T196	Sunhoney(aa) RSC					Aberdeenshire
	(11 stones in circle) 0.333 MR		83'	83.866'	7.4"	
T224	Tullyfourie Hill RSC 2 GF		72' (?)	71.89'		Aberdeenshire
T290	Auldgirth(bb)	1 MY	100.2'	100.64'	5.28"	Dumfriesshire
T346	Blackgate	1.5 GF	53.5'	53.91'	4.97"	Angus

(aa) In 1865 Dalrymple excavated the site; Burl thinks they also reset the stones (?)
(bb) This circle is reported to be a fake, but Thom did not agree.

THE ELLIPSES: PYTHAGOREAN TRIANGLES

Ref	Name	Triangle	Unit	Thom's measures	Calculated	Error	District
T72	Howtallon	3:4:5	1.75 MY	17.5 MY	17.5 MY	Exact	N.Yorkshire
T116	Stanton Drew I	5:12:13	1.5 MY	39 MY	39 MY	Exact	Somerset
	II	5:12:13	1 MY	36 MY	26 MY		
T169	South Ythsie	3:4:5	3 GF	Diam. *c.* 28'	29.14'	1.14'	Aberdeenshire
T190	Loanhead of Daviot	5:12:13	1.5 GF	14 MY (38.08')	37.886'	2.33"	Aberdeenshire
T192	Sands of Forvie	5:12:13	0.25 MR	16 MY	16.25 MY	8.16"	Aberdeenshire
				15.38 MY	15 MY	1.03"	
T250	Boat of Garten	5:12:13	0.666 MY	17.5 MY	17.333 MY	5.44"	Inverness
				16 MY	16 MY	Exact	
T206	Cullerlie(cc) I	8:15:17	0.10 MR				Aberdeenshire
(small ellipse added later)	II		(?)				
T252	Daviot(dd)	12:35:37	0.25 MY		18.5 MY	Exact	Inverness
					17.5 MY		

(cc) These ellipses were added later to an 'old' site.
(dd) This ellipse has an outer circle of stones formed by a hexagram on 18.5 MY.

THE ELLIPSES: ± (NOT PYTHAGOREAN)

Ref	Name	Triangle	Unit	Thom's measures	Calculated	Error	District
T114	Postbridge	16:41:44	0.333 GF	10.5 MY	10.48 MY	0.77"	Devon
				10.05 MY	9.762 MY	9.4"	
T154	Ettrick Bay	23:29:37	0.25 MY	18.5 MY	18.5 MY	Exact	Bute
				14.5 MY	14.5 MY		
T186	Blackhill of Drachlaw(ee)	7:11:13	0.1666 MR	10.25 MY	29.4666'	1.586'	Aberdeenshire
				27.88'	24.933'	2.947'	
T276	Carsfairn	8:9:12	0.5 MR	86.6'	86.6'	Exact	Kirkcud'shire
				60.86'	61.2'	4.08"	

T344	Mickle Findhowie(ff)						
		7:11:13	1 GF		25.26'		Perthshire
					21.37'		
T352	Ballinluig	7:11:13	1 GF	9.5 MY = 25.84'	25.257'	6.52"	Perthshire
				8 MY = 21.76'	21.371'	4.67"	
T372	Penmaen Mawr	13:41:43	1 GF	31 MY = 84.32'	83.54'	9.36"	Conwy
				29.5 MY = 80.24'	79.654'	7.03"	
Small circle nearby = short side of							
the triangle of the ellipse			13 GF	c. 13'	12.63'	4.44"	

(ee) Small rings with comparatively huge stones are always misleading.
(ff) Thom drew a flattened circle B on the plan but said that this was not necessarily the right
     interpretation. All the stones are fallen at the Southern end.

THE ELLIPSES: The square root of 2

Ref	Name	Triangle	Unit	Thom's measures	Calculated	Error	District
T348	Croftmoraig	17:12:12	0.33 MY	11 MY	11.33 MY	10.88"	Perthshire
				8 MY	8 MY	Exact	
T360	Guildtown	12:8.5:8.5	0.25 MY	12 MY	12 MY	Exact	Perthshire
				8.5 MY	8.5 MY		

PAIRS OF CIRCLES: the smaller being part of the larger (illustrated in Section VII)

Ref	Name	Description	Thom's measures	Calculated	Error	District
T110	Ringmoor East Circle with 2 hexagrams		41.4'	41.503'	1.24"	Dartmoor
	West Matching inner East circle		12'	11.98'	0.24"	
T296	The Loupin Stanes Type A flattened circle,					Dumfriesshire
		13 / 21 unit MR./437.7'	37.598'	1.22"		
	Circle enclosing hexagon	44'		43.42'	7"	
T372	Penmaen Mawr Ellipse 43:41:13 GF		84.32'	83.54'	9.36"	Gwynedd
	Small circle nearby		c. 13'	13 GF = 12.628'	4.46"	
T140	Loch Nell	Large circle, 7 star	65'	66.057'	1.057'	Argyll
	(Swan Lake)	Small inner circle	c. 14'	14.7'	8.4"	

PAIRS OF SMALL RELATED CIRCLES: within larger unmarked circles

Ref	Name	Description	Thom's measures	Calculated	Outer hexagram side	District
T342	Tullybeagles Larger circle		32'	31.408'	8 MR	Perthshire
	2 hexagrams touching smaller circle		23.2'	23.556'	6 MR	

	Distance between centres	54'	54.964'	Total length 109.928'

T358	Shian Bank Both circles	27.5'	10 MY = 27.2'	Perthshire
	The 2 marked central circles are identical			
	Distance between centres	70.5'	26 MY = 70.72'	Total length 52 MY (141.44')
	(2 octagons, diameter 26 MY, touching)			

T326	Shin River Larger circle	20.5'	20.46'	Sutherland
	(2 × 11 stars, touching) Smaller circle	13.6'	13.64'	
	Distance between centres	119.8'	119.805'	Total length 239.62'

T234	Carnousie House Larger circle	84' (unit 18 GF)	83.726'	
	(2 × 9 stars, touching) Smaller circle	27' (unit 6 GF)	27.91'	
	Distance between centres	163.1'	163.2'	Total length 326.4'

EGG-SHAPED RINGS

T74	The Hurlers	Pentagram	5 GF	Cornwall
T200	Esslie the Greater	Pentagram	1 MY	Kincardineshire
T212	Kynoch Plantation	Octagram	1 GF	Aberdeenshire
T270	Druid Temple	9 star	1 MY	Inverness
T248	Clava(gg)	Pentagram	1½ MR	Inverness
T288	Twelve Apostles	Pentagram	25 GF	Dumfriesshire
T304	Borrowstone Rig	14 star	¼ MR	Berwickshire
T308	Allan Water	9 star	1 MY	Roxburghshire
T364	Stanydale	Octagram	2 GF	Shetland
T368	Loch Strom	9 star	1 GF	Shetland
T380	Kerry Pole	Hexagram	1 MY	Wales
T392	Maen Mawr	Pentagram	½ MY	Powys
P169*	East Burra	14 star	1 GF	Shetland
P20*	St Pierre	√2		Brittany
P63*	Le Ménec West	9 star	13 GF	Brittany
P64*	Le Ménec East	Pentagram	7 MY	Brittany

(* These last four come from *Megalithic Remains in Britain and Brittany*)
(gg) see: *Megalithic Sites in Britain*, p.62.

UNIQUE DESIGNS

2 Sites with many rings:

T124   The Sanctuary

T130   Woodhenge

3 Sites with the diameter of $10 \times phi$ in megalithic rods

T50   Dean Moor

T216   Broomend of Critchie

T240   Urquhart

Finally, squaring the circle — and the triangle, square and circle —

T264   Gask (Inverness)

Appendix 9

Details of Square Root and phi *Calculations*

Root 2: Plato described how to double the area of a square field (the Meno) by purely geometric means. Yet, early in the megalithic period, they had already discovered a series of numbers that produced a much handier method. The series is 12-17-24-34 — etc.

Thus: $12^2 = 144$; $2 \times 144 = 288$; $17^2 = 289$.

Alternatively, $\sqrt{2} = 1.414$: $17 / 12 = 1.4166$: $24 / 17 = 1.41176$.

So they had discovered how to double or halve the area of a field with an accuracy sufficient for farming purposes. This series was seldom needed for use in the sacred sites; but see the ellipses and the Breton egg-shaped sites.

Root 3: The factor of $\sqrt{3}$ comes into the geometry of hexagons and hexagrams as well as the type D flattened circles. The figure of 1.732 must have been quite impossible either to measure physically or to calculate. But there was a solution, and it is very practical.

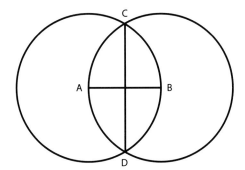

Fig.106

To define $\sqrt{3}$, draw a line $AB = 1$ MR. With centres A and B, and radius 1 MR, draw two arcs that cut at C and D. Then the length $CD = \sqrt{3} \times 1$ MR. (This shape represents a *vesica piscis*). In order to make this length (CD) usable, divide it by 11 in order to relate to their standard foot. This foot, therefore, measures $1.7320508 / 11$ MR $= 0.157459164 \times 6.8$ ft $= 12.848662''$. (Significantly, the 'Northern' or 'Saxon' foot bore an $^{11}/_{10}$

243

ratio to the Imperial foot, and accordingly the Saxon 'stadium' of 600 ft coincided with the standard furlong of 660 ft, and likewise the Saxon rod of 5 yards became the standard rod (pole or perch) of $5\frac{1}{2}$ yards.)

Golden Mean (*phi*): Like $\sqrt{3}$, this figure could not possibly have been accurately measured in ancient times with any known yardstick. Did they proceed in the same way for *phi* as for $\sqrt{3}$? The Fibonacci pairs were used in the megalithic rings up to the 34/55 pair — with the solitary exception of Brogar where they used 89/144, which is two ratios higher.
If AB is thought of as 34 units, then $AC = BC = 55$ units. Again, the divisor is 11.

So 1.618033989 MR / 11 = 0.14709 MR = 0.147094 × 6.8 ft = 1.000239 ft.

Furthermore: 6 MR (40.8 ft) × *phi* (1.618034) = 66 ft = 1 Imperial chain.

This, then, is the golden half-chain that stretches back at least 6 000 years!

Alternatively: 1 rod ($5\frac{1}{2}$ yards) = $1\frac{1}{2}$ MR × *phi* [10.2 ft × 1.618034 = 16.504 ft].

Glossary

APICES plural of 'apex' (cf. 'vertices')

CALENDRICAL relating to the calendar (cf. 'solstitial')

CUNEIFORM wedge-shaped

DECAGON a plane figure having ten sides and ten angles

DECAGRAM a regular ten-sided figure constructed by juxtaposition of triangles — as distinct from the weight of ten grammes! — analogous to 'hexagram'

DECAHEDRON a solid figure having ten faces

ELLIPSE a plane closed curve in which the sum of the distances on any point from the two foci is a constant quantity

ENNEAGON a plane figure with nine sides and nine angles

GNOMON a pillar, rod, etc, whose shadow indicates the time of day; a column or style for observing the meridian altitude of the sun

HENGE a prehistoric circular enclosure

HEPTAGON a plane figure with seven sides and seven angles

HEPTAGRAM a regular seven-sided figure — analogous to 'hexagram'

HEXAGON a plane figure having six sides and six angles

HEXAGRAM a figure formed by two intersecting equilateral triangles, each side of the one being parallel to a side of the other, and the six angular points coinciding with those of a hexagon

ICOSAHEDRON a figure contained by twenty faces

INCOMMENSURABLE having no common measure integral or fractional with another

MESOLITHIC 'Middle Stone Age' — covering early megalithic period

METROLOGY the science of weights and measures

NEOLITHIC 'New Stone Age' — covering late megalithic period

OCTAGON a plane figure having eight angles and eight sides

OCTAGRAM a regular eight-sided figure — constructed by analogy to 'hexagram'

PENTAGON a plane figure having five sides and five angles — also 'pentangle'

PENTAGRAM a five-pointed figure formed by producing the sides of a pentagon both ways to their points of intersection, so as to form a five-pointed star; the five straight lines forming one continuous line or 'endless knot' — also a mystical symbol, called a 'pentacle' or 'pentalpha'

POLYGON a plane rectilineal figure with many (more than four) angles and sides

PHYLLOTAXIS geometrical analysis of arrangements of leaves on an axis or stem

SEXAGESIMAL a sixtieth part or a series by 60s

SOLSTITIAL relating to the solstices (cf. 'calendrical')

TETRAHEDRON a figure contained by four triangular faces

TRILITHON two large upright stones with another resting across their tops

VESICA PISCIS a pointed oval figure, the sides of which are properly parts of two equal circles passing through each other at their centres

Bibliography

Ahl, F.M. (1982). Amber, Avallon and Apollo's singing swans, *American Journal of Philology* 103, 373–411.

Atkinson, R.J.C. (1960, 1979). *Stonehenge,* Penguin, London.

Atkinson, R.J.C. (1982). *Antiquity* 56, 145–6.

Barker, A. (1984). *Greek Musical Writings* I, p.43, note 18, Cambridge.

Barnett, J. & Moir, G. (1984) Stone Circles and Megalithic Mathematics, *Proc. Prehistoric Society* 50, 197–216.

Beaumont, C. (1945). *The Riddle of Prehistoric Britain,* Rider & Co.

Behrend, M. (1976). Discussion of Dr Freeman's Paper, *Journal of the Royal Statistical Society,* JRSS A139, 44.

Berriman, A.E. (1953). *Historical Metrology,* Dent.

Broadbent, S.R. (1955). Discussion of Professor Thom's Paper, *JRSS* A118, 292–3.

Bond, F.B. & Lea, T.S. (1977). *Gematria,* Thorsons.

Boyer & Merzbach (1991) *History of Mathematics,* John Wiley & Sons.

Brown, Norman O. (1969). *Hermes the Thief — the Evolution of a Myth,* Vantage, New York.

Burl, H.A.W. (1971). Two Scottish Stone Circles in Northumberland, *Archaeol. Ael.* 49, 37–51.

— (1972). Stone Circles and Ring Cairns, *Scot. Archaeol. Forum* 4, 31–47.

— (1974). Recumbent Stone Circles of NE Scotland, *Proc. Soc. Ant. Soc.* 102, 56–81.

— (1976). *The Stone Circles of the British Isles,* Yale UP: New Haven and London.

— (1979). *Prehistoric Avebury,* Yale UP, New Haven and London.

— (1993). *From Carnac to Callanish,* Yale UP.

— (1999). *Circles of Stone,* Harvill Press.

— & Milligan (1999). *Great Stone Circles,* Yale UP.

— & Freeman (1977). Local Units of Measurement in Prehistoric Britain, *Antiquity* 51, 152–4.

Butler, A. (1999) *The Bronze Age Computer Disk,* Foulsham.

Childe, V.G. (1955). Discussion of Professor Thom's Paper, *JRSS* A118, 293–4.

Chippindale, C. (1983). *Stonehenge Complete,* Thames &Hudson.

Clarke, D.V., Cowie, T.G. & Foxton, A. (1985). Symbol of power at the Time of Stonehenge, *HMSO,* Ch.3, p.35.

Connor, R.D. (1987). The Weights and Measures of England, *HMSO.*

Cooper, L.C. (1978). *An Illustrated Encyclopaedia of Traditional Symbols,* Thames & Hudson.

Cowan, T.M. (1970). Megalithic Rings, Their Design & Construction, *Science* 168, no.1329, 321–5.

Crawford, G.I. (1976). Discussion of Dr Freeman's Paper, *JRSS* A139, 41-2.

Critchlow, Keith (1979). *Time Stands Still,* Gordon Fraser, London.

Daniel, G.E. (1963). *Megalithic Builders of Western Europe,* Penguin.

Siculus, Diodorus (trans. Oldfather, CH, 1935), Loeb Classical Library: Book II, 47; Book III, 56–57.

Ellis, K. (1973). *Man and Measure,* Priory Press.

Emery, W.B. (1961). *Archaic Egypt,* Pelican.

Fernie, E, (1981). The Greek Metrological Relief in the Ashmolean Museum, Oxford, *Antiquaries Journal,* 51, 255–63.

Fidler, D. (1993). *Jesus, Son of God,* Quest Books.

Fowler, D. (1987). *The Mathematics of Plato's Academy,* Clarendon.

Fraser, Mrs James (1880–83). *Inverness Scientific Society and Field Club.*

Freeman, P.R. (1975). Carnac Probabilities Corrected, *Journal of Historical Astronomy* 6, 219.

— (1976). A Bayesian Analysis of the Megalithic Yard, *JRSS* A139, 20–35.

Freke, T. & Gandy, P. (1999). *The Jesus Mysteries,* Thorsons.

Graves, R. (1960). *Greek Myths,* Penguin.

Hadingham, E. (1975). *Circles and Standing Stones,* Heinemann, London and New York.

Harris, J.R. (Ed.) (1971). *The Legacy of Egypt,* Oxford, 2nd Edition.

Hawkins, G.S. (1963). Stonehenge Decoded, *Nature* 200, 306–8.

— (1964). Stonehenge: a Neolithic Computer, *Nature* 202, 1258–61.

— (1965). Callanish: a Scottish Stonehenge, *Science* 147, 127–30.

— (1966). Stonehenge 56 Year Cycle, *Nature* 215, 604f.

— (1966, 1970). *Stonehenge Decoded,* Fontana, New York & London.

Heath, R. (1999). *Stone Circles — a Beginner's Guide,* Hodder, London.

— (1999). *Sun, Moon & Earth, Wooden Books,* Wales LD8 2NT.

Heggie, D.C. (1981). *Megalithic Science,* Thames & Hudson, London.

James, P. (1991). *Centuries of Darkness,* Jonathan Cape.

Kappraff, J. (2001). *Beyond Measure: a Guided Tour through Nature, Myth & Number,* World Scientific Publishing Co., USA.

Keiller, A. (1934). Megalithic Monuments of NE Scotland, *British Association.*

— (1965). *Windmill Hill and Avebury,* Oxford University Press.

Kendall, D.G. (1971). Review of Thom (1971), *Antiquity* 45, 310–13.

— (1976). Discussion of Dr Freeman's Paper, *JRSS* A139, 37–39.

Kendall, M.G. (1955). Discussion of Professor Thom's Paper, *JRSS* A118, 291.

Knight C. & Lomas R. (2000). *Uriel's Machine,* Century Books, London.

Krupp, E.C. (1977). *The Megalithic Builders,* Phaidon Press, Oxford.

Lawlor, R. (1982). *Sacred Geometry,* Thames & Hudson.

Lewis, A.L. (1892). Stone Circles of Britain, *Archaeology Journal* 49, 136–54.

Lewis, A.L. (1900). Stone Circles of Scotland, *Journal of the Royal Anthropological Institute* 30, 56–73.

Lockyer, J.N. (1909). *Stonehenge and other British Stone Monuments, Macmillan,* London.

Luce, J.V. (1973). *Homer and the Homeric Age,* Thames & Hudson.

Maas, M. & McIntosh Snyder, J. (1989). *Stringed Instruments of Ancient Greece,* Yale.

McClain, E.G. (1976). *The Myth of Variance,* Nicholas Hays, USA.

Macintyre, L. (1994) *Sir David Russell — A Biography,* Canongate.

Mackie, E.W. (1977). *The Megalithic Builders,* Oxford University Press.

— (1977). *Sciences and Society in Prehistoric Britain,* Paul Elek, London.

Marshall, D. (1976–77). Carved Stone Balls, *Proceedings of the Society of Antiquaries of Scotland,* 108.

McKrickard, J. (1990). *Eclipse of the Sun,* Gothic Image.

Michell, J. (1981). *Ancient Metrology,* Thames & Hudson, London.

— (1988). *Dimensions of Paradise,* Thames & Hudson.

Midonick, H. (1965). *The Treasury of Mathematics,* Pelican: vol. I, p.180.

Moir, G. & Ruggles & Norris (1980). Megalithic Science and some Scottish Site Plans, *Antiquity* 54, 37–43.

Muir, R. (1981). *Riddles in the British Landscape,* Thames & Hudson, London.

Neal, J.F. (2000). *All Done with Mirrors* (johnneal@secretacademy.com)

Neugebaur, O. (1957). *The Exact Sciences in Antiquity,* Dover, 2nd Edition.

Newham, C.A. (1972). *The Astronomical Significance of Stonehenge,* J Blackburn, Leeds.

North, J. (1996). *Stonehenge,* Harper Collins.

Patton, M. (1993). *Statements in Stone,* Routledge.

Penhallurick, R.D. (1986). *Tin in Antiquity,* The Institute of Metals.

Piggott, S. (1956). Architecture and Ritual in Megalithic Monuments, *RIBA* Journal, Series 3, 63.

Pliny the Elder. *Natural History,* Section 37, v.35–36.

Renfrew, C. (1976). *Before Civilization,* Penguin, London.

— (1987). *Archaeology and Language,* Jonathan Cape.

Roy, A.E. (1948). The Origin of the Constellations, *Vistas in Astronomy:* 27, 4.

Sachs, C. (1943). *The Rise of Music in the Ancient World,* Norton, New York, p.217.

Schwaller de Lubicz, R.A. (1977). The Temple in Man, *Inner Traditions International,* New York.

Thom, A. (1955). A Statistical Examination of the Megalithic Sites in Britain, *JRSS* A118, 275–95.

— (1961). The Geometry of Megalithic Man, *Mathematical Gazette* 45, 83–93.

— (1961). The Egg-shaped Standing Stones of Britain, *Archives Int. d'Hist. Sci.* 14, 291–303.

— (1962). The Megalithic Unit of Length, *JRSS* A125, 243–51.

— (1964). Larger Units of Length of Megalithic Man, *JRSS* A127, 527-33.

— (1966). Megaliths and Mathematics, *Antiquity* 40, 121–8.

— (1967). *Megalithic Sites in Britain,* Oxford University Press.

— (1968). Metrology and Geometry of Cup and Ring Marks, *Systematics* 6, 173–89.

— (1971). Megalithic Lunar Observatories, Oxford University Press.

— (1977). The Megalithic Yard, *Measurement and Control* 10, 488–92.

— (1978). Distances between Stones in Stone Rows, *JRSS* A141, 253–7.

— & Merritt R.L. (1978). Some Megalithic Sites in Shetland, *J. Hist. Astron. 9,* 54–60.

— & A.S. (1978). *Megalithic Remains in Britain and Brittany,* Oxford University Press.

—— (1979). The Standing Stones in Argyllshire, *Glasgow Archaeological Journal* 6, 5–10.

—— & Foord T.R. (1976). A New Assessment of the Geometry and Metrology of the Ring, *J. Hist. Astron.* 7, 183–92.

Vickers, M. (1984). Hallstaat and Early La Tène Chronology, *Antiquity* 58, Nos.224, 209.

Waerden, B.L. Van der (1983) *Geometry and Algebra in Ancient Civilizations*, Springer-Verlag.

Weeks, L. (1999). Lead Isotope Analyses from Tell Abraq, United Arab Emirates — new data regarding the 'Tin Problem' in Western Asia, *Antiquity* 73, 49–64.

Wiseman, A. & Wiseman, P. (1980). *Julius Caesar — the Battle for Gaul,* Chatto & Windus.

Wood, J.E. (1978). *Sun, Moon and Standing Stones,* Oxford University Press.

Picture Credits

All stone circle diagrams by Richard A. Batchelor based on sketches by Anne Macaulay.

Photographs by Gordon Strachan: Figs. 3, 10, 11, 17, 18, 21, 22, 26, 30, 40, 43, 45, 46, 49, 51, 82, 84, 85, 87, 96, 97, 99

Photographs by Rod Bull: Figs. 24, 56, 57, 105

Index

Sun and Cross

From Megalithic Culture to Early Christianity in Ireland

Jakob Streit

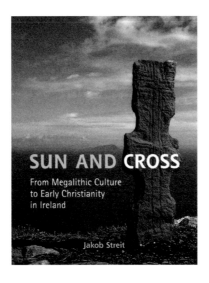

A full-colour edition of this inspiring and fascinating work of Celtic spirituality.

Starting with the ancient sun-oriented monuments of the megalithic age, Streit traces an unbroken spiritual culture in Ireland from the time of stone circles and dolmens, through the Celtic era, into the period of the early Christian stone crosses.

'This is an essential sourcebook for anybody interested in Celtic spirituality and history. Includes a wonderful selection of photographs, illustrations, poetry and quotations.' — *Aisling* magazine

www.florisbooks.co.uk